For Love & Money

For Love & Money

Protecting Family & Wealth
In Estate & Succession Planning

A New Approach Blending Law and Psychology

JOHN W. AMBRECHT, ESQ., HOWARD BERENS, M.D.,
RICHARD GOLDWATER, M.D.,
AND TOM GORMAN

For Love & Money (Unabridged Edition)
Protecting Family & Wealth In Estate & Succession Planning
A New Approach Blending Law and Psychology

The terms Roles and Rules, Rules Crisis, From Roles to Rules, and Maieutic
Consultant are trademarks of Families and Wealth, LLC

Cover design by Cheryl Ambrecht

Library of Congress Control Number: 2007908650
ISBN: Hardcover   978-1-4363-0088-9
               Softcover   978-1-4363-0087-2

This book was printed in the United States of America.

Disclaimer

This book is intended to provide general information on family dynamics and succession and estate planning. It is not meant to be the reader's only source of information on these subjects, and readers are urged to seek advice from other sources, and to use their own judgment.

This book contains the ideas and opinions of the authors and is sold and distributed with the understanding that the authors and publisher are not dispensing legal, consulting, or other professional services in the book. It is also sold and distributed with the understanding that the information in this book is current only to the time it was written and that, while every effort has been made to ensure the information is accurate, mistakes in content and presentation may have occurred.

Therefore the authors and publisher disclaim any responsibility for any liability, loss, or risk incurred as a direct or indirect consequence of the use or application of any of the contents of this book.

To order additional copies of this book, contact:
Xlibris Corporation
1-888-795-4274
www.Xlibris.com
Orders@Xlibris.com
40143

CONTENTS

PREFACE

Nobody enjoys a family feud and, as an attorney, I can tell you that nobody wins one. This is especially true of feuds concerning the assets of a deceased loved one. Family members fighting over an estate rarely feel good about their behavior. Any "victories" come at a high emotional and, usually, financial cost. Warring survivors may feel they're trying to get from the dead what they did not get in life. Some even feel such fighting dishonors the dead. In their lucid moments, family members will often say that the fight is not about money—and they are right. It is about anger, envy, fear, pride, jealousy, resentment, power, love, hate, and regret.

The biggest mistake in estate planning (aside from not planning at all) is to believe that an estate plan can neutralize the emotions that ignite family feuds over legacies. While well-crafted wills and trusts will generally ensure the legal transfer of assets, they will not in themselves ensure a smooth and uncontested transfer. Nor can they guarantee the future growth and profitability of assets that require ongoing management, such as a business, farm, ranch, or real estate. Only a succession and estate plan that considers and addresses family dynamics and emotional issues can do that.

In my experience and in researching hundreds of litigated estate plans, I've found that strong emotions, rather than legal flaws in the documents, drive people to contest wills and trusts. As in divorce, a death in a family often makes money a medium for addressing emotional matters. Divorce is sad and messy by nature. Death is also sad, but the transfer of assets need not be messy *if* emotional issues are properly addressed in the estate planning process.

I have tried several ways of dealing with emotional issues in estate planning, using tools such as the Myers Briggs Type Indicator and various communication models. Only in recent years have I found a truly effective approach to helping families and advisors deal with upsetting emotions and family dynamics in succession and estate planning. This approach applies Roles and Rules, a trademarked model of human psychology developed by psychiatrist Dr. Richard Goldwater, to succession and estate planning. With this approach, I and my associates help family members and other stakeholders plan and implement successful intergenerational transfers of assets. In essence, the method is to help people move from decisions and behavior based purely on family roles to decisions and behavior based more on what we call business rules.

This book explains our approach and shows families and their attorneys, trust officers, accountants, and financial planners how to use it to create effective succession and estate plans. Using straightforward language and real-life examples, we show how to craft a legally sound plan that meets financial and business goals while preserving, and sometimes improving, family relationships. Note, however, that we are not dispensing legal advice or instructions on estate planning in this book. Instead, we are providing a context for creating a sound plan.

Albert Einstein noted that the level of thinking that created a problem cannot solve that problem. The approach described in this book brings a new level of thinking to succession and estate planning, for practitioners and families. In dealing with human emotions and behavior, nothing works one hundred percent of the time. But Roles and Rules works more often and with better results than any other approach to succession and estate planning that I and my associates have tried.

John W. Ambrecht, Esq.
Santa Barbara, California
April, 2008

When they first hear about working with family dynamics in estate planning, many people respond in one of two ways: Either they get it immediately or they say something like, "Why go dragging family stuff into a legal situation?"

Those who get it immediately realize that estate planning *is* a legal situation bound up with "family stuff." Some of those who are wary of dragging family stuff into estate planning just don't see the emotional forces at work in the situation. However, more often they are aware of those forces but fear that trying to deal with them—or even acknowledging them—might make matters worse.

Ignoring psychological issues does not make them go away, nor can legal and financial tools alone address them. But unless they are addressed, strong emotions and psychological agendas, working behind the scenes or out in the open, may undermine the estate planning process. How? By driving people toward behaviors, such as bickering, shutting down communication, failing to provide information, and refusing to sign documents, which prevent timely, satisfactory completion of the plan and which can actually freeze the planning process. Strong emotions also drive people to create wills and trusts that immortalize resentments, power imbalances, or poor relationships in the family. This jeopardizes the implementation of the plan, not to mention family harmony, down the road.

There's a strong business case for addressing emotional and psychological issues in estate planning. I mention this because even today some families, attorneys, and estate planners see this sort of work as "touchy-feely" or unnecessary. Some people "don't believe in psychology" when it comes to financial and legal matters. Yet, as John pointed out above, poor succession and estate plans usually stem from emotional roots. I have seen how long-standing family roles, which have been the honored backbone of a family business, can become major stumbling blocks at the time of succession. I have also seen how powerful family emotions can preclude reasonable business decisions that would facilitate a fruitful succession.

Our goal is not to conduct family therapy or even to create family harmony, although we are pleased when the latter occurs. Rather our goal is to craft a succession and estate plan that will help clients to avoid, or at least minimize, problems generated by poor family dynamics in such situations. In doing so, our larger goal is to minimize difficulties in the implementation of the plan as well as instances in which attorneys and other advisors experience dissatisfaction among clients, trustees, and beneficiaries, and malpractice suits and other actions at law.

Howard Berens, MD
Newton, Massachusetts
April, 2008

INTRODUCTION

Every year hundreds of thousands of families pass their businesses from one generation to the next—or at least try to. Indeed, the available research over the past two decades consistently shows that only about 30 percent of family businesses pass successfully to the second generation, while about 15 percent make it to the third.[1] In the process, thousands of families suffer emotional upheavals, intergenerational conflict, and financial losses. Why should this be the case in a nation with no shortage of legal talent or business acumen?

We trace much of this problem to the limitations of current approaches to succession and estate planning. Most estate planners focus solely on legal and financial issues. They analyze and explain the client's options regarding wills, trusts, gifts, taxes, and insurance, all of which are, of course, vital matters. But clients are also contemplating the end of their lives and the legacy they may leave. Their families are anticipating the loss of a loved one, usually one of the most powerful figures in their lives. These families also have their share of difficult personalities and interpersonal conflicts. These factors, which we sum up under the rubric of family dynamics, generate problems in the intergenerational transfer of family businesses and other significant assets.

Succession and estate planning generally aims to avoid probate, minimize taxes, and ensure beneficiaries' financial security. The typical estate plan comprises documents that will achieve these ends. Yet a five-year study of family businesses revealed that three key factors explain 95 percent of instances of breakdown in the succession process: problems in relationships among family members (cited as the key factor in 60 percent of the cases), heirs not being sufficiently prepared

---

[1] Correlates of Success in Family Business Transitions, Michael Morris, et al., *Journal of Business Venturing*, vol. 12, pages 385-401, 1997, Elsevier Science, Inc.

(25 percent), and issues related to planning and control activities (10 percent).[2] Those are disturbing statistics when compared with the main focus of estate planning efforts. Although problems in family relationships cause 60 percent of the breakdowns, almost no effort goes into addressing those relationships in the planning process. Instead, succession and estate planning efforts focus almost solely on legal, tax, and financial issues.

Most estate planners either assume that a family's dynamics are "okay" (or at least "normal") or assume that poor dynamics won't disrupt the estate plan. Or they see the dangers posed by poor dynamics and assume that legal provisions can neutralize them. Often, those assumptions are valid. Most wills and trusts are not contested, and the assets pass smoothly from testators to beneficiaries. Even in difficult cases, families often deal with negative dynamics in positive ways that produce acceptable solutions.

This book will help when those assumptions are not valid and acceptable solutions remain elusive. It will help when unruly emotions, obstructionist behavior, and bad decisions threaten to overwhelm the estate planning process or the actual transfer of assets. It will help when family arguments, changes of intention, and threats of disinheritance burn up everyone's time and energy.

For instance, a verbal battle broke out among family members in the office of an attorney we know. After thirty very confusing seconds, he threw up his hands and said, "Stop! Stop it! You're all getting into an area that I can't deal with." While that may have been an accurate self-assessment, estate planners must be prepared for such situations. They can't afford to ignore this kind of behavior, nor should they expect it to stop on command. Estate planners and families must know when they need help, what kind of help they need and, when possible, how they can help themselves.

Unfortunately, most planners and families don't know when they need help, what kind of help they need, or how they can help themselves in such situations. That is why we wrote this book.

Two Groups, No Solution

Let's step back to examine the two major groups of professionals that advise family businesses in general:

- On the one hand, we have attorneys, accountants, trust officers, bankers, and various financial and operations consultants. These advisors help families with the nuts-and-bolts of owning and running a business.

---

[2]   Ibid.

In various ways, they help with strategic, financial, and operations management—and, particularly in the case of attorneys, succession and estate planning. These advisors aim to help clients manage the business as a business and either sell it or pass it on to successors.

- On the other hand, we have advisors who take a more "therapeutic" approach to family businesses. These include management consultants who work with family businesses on effective communication, joint decision-making, conflict resolution, leadership, and other so-called soft skills. Often these advisors have backgrounds in mental health or counseling and use personality assessments, communication models, family retreats, and coaching and training to improve clients' effectiveness.

In consulting engagements and in succession and estate planning, each camp views a family business through its own telescope. For instance, attorneys and financial advisors deal with the legal and tax aspects, while management consultants work on communication skills. Practitioners in both camps do good work when they address specific problems in their bailiwicks. But even when they recognize poor family dynamics in family business, neither can do much about them. The first camp gives the entrepreneur and family financial and legal advice, and sometimes management practices to follow. The second camp tries to help family members leave their "baggage and issues" at home so they can run the business like a business.

Even when these efforts succeed, they do so only temporarily. Dad follows management practices, such as sound delegation, and acts like a CEO instead of like Dad for a few days, then reverts to his former behaviors. Junior or Sis leave their family baggage at home and communicate well for a few days, then revert to form. Rather than permanent change, clients achieve short-term modification of undesirable behaviors, at best. The lack of real change is bad enough when the business is operating under established, stable management. But when the challenges of succession and estate planning loom, the family and business require a more effective approach than either camp can deliver.

What would an effective approach to succession and estate planning amid poor family dynamics look like? Let's find out.

An Effective Approach

An effective approach would address both the legal and financial considerations *and* the emotional and family considerations in estate planning in an integrated way. It would encourage sound legal and financial management *and* sound communication practices. Of course, an effective approach would generate a plan that meets the highest legal and fiduciary standards. In addition, an effective approach to succession and estate planning would:

1. Help testators and families address the question of whether to keep or sell the business. Aside from financial considerations and informal judgments about successors, families and advisors have no reliable framework for making this key decision, especially amid poor family dynamics.
2. Promote an objective view of the testator and family, an emotional distance from the situation, and no off-the-shelf solutions. We believe in educating the testator and family to enable them to develop their own solutions with professional guidance.
3. Preserve the value and earning power of the business and position it for growth under the successors, or help the family to extract full and fair value from the sale of the business.
4. Help advisors and their clients to avoid potentially damaging, unprofitable, or hopeless situations. (Yes, there are such things!) Most advisors have no way of assessing a family's dynamics and making that judgment. For instance, attorneys try to ignore family turmoil, isolate the disruptive parties—who may choose to sue later on—or solve the problems with legal provisions, none of which consistently works.
5. Be sophisticated and flexible enough to cover the full range of family issues, including those related to family governance and shared financial assets, yet simple enough for advisors and clients to understand and apply quickly.

Our approach meets these criteria while in no way superceding or compromising the estate plan or its administration. Our approach supplements, directs, and supports the process. It helps attorneys, trust officers, and other advisors to explain difficult situations to testators, clients, and beneficiaries. It provides objective, non-judgmental language, and is therefore client-focused. It is also process-focused as opposed to content-focused.

On that latter note, the legal profession has done a superb job of developing the content of estate plans. Advisors know how to reduce taxes, avoid probate, and so on. What they need are tools that help them explain why the intergenerational transfer of assets can be so difficult, and what to do when difficulties arise. We have found the usual diagnoses to be of little practical value. Things don't go awry just because Dad has unrealistic expectations, heirs don't care, or siblings are at war. Those are not trivial issues and they warrant attention, but they are not root causes. The root causes are underlying psychological forces in the family and the family business. When you identify those forces, you can deal with them, and deal with the estate plan and the transfer of assets, far more effectively.

A Path Forward

In an intergenerational transfer of a business, real estate, or other major assets, people must make a specific type of transition: a transition from family roles to business rules. They must learn to rely less on family roles, and more on business rules, to guide their behavior. Why? Because in most family businesses, people carry their family roles, such as father, mother, son, daughter, brother, sister, oldest and youngest, into the business. Family roles guide and dictate business decisions and on-the-job behavior in ways that they do not in non-family enterprises and, often, not for the better.

Succession and estate planning—and the actual transfer of the business—represents what we call a Rules Crisis. It's an event in which rules assert themselves in a situation that formerly ran on roles. It resembles a society moving from dictatorship to democracy. The Rules Crisis presents an opportunity for growth, development, and the evolution of the business. It also poses the danger that the family or the business, or both, will devolve into disorder, infighting, and destruction. In other words, the difficulties in succession and estate planning amount to developmental tasks. In this book we define those tasks and show how to deal with them productively.

We don't condemn the presence of family roles in the family business. Like most elements in human affairs, family roles in a business produce both positive and negative effects. On the positive side, many family businesses thrive on pride in the family name, trust among family members, and shared economic fortunes. Many benefit from strong historical and personal ties to employees, customers, suppliers, investors, bankers, and the community. If a business succeeds on relationships, then a family business succeeds on family relationships, and family relationships forge strong bonds. On the negative side, a powerful leader oversees most family enterprises. His power emanates from two roles—head of the family and head of the business. In those two powerful roles, the leader can dictate the way the business operates, rather than agree to what we call business rules.

Indeed sometimes the leader of a business sees agreeing to business rules as a form of submission or defeat. He may feel that he has to "submit" to the rules rather than simply agree to play by them. Like dethroned dictators and tribal leaders, these business people perceive a loss of power when their authority gives way to the reality of infirmity, the prospect of death, or the rule of law. In fact, it is a loss of power: the loss of their status as venerated, charismatic leader and of control over the business. In our experience, heads of businesses have difficulty passing on the business to the extent that they see playing by rules as an act of submission and a surrender of power, and to the extent that they have not prepared successors to "play by the rules."

Broadly, business rules are the principles, policies, and procedures that guide and govern a business. These include job descriptions, quality standards, compensation plans, promotion criteria, cost controls, decision-making processes, and a chain of command. In a family business, these are routinely determined, sometimes on a whim, by the owner. If the owner wants to expand or contract the operation, or take an interest-free loan, or hire his inexperienced son-in-law, or promote or fire someone, who has the power to stop him? Managers, employees, and advisors can talk to him, but no one has the actual power to stop him.

We call these principles, policies, and procedures business rules because true rules (like the rules of baseball or the rules of the road) apply to everyone in the situation (be it a playing field or a highway). Rules aim to ensure that everyone in a situation is treated fairly. Legal and business rules—laws and regulations that protect all parties, and policies and procedures that define relationships and expectations—characterize every well-managed company. However, the owner of a family business can "rule" as she sees fit. Sometimes this works, and sometimes it doesn't.

In either case, estate planning presages the inevitable demise of that "ruler," and this can destabilize the business and the family. Introducing business rules to a family business can either disorient and threaten family members or help them get their bearings and move to new, more professional management methods. In fact, the more a business has been running on family roles, the more it will benefit from business rules—and the more difficult the transition to business rules will be. (Note that family members must also make a transition to business *roles*, such as CEO, controller, and vice president of marketing, as well as to business rules. We will examine this transition closely as well.)

Unfortunately, simple knowledge of business rules won't motivate people to adopt them. People don't follow rules just because they know about them. They follow rules because they perceive it to be in their interest to do so. For instance, we all agree to obey traffic signals and assume others will too, to avoid danger as well as traffic tickets. Someone must work with or within the family and the business to facilitate the transition from roles to rules. This book, particularly in Chapter 4, describes the work of that facilitator.

Neither Psychotherapy nor Counseling

None of this involves family or individual psychotherapy or psychological counseling. A family cannot perform psychotherapy on itself. More to the point, psychotherapy and counseling lie outside the field of estate planning and the expertise of estate planners. Even the conditions required for psychotherapy are absent in difficult estate planning situations. People approach psychotherapy with a desire, or at least a willingness, to change and with some goodwill and openness to new ways of interacting. In contrast, family conflicts over estate plans are fraught with hidden agendas, changing alliances, and outright animosity.

While they cannot and should not perform psychotherapy, most estate planners will benefit from a shift in mindset. For instance, attorneys are attuned to the adversarial aspects of legal and business matters, and an adversarial posture can inflame a family feud. Attorneys also bring a rules-based orientation to their work. (After all, the law is an elaborate set of rules.) This orientation has real benefits, but it is also why attorneys tend to believe that wills, trusts, and partnership agreements can, by themselves, effect an orderly transfer of assets. Attorneys are also very client focused. While this focus also has benefits, attorneys must realize that a family is a complex system with issues that may transcend the client's perhaps narrowly defined goals.

We've written this book for both estate planning professionals and their clients. Much of the material speaks to the needs of the attorney, accountant, trust officer, or other advisor to a family business. Yet we believe that anyone in a family or family business involved in a succession and estate plan, keep-or-sell decision, or transfer of assets will find this book valuable. Advisors and families with assets other than an operating business will also find this book useful when they encounter poor family dynamics.

If you are an estate planning professional, we suggest that you approach succession and estate planning amid poor family dynamics with the mindset of a facilitator. Some situations may call for bringing in an actual facilitator, without compromising your position as legal, financial, or business advisor. The essential thing is to recognize when an estate plan—the process as distinct from the content—requires some level of facilitation. In some cases, a skilled member of the planning team or even a trusted friend of the family can act as facilitator. In other cases, a trained facilitator will have to guide the testator and family.

If you are a client or a member of a family in which poor family dynamics threaten the planning process, we suggest that you locate an attorney, advisor, or consultant who can address those issues and act as facilitator. If the planning process is stalled, if the same problems crop up repeatedly, if family members are retaining their own attorneys, take action. If an attorney polarizes the family, make a fresh start with a less adversarial lawyer who will think of the family business, rather than a specific person or faction, as the client. This may require discussion and clarification, because attorneys typically represent only the interests of the party paying their fees. Similarly, the attorney must secure agreement from the family that the business is the client. Indeed, our approach raises a number of practice issues for attorneys, which we address in this book and particularly in Appendix B.

People armed with a knowledge of Roles and Rules are positioned to recognize negative family dynamics in estate planning and are prepared to address them or to find someone to address them. Our goal in this book is to give advisors and families this knowledge and to position them to craft and implement estate plans that meet their needs as professionals, family members, and business people.

The Structure of this Book

This book has eight chapters arranged into three parts, as well as six Appendixes. First, here is the content that you'll find in each part:

Part One, Chapters 1-4: Background, Setting, and Players, explains the Roles and Rules model and the Rules Crisis that every family business faces in succession and estate planning, and examines the keep-or-sell decision. It also explains how Roles and Rules form the structure of a business, and how a facilitator can use our approach to assist a family business.

Part Two, Chapters 5-6: A Case in Point, delves deeply into an actual case in which a family faces a Rules Crisis, fractures into two camps, resolves most of their issues, and moves ahead.

Part Three, Chapters 7-8: Roles and Rules, Goals and Tools, discusses legal devices, such as trust provisions and business structures, that enable advisors and families to address poor family dynamics. It also revisits the keep-or-sell decision, and further explains how to effect a sound plan and deal with intractable situations.

Here is a summary of each chapter and appendix:

Chapter One—From Roles To Rules: An Evolutionary Approach—explains the basics of the Roles and Rules model and its application to succession and estate planning.

Chapter Two—The Rules Crisis: Understanding the Real Challenge in Succession and Estate Planning—examines the difficult situation a family business in succession faces, and how to consider the question of whether to keep or sell the business.

Chapter Three—The Structure of the Business: Roles and Rules at work—shows how to assess Roles and Rules in the business and begin to define new ones.

Chapter Four—The Facilitator: Bringing Law and Order to Town—explores the role that an attorney, advisor, consultant, or family member can play in guiding a family through the plan and the transition.

Chapter Five—The Past Need Not Be Prologue: Analyzing Family Roles—shows how to understand the effects of family roles on the business, in the context of an actual case.

Chapter Six—A Strong Foundation: Generating the Right Rules—shows how to gain the client's and family's cooperation, assist in managing the process, and help generate the optimal Roles and Rules for a given situation, in the context of the same case.

Chapter Seven—Legal and Financial Tools and Techniques—focuses on the most effective legal and business tools for protecting assets, minimizing taxes, and preserving liquidity and capital in the context of our approach.

Chapter Eight—Leading the Family, and the Family Business, Forward sums up and elaborates methods for helping the testator and family identify and work through the key issues they face in the process.

Appendix A: Derivation of Roles and Rules and Its Application to Succession in Business, discusses the theoretical underpinnings of Roles and Rules and establishes the validity of this model of human psychology.

Appendix B: Issues Affecting Attorneys Regarding Professional Conduct and Client Relationships, provides guidance for lawyers considering using Roles and Roles and similar "best practices" in estate work with testators and families.

Appendix C: Sample Communication Rules, provides a sample set of ground rules that we use to bring order and businesslike procedure to family meetings.

Appendix D: Issues in Estate Taxes, Gift Exemptions, and Exclusions, provides general information on estate taxes and some specific information about factors affecting the assets in an estate that are exempt according to the tax laws—a key issue in the goal of tax minimization.

Appendix E: Modifying Trusts with Multiple Trustees to Enhance the Trusts' Stability, explains why trusts with multiple trustees are inherently unstable and provides sample provisions to add stability from a Roles and Rules perspective.

Appendix F: Sample LLC Operating Agreement Procedures, provides ideas and sample language for definitions and provisions for LLC operating agreements that define and reinforce a Roles and Rules approach.

Index

We have taught advisors, facilitators, and clients our approach, and have found that most of them quickly grasp Roles and Rules, see its explanatory power, and use it to improve the outcomes of their estate planning efforts. They even adopt our terminology. We often hear family members say, "Wait! You're playing your family role instead of your business role," and "What rules do we need if we're going to make this happen?" This is not only gratifying for us to hear; it also shows that people make our approach their own and use it to create their own tools and methods. That is as it should be with a model that is both fundamental and flexible.

As a model of human identity and interaction, Roles and Rules applies to a huge range of human situations, in and out of business. But because succession and estate planning deals with issues of family, business, work, money, law, legacy, and death, it has been a rich and fruitful ground for applying Roles and Rules. This book is the result of years of development of this model and its application to this field, and it will give you the guidelines, tools, and tactics that we use in our work in this challenging area. We trust that this book will help others who, for the good of the business *and* the family, want to meet those challenges.

Part One

Background, Setting, and Players

CHAPTER 1

Roles and Rules:
An Evolutionary Approach

At the center of *King Lear*, perhaps the greatest of Shakespeare's tragedies, stands a bad succession and estate plan. In act one, Lear, King of Britain, worn down by the burdens of monarchy and his eighty-plus years, calls his three daughters to him. They are, in birth order, Goneril, Regan, and Cordelia. He asks his daughters, in that order, to profess their love for him so he can divide his kingdom in proportion to their affection.

Despite the fact that she is married, Goneril declares her father to be the greatest love of her life. Not to be outdone, Regan, who is also married, declares the same only more so. King Lear, in turn, bestows one-third of his kingdom on each of them.

He then turns to young Cordelia, his "joy," and says, "What can you say to draw a third more opulent than your sisters? Speak."

Cordelia says, "Nothing, my lord."

"Nothing?"

"Nothing."

Lear warns her, "Nothing will come of nothing. Speak again."

Cordelia says, "I love your majesty according to my bond, no more nor less."

Lear gives her a chance to reconsider. "Mend your speech a little, lest it mar your fortunes."

Cordelia repeats that she loves him as is "right fit" but refuses to join her sisters' flattery fest. Under the circumstances, she sees a simple statement of her love as its truest expression and tells her father that she is merely speaking the truth.

Lear doesn't take this well. "The truth, then, be thy dower."

Against strong advice from the Earl of Kent, a witness to these proceedings, Lear disowns his youngest daughter on the spot. He gives the third of his kingdom that he had reserved for Cordelia to Goneril and Regan to share equally. He also invests his older daughters and their husbands with all the power, revenue, and privileges of government and retains the title of king in name only. Lear states that from then on he will keep one hundred knights as attendants and spend alternating months with Goneril and her family and with Regan and her family.

This being one of Shakespeare's tragedies—none of the comedies centers on an estate plan—things go badly for Lear. During the first of her father's monthly visits, Goneril comes to view his mere presence as a burden. Lear leaves for Regan's palace before the month is out. Goneril, however, gets to Regan first and tells her sister (in so many words) that their father is more trouble than he's worth, and Regan believes her.

By the end of act two, Lear realizes that he has made a mess of things, although he fails to see his immaturity and poor planning as the cause. He calls his older daughters "unnatural hags," swears he'll get revenge and charges into a stormy night to traipse around on a heath. There, in the play's most famous scene, Lear goes into a rage, challenging the elements, defying the wind, and commanding the waves to drown the earth. By the end of the play, Cordelia proves her love by trying to rescue Lear from Goneril and Regan. But, this being a tragedy, everyone winds up dead.

King Lear has endured for more that three hundred years because its themes of sibling rivalry, filial ingratitude, parental foolishness, lost wealth, and misunderstood love are timeless. These themes constantly surface in modern families, and often find their most dramatic expression when parents bequeath their assets to their children.

The Family Plot

As a matter of life and death, estate planning is an important, emotional, and sometimes painful event for most families. Attorneys try to make it neat and orderly by means of the law. When the law fails to make it neat and orderly, it is not a failure of the law or, necessarily, in its application. It is usually a failure on the part of the attorney, client, or family to recognize the limitations of the law.

The law is a set of rules, while a family is a set of roles. We human beings use rules to channel our behavior and interactions so that they are not driven by our emotions. Indeed, that is a major function of rules in society, as we all learn early in life. Rules against hitting in the sandbox tell children that they must "use their words" rather than physical force when they are angry. Parents teach children rules by expecting that they will behave fairly and talk things out rather than hit. Parents set the role expectation that children will learn to play by the rules. In some family businesses, however, parents have not taught their children to play by the rules. Instead, they have taught their children that they are above the rules, that the role of heir apparent or crown prince exempts them from the rules. Often the parents themselves fail to play by rules.

Rules, from the simple convention of standing in line at the movies to the complex system of our courts of appeal, require that we control our emotions and let accepted conventions and standards of behavior guide and govern our interactions. That's a key point: On the ballfield, at the movies, in the courts, in all areas of life, *rules guide and govern our interactions.*

We use roles, on the other hand, to form our identities. Well-known roles comprise a family: father, mother, son, daughter, brother, sister, grandfather, grandmother, uncle, aunt, cousin, step-child, step-parent, ex-spouse, grandchild, and so on. Not every role is filled in every family, but every family is composed of people playing roles.

Some family roles, such as father or mother, are chosen in that people decide to marry and have children. Other family roles, such as oldest sister or youngest brother, are assigned at birth. However, they are all roles, and people associate those roles with emotions. We love, hate, respect, or resent the other people in our role relationships. We often feel ambivalent toward people in our role relationships. The emotions associated with roles—a mother's pride in her child, a son's anger at his father, a brother's rivalry with his brother—generate family drama, in life as they do in books, films, and plays.

Which brings us back to King Lear. Audiences have been asking themselves for fifteen generations: What was he *thinking?*

Well, Lear wasn't thinking. He was feeling. He was feeling lonely, insecure, and unloved. We all want to be loved. We all like hearing that we are loved, and King Lear was no exception. So he called Goneril, Regan, and Cordelia to him and not only asked them to profess their love, but offered to buy it with shares of his estate. Cordelia recognized her father's request as absurd, and it is absurd because Lear is acting completely out of role. He is the King of Britain and their father. Both of those roles place him high above his daughters in rank in the social hierarchy of the time. In those roles he is supposed to love *them* and care for *them*, materially and emotionally. Yet he asks them to compete in expressions of their affection in exchange for shares of his kingdom. It's unseemly at best, and Cordelia knows it and wants no part of it.

Yet Cordelia accepts her father's decision without protest and in precise language. She says, "I love your majesty according to my bond, no more nor less." In this world of roles, she makes what we would call a rules statement. She will not play the role of daughter as dictated by her father and feigned by her sisters. Rather she loves her father as dictated by her tie and duty to him (tie and duty being the meaning of "bond" here). She will not play a false role and instead will speak only to the rule. Cordelia introduces rules to this roles-based situation, but no one around her can accept them. Given these roles running rampant without the benefit of rules, the family breaks up.

After disowning his youngest daughter and dividing his kingdom between the older two, what's the rest of Lear's plan? He renounces his office, retains one hundred knights, and says he'll spend alternating months at his two remaining daughters' homes. Lear should have gotten that last part in writing because both daughters chose not to house him as specified.

King Lear was, at this point in his life, not a wise ruler. Presumably he was sharper in his earlier years or he would not have a kingdom to divvy up in his eighties. However, he made a hash of his succession and estate plan. Instead of enjoying a carefree retirement in Tuscany, Spain, or the south of France, Lear wound up out in the wind and the rain on a heath somewhere in England.

How can the rest of us avoid a similar fate?

By understanding and addressing the Roles and Rules at work in succession and estate planning situations. Let's take Roles and Rules, one at a time.

Roles = Identity

In the Roles and Rules model, we define a role as a set of actions that one person performs more for another person than for oneself. A role is defined by the needs of the person for whom the role is played. Thus a husband plays the role of husband for his wife. A wife plays the role of wife for her husband. If a spouse dies, the survivor ceases to be a husband or wife because he or she no longer has anyone to play that role for. We also play our professional roles for one another: A manager plays the role of manager for her subordinates. A teacher plays the role of teacher for his students. A physician plays the role of physician for her patients.

All roles come in pairs. That stands to reason in that a role is a set of actions that one person performs more for another than for oneself. Thinking of roles as existing in pairs simplifies the Roles and Rules analysis of relationships. Although a manager may have many subordinates or a teacher many students, the relationship between the manager and a given subordinate or a teacher and a given student is still a dyad. (The psychological origin of roles in human consciousness goes back to the original mother-infant dyad. See Appendix A for in-depth background information on the Roles and Rules model itself.)

Every role is larger than the person playing it. Every role—spouse, parent, manager, teacher, and so on—has its own demands, which transcend the needs of the person playing the role. For instance, the roles of king and father are larger than Lear. As king, he is supposed to be strong, powerful, and secure. As father, he should see to his daughters' need to be loved, not worry about whether they love him. Perhaps when Lear puts forth his absurd proposal, Goneril and Regan lose all respect for him. Cordelia also sees the deep flaw in her father, but loves him too much to take advantage of it.

There is a selfless aspect to performing a role well. All good actors know this. They give up a bit of themselves in order to identify with their roles. In doing so, they create their characters. To play their roles in character for one another and for the audience, they respond to scripted situations the way their characters might, not the way they themselves might. Something similar occurs when we assume our various roles in life. When a couple takes on the role of parents, they realize (sometimes suddenly) that they cannot impulsively leave the house for a night on the town. They have to stay home and care for the infant. They sell the sports car and buy a minivan. They leave the city and move to a suburb with good schools. They give up some of their individual selves in order to play the role of parents for their child.

It is through our roles that we build our identity. We build our identities in the ways we play the roles that we are born into, such as male, female, Briton, Brazilian, oldest, youngest, grandparent, or widow. We also build our identities in the ways we play the roles that we assume, such as husband, wife, parent, doctor, teacher, ball player, or bond trader. We all play our roles differently, because each of us brings different intellectual and physical gifts to our roles. However we go about it, we invest ourselves in our roles and in doing so we each develop a unique identity. Most psychologically healthy adults learn to play their roles reasonably well and in doing so develop a reasonably strong identity and a reasonable amount of character. In contrast, people with "character" disorders cannot function in role well enough to do anything for anyone in a sustained way. They are too self-centered, out of touch with others' needs, or otherwise disordered to play roles properly.

Emotions generate roles because our identities are wrapped up in them. People often *identify* themselves with one group in opposition to others who are not in that group, and that identification generates an emotional connection. For example, when people identify themselves as fans of the New York Yankees or the Boston Red Sox, they identify with the team. The team's victories and losses become the fans' victories and losses. Red Sox fans (and baseball fans across America) hate the Yankees. But nobody gets emotional about the infield fly rule.

Speaking of emotion, most people derive happiness from playing a role for another person. Many people, including some of history's most profound thinkers, believe that true happiness can be found only in playing a role well for another person. The gratifications derive largely from altruism, from bringing happiness to another person, and from executing the role well almost for its own sake.

Parents have children, do for them, and see them into adulthood out of love for the children, long before they know whether it was "worth it" or not. Soldiers go into battle partly or wholly for altruistic reasons: self-sacrifice and love of country. They enter life-threatening situations to play the role of soldier for their leaders, fellow citizens, and one another.

If happiness comes from truly wanting to play a role that another person needs one to play, then misery comes from unfulfilled role expectations. If a husband or wife firmly expects certain things which his or her spouse cannot or will not deliver, they are both doomed to unhappiness. Many children, including many in family businesses, spend their lives trying to get a parent to play the role of the parent that they need, to their everlasting disappointment. Some parents become angry with children, even to the point of disowning them (as did Lear), for not playing the roles they expect them to play. All the world over, people clash over the ways in which they play their roles for one another.

Roles and Rank

As noted, a role is larger than any person who fills it. The role of father or mother is larger than any man or woman who happens to be one. The role of president is larger than Lincoln, FDR, Reagan, Clinton, or Bush. The role of king is larger than Lear, and the role of King Lear is larger than any actor who plays it. The needs of the role outrank the needs of the person filling it. Roles also outrank one another and always have hierarchical ranks associated with them. Within the role relationship, higher rank enables a person to impose his will on, or at least strongly influence, people in roles of lower rank. Parents outrank children. Presidents outrank senior vice presidents, who in turn outrank vice presidents. Managers outrank employees. In a matriarchal society, mother outranks father, while it's the reverse in a patriarchal society.

The way people handle their rank in a role is a force for good or ill in a family business as in other situations. In general, the more altruistically a person plays a role, the better he'll play that role for others. In fact, if you take on a role because of what you can get out of it, rather than what you can give to it, you stand little chance of playing the role well. Similarly, if you let the power of higher rank go to your head, you won't be able to play the role well.

In a business all managers, regardless of their level, must play the role of manager for their subordinates. They must give them the training, resources, and compensation that they need to do their jobs well. They must support, guide, praise, and correct their employees' performance and help them to improve. If all managers in a business did this, the result would be a kiss-down organization, which differs sharply from the far more common kiss-up organization. In a kiss-up organization, a manager expects his employees to support him and reinforce his sense of importance. Kiss-up companies are so common that the Yes Man and the Apple Polisher are familiar figures in corporate life. Other familiar figures include the tyrant, bully, and autocrat as well as the manager who will not correct an employee or make a decision.

People of higher rank must, for the good of the outfit and everyone in it, play their business roles for the people lower in the organization. Occasionally, you will hear of autocrats or tyrants who have built fabulously successful businesses. Very rarely will you hear that the businesses prospered after their tenure. They see little need to groom successors or build structures that will outlast themselves. Unconsciously or consciously, many hard-driving entrepreneurs do not want their businesses to survive and prosper without them. If the businesses did survive, it would prove that they were not indispensable after all.

So, a role is a series of actions undertaken for another person and roles are the means by which we build our identities. A role is larger than the person playing it—meaning, the demands of the role outrank the needs of the person playing it—and roles imply rank in a hierarchy. With that in mind, let's turn to rules.

Rules = Interaction

By definition a rule is a condition—a requirement or prohibition—that applies equally to everyone regardless of their role or rank. A rule operates in the same way among all parties *by explicit or implicit agreement*. All parties to a true rule agree to abide by the rule. Boxers agree to hit one another above the belt, and not below the belt. Baseball players agree to hit only the ball. A household rule about knocking on the bathroom door applies to Mom, Dad, and the children equally. In contrast, a "rule" that the children must be in bed by nine o'clock isn't a rule as we define the term, but rather a role expectation that the parents place on the children. We are not saying it's bad to have role expectations, only that they are expectations rather than rules because the children do not agree to them and the parents are not subject to them. That's why children say things like, "Mom, why do you get to go to bed whenever you want?"

Rules are the great equalizers in the natural order of things, as well as in human affairs. The rules of multiplication and division apply equally to all numbers, regardless of their size. There is no true rank among numbers, and no number is better or worse than another number. Similarly, in physics, a proton doesn't outrank a neutron. In astronomy, Jupiter doesn't outrank Saturn. They are all subject to the same laws of the physical universe.

Rules should work with similar evenhandedness in human affairs. As a society, we agree on the rules that we call laws. We also agree on the way the laws will be changed if we stop agreeing with them. For instance, under the democratic system of government in the United States, the laws apply—or are supposed to apply—to everyone equally, as the doctrine of equal protection under the law states. Of course human beings, being what they are (emotionally invested in their roles and obsessed with rank and status), often undermine the evenhanded functioning of the law. But that does not do away with the intent of the law or the nature of rules.

Rules facilitate participation in a system. For instance, people can participate in a game only when they know the rules of (interaction in) that game. What's the objective? Who are the players? Where are the boundaries? How do we keep score? What is a foul? What happens if you commit a foul? Who wins and who loses? Rules ensure fair interactions for everyone, regardless of their rank. A game in which one powerful person, such as the owner of the ball, makes up "rules" as he goes along is unfair and not worth playing. Real rules, like the rules of baseball, apply to everyone in the game and allow everyone to participate.

Money runs on rules because the value and behavior of money are the same no matter who holds it. Ten thousand dollars in an account paying five percent interest a year will pay $500 a year to whoever deposited it there. A corporate CEO and a file clerk each need $2 to ride the New York City subway (as of this writing). If a senator has two million dollars and a lottery winner has ten million, the lottery winner can buy more goods and services than the senator. Money does confer rank of a kind, and this can complicate family situations. But money doesn't change one's role, and role is what determines true rank. Often a star salesperson will earn more money than the sales manager. However, because of her rank in the organization, the sales manager can assign the salesperson to a new territory or reassign an account to a new salesperson. Money operates at the level of rules. Roles operate on a separate track.

Rules are not better than roles, nor are roles better than rules. People need both in order to create human, and humane, systems. Together, Roles and Rules add up to the structure of a system: the identities and the interactions in the system. No system, business, or nation can endure without a strong structure. For example, the U.S. Constitution defines executive, legislative, and judicial roles for people to play as well as rules for interactions among these three branches of government. This durable structure has enabled the United States to prosper amid waves of immigration, major wars (including civil war), poor leadership, and internal unrest. In contrast, dictatorships are inherently unstable because they rely mainly on the role of the leader. Dictators forbid people's participation in government because it would diminish their power. However, their disdain of rules dooms their government because they create no structure to pass on to later generations.

When such a situation develops in a family business, as it does in many, the business must move from operating on family roles to operating on business rules. The people in the business must also move from behavior derived from family-based roles to behavior in keeping with business-based *roles*. Dad must play the role of, say, chairman emeritus, not Dad. Sis must play the role of president, not Sis. The family business needs well-defined roles, such as director, manager, and bookkeeper, as well as rules, such as performance standards and compensation policies, if it is to have a sound structure.

Why Roles *and* Rules?

Roles and Rules describes human development at both the individual and collective levels. As individuals we are born into a world of roles. We start as infants and children ranking far below our mother and father. We perceive our lower rank, although at that time we have no idea what a rule is. Learning the rules is a gradual process that takes place at home, in school, on the playing field, and then later on the roads, in the legal system, and in academe, business, finance, and other fields of endeavor. As we grow into adulthood, we form identities in the context of our roles and interact with others in the context of rules. Development occurs when people learn to play by rules, for example, when a feudal society adopts democratic laws or when children learn the rules of fair play. Rules effect interaction between people. That interaction enables people to develop perceptions, skills, and knowledge beyond that which they can gain functioning only in their roles-based relationships.

Entire societies and organizations can undergo a similar process. For instance, Europe and Japan were once feudal societies ruled by overlords, which eventually made the transition to democracies ruled by laws. Kings and emperors rule by divine right while presidents and prime ministers are elected by the one-person, one-vote rule. Just as individuals and societies grow and develop by moving from roles to rules, so can a family business. Notice that roles are not abandoned in this process. Instead, rules modify interactions and mitigate the effect of certain roles. For instance, the monarchy in the United Kingdom still exists and people still play the roles of the royals, but they have no governing power. Similarly, in a family business the father-founder may become chairman emeritus, an honorific without real power, provided the father-founder can relinquish or accept modification of his father-founder role.

Regardless of the specifics, a family business develops into a "real" business when people move into business roles and adopt business rules. Those rules—management policies, practices, and procedures—modify the effect of family roles and professionalize the business. When that happens, people on the job operate in their business roles rather than their family roles. But, as with most developmental tasks, this is rarely easy.

Identifying Roles-Based Behavior

The tendency of family businesses to operate more on family roles than on business rules can generate certain negative behaviors. These behaviors may intensify as the task of estate planning and the transfer of assets and control looms. Therefore, families and estate planners should recognize family-role behaviors in business settings. Here are a baker's dozen of the most common of those behaviors, along with illustrative quotes:

1. Parental role expectations being placed on children, whether or not the parents and children work in the business. *("I don't want my son going into the business after what it's done to his father.")*
2. Family members, particularly parents and older siblings, pulling rank in the business. *("We'll do it my way because I'm your father and I started this business.")*
3. Lack of clearly defined functions, responsibilities, and job descriptions. *("Around here, we all just do whatever needs doing.")*
4. Lack of job performance standards and regular performance appraisals. *("Of course you're doing a good job. I'll tell you when you're not.")*
5. Lack of compensation policies; salaries doled out almost as allowances rather than compensation. *("I've always taken care of you, haven't I?")*
6. Tendencies to ignore or override the formal chain of command, if there is one. *("I don't care what Jerry told you to do. This shipment has to go out now!")*
7. Hidden agendas and secret lobbying rather than open discussion. *("Unless you stop him, Dad will borrow much more than we can pay back.")*
8. Resentments, disputes, and alliances carried from the family into the business. *("Your sister may have a degree in finance, but she still doesn't know what she's talking about.")*
9. Insular environments that fail to employ current best practices. *("Don't tell me how it's done. What we're doing has been working since 1972.")*
10. Second-class status or unfair treatment of non-family members. *("I'll never own a piece of this business no matter how much I contribute, because I'm not family.")*
11. Second-class status or exclusion of women or, in some industries, men in the family due to gender stereotypes—often with the tacit consent of those being stereotyped. *("I just vote my shares the way my brother tells me to. Men know more about that stuff.")*
12. Failure or refusal of a parent to play his business role, especially the role of leader. *("I can't fire Louis, even if he's on drugs. He's my brother's son!")*
13. Cultivation of a kiss-up company culture. *("I have to let her think she's right. She's the boss's daughter.")*

Role-based behaviors die hard. Rarely do people change engrained role-based behavior just because it's been pointed out to them. This goes double for people in positions of power. But pointing it out is a start. Moreover, the succession and estate plan presents a golden opportunity to write these harmful behaviors out of the business, and to develop rules that encourage people to play their business roles properly.

As we explain in detail in Chapter 2, an intergenerational transfer of wealth represents a Rules Crisis—a need to establish rules that modify family roles and that introduce or reinforce business roles. We will explain the Rules Crisis in more detail, but basically it occurs when people are unprepared to move into business roles and follow business rules. Such people don't understand business roles and rules. They also usually fear the loss of their family roles-based power or perquisites, and thus want to hang onto their family roles.

For instance, four brothers who were close in age owned a multimillion dollar marina, which they operated mainly on the basis of their family roles. Sales, storage, repairs, and other work occurred on well-established schedules and the accounting system had been formalized. However, decisions regarding suppliers, purchases, pricing, hiring, firing, and expansion were made informally by the brothers. This system worked for more than twenty-five years. Then, as their children came of age, flaws became apparent. The brothers had not given the next generation specific responsibilities, performance standards and appraisals, or management training. Salaries were decided on the age, rather than the contribution, of the children, who were taking three-hour lunches and hadn't earned the respect of the staff. They wanted more responsibility, but they weren't ready for it. Each child would lobby his or her father, which sowed discord among the brothers, each of whom protected his own children.

This was a case where the family—initially, the four brothers and their spouses—listened politely to our presentation on wills, trusts, taxes, and liquidity management, then came alive when we talked about the Rules Crisis and the need to move from Roles to Rules. By this time, friction among the brothers, their children, and the staff had intensified, but they didn't know why. They thanked us warmly for explaining what was going on and how to fix it.

Fixing the business meant defining a true structure. Instead of managing as a loose team, the brothers defined the roles of CEO, chief of operations, and chief of administration. The latter two each had their own staff, with the children assigned to specific positions. With the help of a facilitator (whom you will meet in Chapter 4), the brothers developed a strategic plan for the first time, as well as job descriptions, performance standards, appraisal policies, and a formal compensation plan. They also openly discussed their children's strengths and weaknesses for the first time and adopted mentoring roles for the next generation.

None of this happened overnight. We'll come back to this case occasionally, but it's worth noting now that the brothers had to see someone—the facilitator—playing the role of leader and mentor *for them* before they could become leaders and mentors themselves. After the new structure was defined, they needed someone to act as leader, mentor, and "rules enforcer" to guide them through the transition. (Even when you have rules, you need someone to play the role of enforcer or umpire; that's why we have judges in courtrooms and referees on football fields.) The four brothers made the transition, and today they run the marina as a "real business." Each brother sees a clear, orderly path to retirement, and their children are learning competence and cooperation, earning the respect of the staff, and developing their own ideas and plans for the future of the business.

The Evolution of a Business

For a family business to evolve in this way, the senior generation must allow the next generation to form its own vision of the business—that is, their own version of the Roles and Rules that constitute the structure—and let them work to achieve that vision. This doesn't mean that the next generation jettisons the existing structure and casts aside the senior generation. It means that the senior generation leaves the field so the new players can play the game their way. It means that the senior generation adopts mentoring roles, or perhaps umpire roles, while allowing the next generation to assume leadership roles, as the brothers with the marina did. It also means leaving the next generation a structure to build on, in the form of Roles and Rules, and not just a collection of assets and employees. Moving from roles to rules and integrating Roles and Rules into a new structure facilitates the evolution of a family business into a real business.

Most business and consulting initiatives fail to consider the identities and interactions that constitute the organization. Most try to change *either* the system's roles (most "therapeutic" consulting) *or* its rules (most legal, financial, and management consulting—and estate planning). Roles and Rules deals with both the identities *and* the interactions in a system.

As you will see, Roles and Rules provides a theme, framework, or template for succession and estate planning, rather than a recipe or formula. Wills, trusts, partnerships, gifts, bequests, insurance, and taxes still hold the central place in the estate plan. But they can be used more effectively within the framework of Roles and Rules. Similarly, other methods, such as Myers Briggs Type Indicators and various models of communication, work better with Roles and Rules as an underlying theme. In that sense, other tools and methods can be downloaded to the Roles and Rules "operating system" and work better. Also, we've found that attorneys and estate planners who grasp Roles and Rules soon develop a new understanding of the difficult cases they have seen in the past. They also see ways to modify their approach to generate better outcomes in the future.

We've pointed out that movement from roles to rules represents a developmental task for a family business. While it's possible for this transition to occur gradually over time, the need for it generally arises with the need to craft a succession and estate plan. This gives rise to the above-mentioned Rules Crisis, the subject of Chapter 2.

Bear in Mind

- A role is a set of actions taken on behalf of someone else. A role is larger than any person who plays the role, and roles determine rank in a hierarchy. People use roles to define and build their identities.
- Rules are conditions that, by explicit or implicit agreement, apply to everyone in a situation equally regardless of their rank. People use rules to guide and govern their interactions.
- Money operates by rules. Its value and other attributes are the same regardless of who owns it.
- Roles *and* Rules make a world. Both are always at work in our lives and relationships. Neither is better than the other, and you have to examine both the roles and the rules in a situation or organization to truly understand it.
- In most family businesses, family roles drive decisions and behaviors of key people. For the business to evolve, people must move from behavior based on family roles to behavior based on business rules. However, roles don't go away. Instead, people develop new, stronger, business-based roles in the organization.
- Every structure is composed of Roles and Rules. The senior generation must pass on a sound structure in which Roles and Rules are well-defined, understood, and accepted. Otherwise, they are passing on a bunch of assets rather than a business.

CHAPTER 2

The Rules Crisis:
Understanding the Real Challenge in
Succession and Estate Planning

Now, with Roles and Rules in mind, we turn to the central challenge in succession and estate planning for families with businesses or other significant assets—the Rules Crisis. If you accept that individuals and societies develop by moving from behavior based on roles to behavior based on roles *and* rules, it's a small step to see that a family business develops the same way. Just as a society goes from feudalism to democracy, a person goes from roles-based behavior, as an infant, to more rules-based behavior as an adult, while moving into adult roles. A family business also develops by moving from behavior based more on family roles to management based on business rules. Family members move into business roles and largely leave family-roles-based behavior out of the business.

In this way Roles and Rules amounts to a universal human narrative. Every society and every person has a story, and so does every family business. Our lives start in infancy in the basic, universal, roles-based hierarchy of mother and child, and they end in death—the basic, universal, and inescapable rule. As you will see in Chapter 5, the narrative of a family business starts as a story of roles. It starts as a story of the founders and the sacrifices they made, working round the clock, with everyone betting their futures on the business, feeling the energy and excitement that comes with creating something new.

Then gradually or suddenly, rules enter the business. The family way of working no longer seems effective, signaling the need for more organization. Finances become so complex that the business needs a controller and financial reports, along with rules for salaries, raises, benefits, profit sharing, and ownership. The outfit grows to where it must conform to certain laws that govern businesses of a certain size. It may evolve from a sole proprietorship to a partnership, limited liability company (LLC), or corporation. The more any human organization grows and evolves, the more it is subject to—and requires—rules to ensure the fairness and order that people need in order to function well amid complexity.

Despite whatever rules a family business adopts, family roles die hard when they die at all. Many founders adopt only the rules required for the business to operate on a sound legal and financial footing. After all, they cannot ignore laws, regulations, and tax codes. But they're often slow to adopt standard management policies, practices, and procedures and even slower to observe them. They often eschew written job descriptions, performance standards, and compensation guidelines. Many ignore managerial basics, such as planning, delegation, and the chain of command, in favor of seat-of-the-pants methods. In other words, most founders like to preserve their roles-based control, and they do that by not adopting true rules. (Remember, true rules apply to everyone.)

As a result, most family businesses operate on a tribal level. That's no secret. Academic literature and popular books on family business widely acknowledge that family roles carry over into the business. As we've noted, that's not a wholly bad thing. However, when the senior generation retires from a business that has been running on family roles, things are bound to get complicated.

The Rules Behind the Rules Crisis

What we call the Rules Crisis occurs when rules—tax laws and laws of probate, wills, and trusts—assert themselves in the family business with irresistible force. That force emanates from three sources: First, tax and probate laws are (1) seriously enforced and have serious financial consequences. Second, when the senior generation retires or dies, the roles they were playing disappear. That (2) disrupts the established order and can create chaos. Third, the ultimate rule is (3) that everyone dies, which means that the Rules Crisis is inevitable. The founder, no matter how benevolent or malevolent, skilled or incompetent, will not be around to play his or her role any more, nor, eventually, will other members of the senior generation.

The following point, noted in the Introduction to this book, warrants repeating: The rules in wills, trust agreements, and other legal documents are not sufficient to preclude the Rules Crisis or to neutralize its effects on the family and the business. Indeed, some of those rules—probate, tax laws, and so on—are the very rules that foment the crisis.

Allow us to explain.

The Rule of Law

Throughout the narrative of the family business, the founder has been playing a role largely unfettered by rules. Numerous surveys have shown that many people go into business for themselves to be their own boss, an oxymoron that describes a hierarchy of one, which is impossible. Submission to rules is antithetical to the entrepreneurial personality, which is creative and charismatic—qualities associated with roles. Hence, the prevalence of seat-of-the-pants, roles-based management in family businesses.

In the absence of rules, roles will prevail. This is true in all situations. Human beings fall back on roles (a Freudian might say, "regress to roles") when there are no rules to guide behavior. For instance, when the schoolyard bully resists a rule in a game, his ultimate position is, "Make me!" He asserts his role as the physically larger or more violent party, and in that role insists on his way rather than submit to the rules.

Fans of western movies might recall that in *The Man Who Shot Liberty Valance*, Ransom Stoddard, the eastern-schooled attorney played by Jimmy Stewart, arrives by stagecoach in a lawless territory. During a holdup, he tries to explain the law to the eponymous outlaw played with scenery-chewing relish by Lee Marvin. Valence repeatedly whips Stoddard with a riding crop while saying, "I'll teach you law: Western law!" By the end of the movie, Ranse has been elected Senator Stoddard and, thanks to Tom Doniphon (John Wayne), Liberty is dead. On the larger canvas of this terrific John Ford film, the rule of law prevails and the territory becomes a state, with Stoddard its representative in Washington. Indeed, the movie points out that Wild West territories became states only by adopting the rule of law; otherwise, they were viewed as barbaric by those back East and unfit for statehood.

Although few family businesses are headed by Liberty Valences, some are headed by men and women with a similar view of rules. Yet they know that when they are dead, all that's left will be the rules in the succession and estate plan. That's the source of the Rules Crisis. The irresistible force of legal and business rules meets the immovable object of family roles. The results can range from detrimental to devastating *unless* the testator, family, and business are prepared for the crisis. Practitioners and families who use our approach can prepare for it, and learn to view it and use it as the developmental task that it can be, and should be, in the evolution of the family business.

Face the Crisis, and Evolve

In prehistoric times, as the oceans got warmer and trees grew taller, certain species faced and dealt with the resulting developmental crises. That's why we now have amphibians and giraffes. Other species couldn't deal with developmental crises, which is why they are found only in science museums.

The movement of a family business from family roles to business rules holds several implications:

- Family members cannot and do not abandon their family roles. Instead, those who own, work in, or benefit from the family business must eliminate or at least minimize *behavior* based on family roles.
- Business rules—management policies, practices, and procedures as well as legal rules—make a business a true business and empower people to run the business as such.
- Business rules define business roles, such as president, controller, vice president of marketing, operations manager, and so on. These positions are, or at least can be, defined in terms of their function and scope, just as the rules of baseball define the positions on the playing field.
- Business rules foment a crisis for the family because roles and rules are not naturally compatible; they are at right angles to one another. This is particularly true of family roles. For instance, when a middle-aged father and his eighteen-year-old son play one-on-one basketball, there are family roles and basketball rules at work. As a result, there's more going on in that game than there would be in one between two middle-aged men or two teenagers.

Like every crisis, the Rules Crisis poses danger and opportunity. It's an inflection point that pushes people to evolve. You cannot simply slot the successors into positions on an organization chart, give them management guidelines, and tell them to do their jobs. As in that father-and-son basketball game, there is more going on. There's a real need for growth and development. Even without family roles as a factor, legions of people have failed in business because a superior said, "Okay, you're the manager," or "Congratulations, you're the new national accounts rep," and left it at that. People need training, coaching, mentoring, and modeling of the roles they are expected to play.

A business comprises more than assets and accounts, and employees and customers. The actual business consists of its structure, and in a family business that structure has been determined largely by family roles. Those roles cannot be passed on. They are bound up in identities, and identities cannot be replicated because we all bring our own gifts and shortcomings to every role we play and thus to our identities. Therefore, the Rules Crisis calls for the senior generation and successors to reconceptualize the Roles and Rules that constitute the structure of the business, so the successors can take the business into the future.

The Rules Crisis comes uninvited, yet it can be anticipated, mitigated, and used to good advantage. We believe there is no better tool for doing this than a knowledge of Roles and Rules and how they work in a family business. We also believe that the alternative is tension, chaos, and perhaps financial loss and emotional turmoil for the family.

The Linchpin Question

We'll look more closely at the developmental tasks posed by the Rules Crisis in a moment. First, however, we want to pose the key question on which the entire succession and estate plan hangs:

Does the testator want to sell the business or keep it in the family?

We are not recommending that anyone ask—let alone try to answer—this question without background on the situation. (Of course, a firm decision to sell the business may have already been made, in which case the question does not apply.) The importance of the question is this: If the testator decides to sell the business, there is much less need for Roles and Rules because family members' roles in the business usually become moot. The family will require rules regarding valuation, distribution of the proceeds of the sale, and who has the power to accept a price and terms, if the testator lacks sole discretion. Potentially serious tax consequences must also be addressed. Moreover, if wealth and assets are to be shared among beneficiaries, Roles and Rules must be applied to family governance issues, which can be thorny but which differ from those of business succession.

Thus, before making the keep-or-sell decision, the testator and family must assess the Roles and Rules at work in the family and the business. That assessment, along with tax and financial considerations, should drive the decision. Most testators and families make the keep-or-sell decision either implicitly or financially. Instead, they should explicitly consider the finances *and* the family's willingness and ability to address the Rules Crisis and manage the business going forward. For instance, implicitly, the testator may assume that Junior will assume the leadership role; financially, the family may want to retain their source of income. But if the testator or family decides to keep the business when it should have been sold, financial ruin, rather than security, may result.

We'll examine ways of making this decision in detail in Chapter 8. For now, the key point is that once the testator decides to sell the business, you need only rules in the form of a sound will and trust agreements, because you are passing on money and securities. Money can be professionally managed by a trust officer or portfolio manager in keeping with the fiduciary rules. The fiduciary rules govern the conduct of people, banks, companies, and other entities that hold assets in trust for a beneficiary. Laws regarding what a fiduciary can do with beneficiaries' assets vary by state. However, in general a fiduciary cannot take funds for his own use, must invest to achieve a reliable return on assets, and must place beneficiaries' interests first. Every state maintains a legal list of securities in which fiduciaries may invest or specifies that fiduciaries must apply the prudent man rule to investments.[3]

In any event, if the testator decides to keep the business in the family, a Rules Crisis looms. This crisis has various facets, all of which should be considered before making the keep-or-sell decision.

Facets of the Crisis

The Rules Crisis manifests itself mainly in various forms of conflict. One major benefit of Roles and Rules is that it enables advisors and families to see beyond "personalities" to the root causes of the conflicts. Essentially, these are conflicts between roles-oriented viewpoints and behavior, on the one hand, and, on the other, rules-oriented viewpoints and behavior. The chief areas of conflict are:

- Conflict between and within the generations
- Conflict within the business
- Conflict between the business and the trust

These conflicts are every bit as important as financial considerations in the keep-or-sell decision. We are not saying that if these conflicts or the potential for them exists, the family should sell the business. We are saying that the family will have to anticipate and address the Rules Crisis underlying these conflicts.

Conflict between and within Generations

As you will see in a number of cases that we'll cite in this book and in the major case we present in Chapters 5 and 6, the Rules Crisis can ignite both intergenerational conflict and conflict within each generation. Intergenerational

---

[3] The "prudent man rule" states that a fiduciary or trustee can make only investments that an intelligent man or woman exercising discretion and prudence would make. This is open to interpretation but certainly prohibits speculative investments. In contrast, the "business judgment rule," which applies to business executives and corporate directors, calls for a person to act in good faith and with reasonable care. That represents a lower threshold of responsibility than the prudent man rule.

conflict and factions within families are hardly new, but Roles and Rules provides a new way to understand them. For example, we usually show the pie chart and checklist in Figure 2-1 to family members in early meetings and ask them to rate the importance of the issues on the chart. While our results are anecdotal, we have consistently found that the testator and the senior generation place relatively high priority on rules issues, such as taxes, liquidity, and asset protection. In contrast, the next generation places relatively high priority on roles issues, such as maintaining family harmony and avoiding conflicts.

Figure 2-1

Estate Planning: Issues of Importance

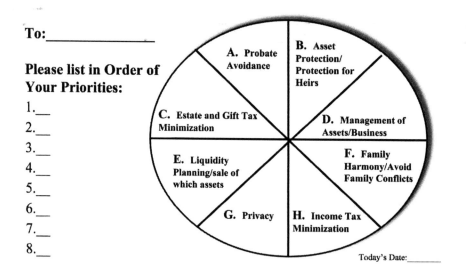

Why would generational priorities tend to fall along these lines?

The older generation tends to focus on rules because they know that after their deaths they will not be around to play their roles any longer. Rules are all they will leave behind. Some testators try to design rules to somehow compensate for their failure to play their parental roles well for their children. They also focus on rules for the practical purpose of transferring wealth with minimal taxation. Meanwhile, the next generation often wants to be taken care of; they want the older generation to continue to play their roles for them. Members of the next generation are often trying to get their parents to play the roles of parents that they've long wanted them to play, but haven't been able to get them to play. Their desire to preserve the current family roles, whatever they are, reflects their fear of change. Whatever the current situation, it is at least a known quantity. Yet a crisis always demands change, with failure, inertia, or chaos as the alternatives to successful resolution of the crisis.

We have repeatedly seen conflicts break out along clear fault lines demarcating two camps—roles-oriented family members, and rules-oriented family members. You can readily identify them. Roles-oriented family members express a desire to be taken care of and oppose most efforts to professionalize the business. They resist business rules because those rules threaten their status in the business and their roles-based power. They resist the objective accountability that characterizes a real business, especially if their competence is open to question. For instance, if the founder's son manages people poorly, he will resist a policy of conducting periodic 360-degree evaluations, in which superiors, subordinates, and colleagues evaluate a manager. Why should he subject himself to such an evaluation when he's the founder's son?

In contrast, rules-oriented family members want to professionalize the business and will base their arguments on growth potential, increased revenue and earnings, improved competitiveness, and the like. They want written policies and procedures, explicit reporting structures and duties, and transparent ways of assessing and rewarding performance. They usually oppose efforts to include family members in the business unless they possess the requisite expertise and competence. Indeed, they often don't understand why such family members would think they deserve, or even want, a part in the business.

Roles people and rules people speak two different languages from two separate viewpoints. Roles and Rules enables everyone to stop examining these situations through the telescope of roles or the telescope of rules and instead view the entire picture through binoculars. Moreover, because Roles and Rules is objective and non-judgmental, it recognizes the legitimacy of everyone's needs. It's natural for some people to want to be taken care of, especially if someone has been taking care of them all their lives. Such people have rarely been required to play by rules. It's also natural for people with business skills to try to limit the involvement of those who lack them. Understanding, let alone resolving, these issues isn't easy, but there's no substitute for doing so.

Conflict within the Business

The Rules Crisis can also foment conflict in the business, for most of the reasons cited above. In addition, however, there may be non-family members in the mix. For instance, when non-family members see the boss's son keep his job despite his incompetence, they may undermine the business in large and small ways. High performers will move on to companies that reward people for their performance rather than for their roles in the family. Others may turn in sub-par performance or build up resentment that comes out in destructive ways. Similarly, conflict often arises between a professional advisor, such as a consultant, who operates on rules, and a founder or a family member who operates on roles.

The more a family member sees himself as exempt from rules, the greater the potential for conflict when rules assert themselves, as they do in a Rules Crisis. Although they don't realize it, parents almost never help their children when they shield them from the world of rules.

Another source of conflict within the business is disparity between its official structure and its actual structure. For instance, the official structure may call for the controller to sign off on all purchases above a certain amount; however, that might not be happening for any number of reasons. Similarly, certain jobs may require certain qualifications, which might be routinely ignored. Disparities between the formal and informal structure indicate areas potentially requiring attention if the business is to be managed as a business. We'll examine the issue of structure in detail in Chapter 3.

In situations of conflict within the family or within the business, you can identify people's viewpoints by listening to what they say. The following statements are typical of roles-oriented people:

Typical Roles Statements

- All you care about is money.
- What will Cousin Charlie *do* if he's not in the business?
- Dad (or Mom) would have wanted it like this.
- So-and-So *deserves* a role in the business.
- I don't care about policies and procedures.
- We should ask ourselves what Dad (or Mom) would do. (or: Dad always said . . .)
- The important thing is that everything continues the way it's been.
- This isn't a democracy.
- Because I said so.

The following statements are typical of rules-oriented people:

Typical Rules Statements

- We will be able to increase revenue and income if we do the following.
- We have to run this organization like a business.
- We need written guidelines, policies, and procedures.
- So-and-So may be a family member, but that doesn't qualify him for a role in the business. (or: What are So-and-So's qualifications?)

- Here's what the trust agreement says.
- Here's what the numbers show.
- Accepted managerial practice would call for the following.
- We have to be able to change and be flexible.
- Because that's what the agreement (or policy or procedure) says.
- What are the legal and regulatory ramifications?

One of the reasons that these conflicts can become intractable is that roles people and rules people have difficulty understanding one another's viewpoints. Roles people may sacrifice revenue or earnings to give a family member a place in the business; after all, we're a family. Rules people will tend to fire a family member to fill a position with someone who will generate or save more money; after all, it's a business. Dealing with such issues is the stuff of Roles and Rules.

Conflict between the Business and the Trust

This third area of conflict truly complicates the situation because there are inherent conflicts of interest between a business and a trust. For example, testators and advisors will sometimes try to design a trust to ensure that the business stays in the family and be managed in certain ways. Such agreements assume, incorrectly, that the trustee, armed with the trust agreement, can play the role of alter ego of the testator for the beneficiaries and the business. However, this puts the beneficiaries and the business at loggerheads.

The conflict between the trust and the business stems from the nature of a trust and the fiduciary rules. A trust is set up for the beneficiaries, not for the business. The trustee therefore must place the needs of the beneficiaries above those of the business. The fiduciary rules—the rules governing the behavior of trustees—call for the trustee to invest the assets of the trust so that they earn a reasonable return. The prudent man rule implies that funds be invested in a diversified portfolio rather than a single business. Even if the trust were written to hold only the business, if that business were to hit a few unprofitable quarters, what is the trustee supposed to do? Generally, she's supposed to see to the financial security of the beneficiaries. Under the circumstances, selling part of the business or pulling money out of it may be the prudent course of action. That might not, however, be in the best interests of the business.

At first blush, the solution might appear to be to structure the trust such that a) its sole or chief asset is the business and, b) the trustee or the beneficiaries (or both) have decision-making power in the business. This does in fact offer a potential solution, but one fraught with difficulty. That's because the fiduciary rules and the nature of a trust tend *not* to favor keeping a business in the trust if the purpose is to provide for the beneficiaries' financial security, unless they work in the business.

The fiduciary rules and trust law basically call for diversification of the assets in the trust. In most states, you cannot have concentrated assets in a trust without putting the trustee at risk for being sued for losses. So if the family business represents a major portion—say 30 percent or more of the assets in the trust—even if the trustee is directed in the trust instrument to keep the business in the trust, the trustee is not necessarily protected in many states. A number of courts have either ordered trustees to diversify the assets in a trust or held them liable for not diversifying assets in a trust. Indeed, in some cases testators have explicitly directed that the trustee *not* sell a certain asset, such as stock in a particular company; then, after the value of the stock fell precipitously, the beneficiaries successfully sued the trustee.

On the other hand, if the beneficiaries and heirs work in the business, then they are not simply beneficiaries and heirs but also successors. That means that they must address the Rules Crisis, assume their business roles, and observe business rules, while balancing the needs and interests of the family and of the business going forward.

Problems of Professional Trustees

Even professional trustees at financial institutions face problems due to the conflicting nature of their roles as trustees and the rules governing trusts. Here we look at the advisor's side of the situation to get a sense of the problems they face, and use Roles and Rules to understand their point of view. In many, if not most, cases the client has little or no knowledge of the issues described here. In some cases, even after the initial discussion between client and advisor, the client fails to hear the advisor's advice or cautions. Often the client simply has obtained a boilerplate set of documents which, as you will see, can create difficulties for the trustees who manage the situation after the testator's death.

The following discussion occurred with trustees who manage trusts they have been assigned upon the death of a testator. Usually the surviving beneficiaries, spouse, and children need income from the trust, and problems may arise around this fact. At times the children are in conflict over how much money is spent on their surviving parent and how much will be left for them. At times the surviving spouse needs a compassionate trustee who can do more than send money because they have little experience in financial management or even in bill-paying. They turn to their trustee to do what their spouses did in the past. In the conversation reported below, the trustees have been discussing how difficult this can be in that they feel they need to be good "social workers" yet must abide by the law and the trust documents.

Michael, a senior trustee with many elderly clients, describes what happens once the testator dies and he becomes the trustee, using the example of a testator,

Mr. Smith, who was a partner with Mr. Brown, in a successful small company. Mr. Smith died unexpectedly at a rather early age and left his partner lacking a good friend and valuable business asset, particularly because he had played Mr. Outside to Mr. Brown's Mr. Inside. Instead of this very competent partner, Mr. Brown now faces his former partner's spouse, Mrs. Smith, who as a result of the trust documents owns half of the business, although she possesses no management skills. Indeed, instead of contributing the skills and making the sacrifices her husband made as co-owner, Mrs. Smith requires an income that will drain funds from the business.

Michael explains: "In the case of Mr. Smith and Mr. Brown, there would ideally be some provision in the trust agreement to pay the salary of the decedent's replacement. For the good of the business someone must perform the decedent's function. As Mr. Outside, he excelled in finding new customers and selling the company's services. Using funds to hire this person would represent a case of the trust supporting the business. Yet we also face the potential need to withdraw assets from the business to protect Mrs. Smith's finances by diversifying her investments in the stock market.

"What corporate trustee would keep the investment in the business? We have an obligation to act in the best interests of the beneficiary—if necessary at the expense of the business her husband and his partner spent their lives building. Mrs. Smith's needs come first because the [fiduciary] rules require that we maximize her security and minimize her risk. If we look at the business in the context of her risks and needs, we would *have to* diversify her assets. That may well mean withdrawing support from the business and investing her funds in a diversified portfolio of securities. We knew these folks for many years and we know their business, but we walk a thin line if we try to help the business, when the rules require us to act in the best interests of the beneficiary. If we leave all of her assets in the business and it fails, she will be out of luck."

Michael goes on to say: "How can a trust document be drawn up to protect the business? If it is not drawn up to do so very specifically, then the effect is often detrimental to the business."

Nick, his associate, carries the discussion forward: "The question, in Roles and Rules terms is, How do you draft a role? That's the problem. You are introducing divided loyalties to the trust agreement itself if the trustee has an obligation to beneficiaries and to the business. It can place a trustee in the position of protecting an asset of the trust which no longer serves the purposes of the trust. If we try to play a role for the business, then the trust is serving the purposes of the entity, which is not what the trust has been legally created to do."

Nick goes on to ask, "How do you draft those roles that we may feel we need to play for the beneficiary and for the business as well? The client should state in his trust document that he intends that the trust will continue to hold the business interests, whether it is a partnership, LLC, or another entity. The testator had better make it clear because the bias in the trust business is to not hold something that is not publicly traded. There is a bias against holding a privately held interest in a business."

The Roles and Rules View

Here Roles and Rules are well represented as antagonistic because a trustee wants to play a role, but the trust is a set of rules (governed by the fiduciary rules). *A trust cannot play a role.* A trust runs on rules and the trustee must follow the fiduciary rules and common law, as well as the provisions in the trust documents. That is why the provisions in the documents are so important. That is why the provisions should, to the extent possible, integrate both dimensions—Roles and Rules—so that the trustee, as a human being, has legal permission to play a role *within the boundaries of the legal rules.*

Unfortunately, the rules in this area are not entirely clear or consistent. That is partly because estate law is in some respects inconsistent from state to state. In some states, such as Delaware, the courts tend to follow the language of the trust very closely because it represents the intent of the deceased. Others, however, tend to seek equity for the beneficiaries under the fiduciary rules and will in some cases even override the clearly expressed wishes of the testator in the trust documents in order to achieve that equity.

As noted earlier, in actual cases brought by trust beneficiaries, trustees have been held accountable for loses incurred when they continued to hold in the trust a stock that decreased in value, even though the trust provisions stated that the stock should not be sold. Those courts have held that the trustee should have exercised his judgment under the fiduciary rules and sold the stock for the benefit of the beneficiaries. Other courts in other states, however, have held that the trustee cannot be held liable for following the intent of the testator as expressed in the trust agreement, even in cases like these. But again, there are no real guarantees except that, in terms of Roles and Rules, a trust cannot play a role.

Everyone Needs an Education

In our approach it's essential that the advisor bring no preconceived notions, let alone solutions, to the Rules Crisis. All decisions, from the keep-or-sell question to the choice of successors and business structures, rest with the testator and the family. The advisor or facilitator truly works with them to develop the plan that best suits them, whether that is to keep the business or sell it, or to pass it on to family members or hire professional managers. A key theme thus becomes educating the testator and family about ways to plan for retirement and death in light of their personalities, skills, and relationships, the needs of the business, and the need to minimize taxes, provide liquidity, and protect assets. This educational process can be difficult, given the personalities of some testators and families, but it's essential. In fact, the more driven and opinionated the testator and the less prepared the potential successors, the lower the chances of a successful plan. So, they should know what they are getting themselves into.

How do you go about broaching these topics?

We use four basic tools and tactics, which are to:

- Discuss statistics, stories, and priorities
- Explain the Rules Crisis
- Explore the testator's intentions
- Assess the business structure

We cover these tools and tactics in the following sections. Note that while these sections address advisors, they apply equally to testators and family members.

1. Discussion of Statistics, Stories, and Priorities

One of the first things we do in cases involving a family business, farm, ranch, or real estate holdings and poor family dynamics is to establish the right atmosphere, focus, and sense of urgency. Few testators and families (or attorneys) realize that estate planning in such situations goes beyond legal and financial issues. Therefore, we quote statistics like the ones presented in the Introduction to this book, including the finding that problematic relationships among family members is the key factor in 60 percent of faulty successions, and unprepared heirs are the key factor in another 25 percent.

The attorney on our team will point out that when an estate plan fails to convey the assets smoothly or results in a lawsuit, it's not because he doesn't know the law. It's because the family didn't understand the dynamics in their relationships and the potential effects on the business. He mentions that this is not therapy, but that any testator must consider both the family and the family business. He then discusses a few cases in which estate plans have gone horribly awry and notes that court records are full of such cases.

We describe a few other "horror stories" while pointing out that the testators and family members in these situations are not bad people. They simply misunderstood how family relationships affect a business and how things change once the senior generation is gone. If this sounds as if we are, in a way, trying to scare the testator and family, that's because, in a way, we are. We have learned that unless we make families aware of the seriousness of these problems and prompt them to consider whether they have them, they won't take family dynamics seriously. They might not even adequately consider the keep-or-sell decision. These aren't scare tactics but rather facts with scary implications. Lack of awareness of these facts is even scarier.

2. *Explanation of the Rules Crisis*

How deeply we explain the Rules Crisis and Roles and Rules depends on the testator and family and their situation, sophistication, and openness. We've found that some families resist almost any discussion that ventures beyond taxes and finances. Yet we've also seen a lot of genuine interest in family issues. Even when people don't relish dealing with them, they will at least listen when they think that their issues could create financial or emotional pain for them or their heirs.

As you will see in the section immediately below and in subsequent chapters, you can discuss these matters without ever mentioning Roles and Rules. Instead, you talk about creating a business that will run like a business, helping the next generation to assume their business roles, and positioning the business to grow and evolve. These things don't happen by themselves. It takes real work to create a business that runs without the senior generation and with successors using true management practices. If both generations are not prepared to see themselves and the business through this developmental crisis, then it may be best to sell it.

What about creating a sense of urgency? Clients and families must realize that preparing for the Rules Crisis takes time. It takes years or decades to build a successful business. Thus it is only logical that it may take a few years to see it through its next stage of development. To create a sense of urgency, we sometimes recount the following anecdote, which John F. Kennedy used to tell:

> The great French administrator Marshal Louis-Hubert Lyautey once asked the gardener at his estate to plant a tree. The gardener objected, pointing out that that type of tree grew very slowly and would take one hundred years to reach maturity. Lyautey told him, "In that case, there's no time to lose. You'd better plant it this afternoon."

We all know that it's easy to postpone things, especially things having to do with one's demise (which most of us also want to postpone). That's one reason that succession and estate planning presents a great opportunity for a family business; it forces people to deal with potentially unpleasant facts. Better they should do so when they can plan and decide without the added burden of grief and perhaps even more disruptive emotions.

3. Exploration of the Testator's Intentions

An exploration of the testator's intentions must go beyond minimizing taxes and establishing financial security. Yet we're not suggesting an excavation of the testator's psyche. We are suggesting a talk with the founder about the business, about the next generation, and about what he wants for both the business and heirs. You ask what the business means to him, how he views it, and what he wants to do with it. You discuss the interests and qualifications of the next generation. Then you assess his responses and the discussion of interests and qualifications in terms of Roles and Rules.

This entire discussion has to be conducted in objective, non-threatening language. Roles and Rules facilitates this because it recognizes the legitimacy of all points of view. For example, we don't think or talk in terms of the testator "building a monument to his ego," or of a child "not giving a damn about the business." Rather we recognize that the business has a certain meaning to the testator and to the child. The testator may want to lend meaning to the child's life, given that the business meant so much to him. To the child the business may mean very little because she has seen it only as "Dad's job." Her gifts, skills, and interests may lie in other areas. That doesn't mean she doesn't care about her father or the business. The rule is that she gets to choose her own line of work in life. If her father cannot play the role of father without placing role expectations on her and she cannot play the role of daughter the way her father wants her to, then perhaps like Cordelia in Macbeth she should tell her father. That way, he can make an informed keep-or-sell decision and if necessary choose another successor so she can get on with her life.

The language of Roles and Rules is <u>non-judgmental</u> because Roles and Rules are simply two different ways of knowing about the world. Roles-oriented people and rules-oriented people may talk at cross purposes and fail to understand one another's points of view. They may even harbor ill will or somehow be corrupt. But unless there's evidence of ill will or corruption, in which case other measures (such as isolating them or paying them to go away) may be in order, we stick with non-judgmental language and an objective point of view. <u>Our goal in doing so is to understand the client</u> and family and their points of view and their true intentions. We use this language, which we'll demonstrate in subsequent chapters, for business reasons, yet it tends to foster intimacy, candor, and trust. Moreover, it enables any advisor to interact with clients and family members without taking sides, becoming confused, or getting caught up in family conflicts. It enables advisors to observe, understand, and even empathize with the players in the family drama without becoming part of it. And that's essential if they are to do their jobs.

4. *Assessment of the Business Structure*

Roles and Rules come together in societal and organizational structures. Some societies and organizations are weighted more heavily toward roles (dictatorships, families) and some toward rules (democracies, corporations). Most of us think of a business as a collection of assets, such as accounts receivable, inventory, and plant and equipment. However, we think of the business as its structure, that is, as the configuration of Roles and Rules in the business. The structure is the way in which Roles and Rules come together and operate in the organization.

The topic of assessing the business structure warrants a chapter of its own, and that is Chapter 3. It's important because without the structure as embodied in the Roles and Rules of the organization, there really is no business to pass on. Without the structure—without the Roles and the Rules—it's just a collection of assets. As any bankruptcy judge or liquidator can tell you, the value of the assets alone is a tiny fraction of their value as a business. The business is not just its people (managers and employees) nor is it their relationships as depicted on the organization chart. The business is the structure composed of Roles (business roles and the people who fill them) and Rules (the *de jure* and *de facto* interactions, policies, practices, and procedures). Clearly, the Roles and Rules in some businesses are more well-defined and more effectively executed than in others. Yet every organization consists of Roles and Rules, and truly assisting a business calls for understanding them.

The Rationale for Roles and Rules

It quickly becomes apparent to a client and family that our approach to succession and estate planning differs from the usual approaches. We therefore explain our approach and its costs and benefits openly. As explained in Chapter 8, we offer various levels of involvement and service. It is essential that the client and the family, the senior generation and the next generation, buy into our approach. Sometimes they don't, and we are at peace with that, provided we've had a chance to present it.

The rest of this book explains our approach and how it works with clients. Candidly, sometimes it doesn't work in the usual sense of the term. We do not set out to save the business or cure the family, but rather to help the family to establish rules, such as rules for family meetings, and to make *their* decisions regarding their future. If a testator wants to wreak havoc in his family or business, a rogue child is determined to launch a lawsuit, or successors insist on remaining unprepared, we cannot change that. We can, however, understand it, explain it in a mature manner, and when possible limit the damage to the family, the business, and ourselves.

On a brighter note, most people want family harmony and a secure financial future. Most people will listen to reason, even if they find it difficult to behave reasonably. Roles and Rules taps these positive motivations and capitalizes on people's desire to grow and develop as individuals, and as a family and a business. Those are the opportunities that our approach offers, in both direct and indirect ways, when the Rules Crisis looms. They are also opportunities that remain unacknowledged in most succession and estate planning methods.

Bear in Mind

- The testator should consider the decision to keep the business in the family or to sell it in light of the Roles and Rules at work in the family, the successors' preparedness for the Rules Crisis, and the potential for unresolvable conflicts.
- If a testator decides to sell the business, then the need for Roles and Rules diminishes. Yet sound rules are still necessary regarding valuation of the business, power to accept a price and terms, and distribution of the proceeds of the sale. Even in the absence of a business, sound family governance demands a sound governance structure, which Roles and Rules can be used to develop.
- The differing viewpoints of roles-oriented people and rules-oriented people fuel conflicts in family businesses and in the estate planning process. These conflicts occur mainly between and within the senior generation and the next generation, within the business itself, and between the business and the trust.
- We make an effort to educate clients about the Roles and Rules at work in their family business. To broach these topics we discuss statistics, stories, and priorities in succession and estate planning, explain the nature of the Rules Crisis, explore the testator's intentions, and assess the structure of the business.
- As an approach, Roles and Rules respects all viewpoints, employs non-judgmental language, and seeks to reconcile and integrate viewpoints to the extent possible. If reconciliation isn't possible, then we seek the best possible outcome for both the family and the business.

CHAPTER 3

The Structure of the Business: Roles and Rules at Work

In the course of an engagement with a family-owned, retail housewares chain, one of our associates asked the company's CEO who reported to him. The CEO, whom we'll call Fred, smiled, rolled his chair back away from his desk, opened the middle drawer, and pulled out a large sheet of heavy paper. This was the organization chart, complete with job titles in fourteen-point font and neatly drawn boxes and reporting lines. The chart showed the CEO at the top and four district managers reporting directly to him and, reporting to the district managers, some thirty store managers. Beneath each store manager were several department heads. It was a picture of a well-ordered hierarchy.

However, subsequent interviews with employees at all levels revealed that while the org chart was a pretty picture, it did not portray reality. In reality, Fred constantly issued orders not only to the district managers but to everyone else in the company, from the store managers and department heads to the workers on the loading docks and in the stockrooms. Everyone took orders from the CEO, and took them often. Indeed, the org chart could have been drawn as a mandala, one of the fascinatingly complex circular designs that Hindus and Buddhists use to symbolize the intricacies of the universe.

Fred's micromanagement rendered any succession plan moot, given the turnover in the executive ranks. The district managers and store managers had lost their authority and their initiative. They felt that they lacked clear goals and that planning was impossible, because at any time Fred might countermand any directive they had given to their employees. People would barely start working on one priority before hearing about another, more urgent, often contradictory one.

We'll discuss how we worked with this organization in this chapter. A key point, however, is that every organization has two components: a formal structure and an informal structure. The formal structure defines the official reporting relationships and operations. The informal structure describes the way people *influence* one another and work with one another in practice. In an ideal world, the two components of the organization would be congruent. There would effectively be one structure. But in most businesses the two structures are not congruent, although there is usually a lot of overlap.

The formal structure need not be very formal. It is simply the way the company is "supposed" to work—who supervises whom, who is assigned which tasks, and so on. Meanwhile, the informal structure describes the actual day-to-day, on-the-job functions and relationships. In a family business, this informal structure typically reflects the effects of family roles. In general, the greater the congruence between the two structures the better for the organization, assuming that the formal structure is sound. Usually, however, there are significant disparities between the formal and the informal structures.

The key people in a family business can strengthen the structure by more closely aligning the formal and informal structures. In some cases, this is necessary to ensure the survival of the business. How can strengthening the structure ensure the survival of the business? Because in a sense the structure *is* the business. To leave a business to successors, the retiring generation must transfer a durable, flexible, financially and operationally sound structure to those successors. Without such a structure, there is no business; there is only a collection of people and assets.

In this chapter, we use Roles and Rules to examine organization structure and to begin defining a durable structure in the context of a succession and estate plan.

Roles + Rules = Structure

Recall the definition of Roles and Rules. A role is a set of actions that one person performs more for another person than for oneself, and a role implies rank. A rule is a requirement or prohibition that applies to everyone equally. A rule operates in the same way among all parties, by agreement.

That said, in hierarchies distinctions usually arise in how rules apply. For instance, the rule in a business is that everyone gets paid. (In fact, it's the law.) However, some employees are paid more than others. Similarly, everyone has access to a restroom and a lunchroom, but senior managers have access to the executive washroom and executive dining room. Although some rules, such as those against sexual harassment or misuse of company funds, apply equally to everyone, others, such as those regarding pay and restrooms, apply to everyone *at a certain level.* For example, the rule might be that all vice presidents can authorize purchases up to $5,000, while all senior vice presidents can authorize purchases up to $10,000.

As we will see, business rules inform business roles by defining how roles in the business are assigned, attained, and performed. Indeed, business rules define business roles. Both in general and in any given company, certain business rules—that is, policies and procedures—define the authority, scope, reporting lines, and duties of the chief executive officer, chief operating officer, chief financial officer, comptroller, chief marketing officer, sales manager, chief information officer, purchasing manager, salesman, supervisor, and so on. These roles are positions analogous to the positions people play in a team sport. Of course, there are no analogous rules that define how people should play their family roles, which is one reason that interactions between family members are so emotional and messy.

In a business, Roles and Rules define the organizational structure. Roles define the hierarchical or vertical elements of the structure; rules define the equalizing or horizontal elements of the structure. To visualize these dimensions, picture a corporate headquarters housed in a skyscraper. To visualize roles, imagine you are standing on the roof and, with X-ray vision, you can see down through each floor and down through the company's hierarchy. The CEO has the top floor to himself. You look through that floor and, on the next floor, you see executive vice presidents at work. On the floor below that, you see senior vice presidents and so on through the hierarchy of vice presidents, assistant vice presidents, managers, and assistant managers, each on their own floor, with their own roles and places in the hierarchy. That hierarchy—and those roles—define vertical, rank-related relations and interactions in the organization.

Now picture yourself in the corporate helicopter, hovering alongside the top floor of the building. From this perspective, you can see through the office walls and across each floor. As you descend alongside the building, you can see the furnishings and décor on each floor. You see the mahogany desks and chairs adorning the executive vice presidents' offices, the maple that the senior vice presidents enjoy, the oak that the vice presidents rate, and the pine that the assistant vice presidents have to settle for, and so on down through various grades of veneer, metal, and polymer. The carpets, fixtures, and wall-hangings are also of a uniform grade across each floor.

The rule here is that everyone at headquarters gets an office, but the type of office depends on your rank. Everyone of a certain rank gets the same type of office, on the same floor, with same square footage and furnishings. This is how rules ensure fairness even though they apply somewhat differently at different ranks. This point confuses some people, but make no mistake: Rules are in effect at all levels of the hierarchy. The CEO cannot give his son-in-law who is a vice president an executive vice president's office, without breaching the company's rules. Such a breach would sap morale and undermine the business.

Every building possesses vertical and horizontal elements, and so does every organizational structure. In an organization, roles define the vertical, rank-related elements and rules define the horizontal, equalizing elements. Note, however, that rules also affect the ways a role interacts with the roles above and below. Moreover, businesses and their owners and managers are subject to legal rules, such as the minimum wage, labor, and tax laws. Management principles, policies, and procedures, such as the principles of delegation and the chain of command, also inform the ways in which business roles interact within the hierarchy.

The facilitator (whom we'll discuss in Chapter 4) must understand and guide the family and business to understand the Roles and Rules at work in the organization, and help the testator, owners, and managers create a workable, durable structure to pass along to the next generation.

What Works?

In a durable organization structure, business Roles and Rules function properly. What does that mean? It means that people play their business roles, particularly management roles, *for* the people they are supposed to play them for, and operate by accepted business and management principles, policies, and procedures. When people fail to play their business roles properly and fail to operate by business rules, they undermine the business, and its structure. When people on the job act outside of their business roles, they create disparity between the formal and the informal structures and that disparity generates confusion and inefficiency.

Of course, we recognize that people often exert influence in an informal structure because they perceive deficiencies in the formal structure. Those deficiencies often arise from managers failing to play their roles well. In a sound structure, people play their roles well by playing agreed-upon roles by agreed-upon rules.

On that subject, let's return to our example of the retail housewares chain. In that organization, Fred's role was defined as CEO with four district managers reporting to him. Under the business principles (or rules) of delegation and chain of command, Fred should give direction *through* the district managers, who would in turn give direction through the store managers and so on. However, Fred brought his role as head of the family into the business. He started the business from a single store and, for better and worse, had always taken a paternal approach to managing it. This led him to ignore the rules of delegation and chain of command and to give directions willy-nilly, which undermined his managers' roles and their participation in the business.

It also undermined his role as CEO, and the business itself. A CEO who's directing workers on the loading dock and in the stockroom isn't doing his job. His job is to have someone else oversee the loading and stocking so he can deal with higher-level strategic, operational, and financial matters. Fred was not playing the role of CEO for the people in the business; he was playing the role for himself. He liked giving orders, being in the trenches, and solving everyday problems. He liked to see people jump at his command, enjoyed the excitement he stirred up, and reveled in his sense of importance. In every troubled organization, there are either unfilled roles or, as in this case, people failing to play their roles well. As you will see, discovering which roles are unfilled or poorly played is a key to helping a family business out of its troubles.

A facilitator employing Roles and Rules does not necessarily ask people about the roles or the rules in the business: "What's your role? Do you think that you're playing it well? What are the rules around here?" People might not comprehend Roles and Rules as we define them. Yet these may be useful questions to ask, and some people intuitively grasp or can quickly understand the meaning. In any event, a facilitator using Roles and Rules does not approach an organization with the goal of having it conform to preconceived notions of structure, efficiency, and effectiveness. Instead, the facilitator asks questions that draw forth people's descriptions of what they do. It is those descriptions that reveal the workings of Roles and Rules in the organization.

The more an organization is run on the basis of family roles, the less likely it is to survive across generations. That's because the family roles, such as charismatic founder or unquestioningly supportive spouse, are going to change or disappear. As will be seen, family roles often repeat themselves, but typically play out differently from generation to generation. Incidentally, many readers may notice that our analysis of structure would apply to and probably benefit a family business not preparing for succession. However, our focus is on preparing the business for intergenerational transfer, unless the family decides to sell it, in which case the official structure should probably be firmed up. Savvy buyers will know when a business lacks structure and will value it accordingly.

Analyzing Rules: Input and Output

Rules describe and guide interactions between people, in a game ("The pitcher throws the ball to the catcher, and the batter tries to hit it.") or in a business ("The inspector receives a widget, tests its quality, passes or fails it, and sends it on to shipping or back to production."). Recall that rules have no emotional component—nobody gets excited about the infield fly rule. Rules are in a sense purely descriptive: We stop at stop signs. We give correct change. We direct employees by delegating responsibilities through a chain of command.

We've found that the best way for a facilitator to learn about the interactions in an organization is to interview people about the work they perform, by discussing it at the level of input and output. Every person in a job receives certain input, performs certain work on that material, then sends the output to other people inside or outside the organization, who view it as their input. Production workers take raw materials, make widgets, and send them to inspectors, who send them to shipping. Shipping workers take the widgets, package them, place them in cartons, and load them on trucks. Accountants take data on transactions, create financial reports, and send them to managers, who review the reports and make decisions based on them. Salespeople take prospects, transform them into customers, and hand them off to customer service. In fact, the entire organization is one huge entity that takes inputs, transforms them, then distributes them as output.

A facilitator can interview people about their input and output, but it's best to avoid those somewhat technical terms. Instead, simply ask: What do you work on? Where does it come from? How often? What do you do with it or to it? How long does that take? What else do you do with it? To whom do you send it? What information do you track? Into what form do you put that information? To whom do you send it? How often?

These questions must get at the hierarchy—who assigns work and how—and the interactions with peers that facilitate success. So, good questions include: How are people selected for tasks, and how is work assigned? Who does that? Is it the same person who evaluates your work? How do peers compete for work, or work together? And so on. It's useful, but potentially difficult, to learn who decides which work comes to an individual. Does it come from above or from a lateral position—or from below? Is the work assigned fairly? How is performance judged? The answers to these questions often involve roles aspects of the structure, which we'll address later in this chapter.

This discussion of rules should be free of emotion: At this point, a facilitator just wants information about the interactions and flow of work, and about who does what. She doesn't ask people, "How did you feel about that?" or "Didn't that make you angry?" (Those questions are for psychotherapists, and this is not psychotherapy.) In fact, at this early stage in the Roles and Rules process, if a employee/son says that his boss/father told him to jump in the lake, the question to ask would not be, "How did you feel about that?" but rather, "What did you do then?"

You want to understand the person's point of view, not in an emotional way but from the organizational standpoint. It's like asking a third baseman what he does. He would say something like, "Well, I stand over here and catch the ball when it comes my way and throw it to the first baseman or second baseman," and so on. That way, you understand the ballgame from that particular point of view. (If you were interviewing the third baseman about how the game is played and he told you that he can't stand the shortstop, you'd see that as off the subject, right?) If you were to interview the people playing all nine positions on the baseball field, you would have a very good idea about how the game of baseball is played, what each player does, how the ball comes to him, and what he does with it. You would not know how the third baseman and the shortstop get along, and that would be fine. You are only trying to understand the interactions, the rules, that comprise the game—or the business. (This, of course, applies mainly to owners, managers, and key employees, and as dictated by the scope of the consultation or engagement, as we'll discuss later.)

At every position in the business there is input and output, and that's where to stay focused at this point. This initial effort has nothing to do with role, rank, hierarchy, or emotion. That is why it generates a clear picture of what people do in the business.

Talking about Roles

If emotions do arise in an input-output discussion—if people express anger or irritation or tell you that things aren't fair—those feelings are associated with roles. Emotions emanate from the hierarchical aspects of the organizational structure, not from the rules. (Perhaps the third baseman sees the shortstop as an arrogant, superior superstar.) At this point, a facilitator may be tempted to judge the validity of an interviewee's feelings or even tempted to empathize. Neither response would be useful, nor would it be useful to make or encourage judgments about co-workers or decision-makers. It's far better to ask, "What do you know about how that decision is made?" and "How are you notified about a decision?"

As with rules, it's best to discuss roles in terms of the interviewee's position in the hierarchy. Useful questions for uncovering the roles in a business include, "Who assigns you your work? Who do you report to? Who do you look to for guidance? How do you know whether you've done a good job? Do you get feedback on the job you've done? From whom and how often? Who performs your performance review? When do they do that? What happens to the appraisal? Who do you turn to for help? Who, if anyone, reports to you? Who looks to you for guidance? Whose performance do you review? How often do you do that?"

These roles-related questions reveal the interviewee's place in, and the nature of, the organization. If the person doesn't have a regular boss, has more than one boss, or never receives a performance appraisal—that tells you something about the organization. It tells you that someone is not playing the role they should be playing for this individual. In discovering the roles and how roles operate in an organization, you will notice still more disparities between the formal and the informal structure.

Moving to a New Role

In the case of the retail housewares chain, interviews with the district managers, store managers, and employees revealed that Fred gave orders to everyone and that this kept people from getting their work done. The questions had nothing to do with fairness, feelings, or personalities; they had to do with how work got done or didn't get done.

The questions posed to people in the retail chain also revealed the disparity between the formal structure on Fred's organization chart and the informal structure described by the managers and the workers. For instance, the buyers were an extremely important element, as they are in most retailers. The buyers visited manufacturers, suppliers, trade shows, and importers in search of merchandise and, by picking, choosing, and bargaining, created the output of salable inventory. But they were also supposed to generate output in the form of reports about what they had purchased: item descriptions, stock numbers, wholesale prices, and so on. They were supposed to enter these data into hand-held computers so the inventory could be updated and tracked by people in the warehouses. However, the buyers did not enter this data in an accurate and timely manner, which generated problems. The warehouse and inventory managers needed the authority to tell the buyers that they couldn't purchase more merchandise until they provided proper information. Yet this would create an upheaval among the buyers.

Fred, as CEO, had the role of settling the matter. He found this difficult, partly because he had been a buyer and, like the current buyers, had little tolerance for administrative detail. Yet he stepped up and did settle it. He began holding weekly meetings, facilitated by our associate, to establish the procedures for accepting deliveries and entering inventory data. At similar meetings they also started to resolve the problem of Fred's random directives, which the district managers and store managers had raised.

On a deeper level, Fred gradually learned to distinguish between his role of founder, father, and former buyer and the role of CEO. He learned the business rules of delegation and chain of command, and these rules helped define Fred's role as a real CEO and helped him grow into that role. That is how Roles and Rules typically operates: The business rules help people grow into new business roles.

What to Learn about Structure

You learn about the organizational structure over the course of the succession and estate planning process. A facilitator or a planning team can rarely say, "Okay, we understand the structure completely, let's move on." An organization is too complex. Moreover, at this point the family business is evolving a new structure, or contemplating such an evolution. In applying Roles and Rules to a succession and estate plan for a business fraught with family issues, you learn about the structure by asking questions about input and output (Rules) and the reporting arrangements (Roles) and listening to what people say. What they say will determine your understanding of the situation, which will continue to evolve.

The kinds of things that you want to determine about the structure in the initial and subsequent interviews with management, administrative staff and workers include:

- The work that people are assigned and are actually doing
- People's understanding of their contribution to the organization
- The business rules that guide people's interactions, and their understanding of those rules
- The key roles in the business and who is filling them, and any roles that are not filled or not being properly played
- People's understanding of their position in the organization and of who is above, below, and lateral to them
- The extent to which people, particularly people in management roles, are playing their business roles for others or for themselves
- The extent to which family roles are affecting the way people play their business roles and whether this a kiss-down or kiss-up hierarchy
- The disparities between the formal structure and the informal structure

This last item is the main reason for examining the structure. The disparities between the formal and the informal structures will indicate the kinds of problems that may arise in the succession. The informal structure runs on influence that emanates from roles. It's made up of roles without many rules. In troubled family businesses, the official structure is poorly defined, weak, or composed of roles not being properly played and rules being ignored. Therefore, this analysis will also indicate the kinds of business Roles and Rules that may strengthen the structure.

Note that we do not enter the situation with a clipboard and checklists and grids to fill out. Rather, we ask questions and listen to the owners and senior managers to gain an understanding of the origins and flows of power in the organization. That's because formal and informal structures are ways of defining and directing power in an organization. While informal structures exist in any organization, a rational, transparent, and fair formal structure will do the best job of defining and directing power. It does this by defining the business Roles and Rules in the organization in a rational, transparent, and fair manner for everyone to see and navigate.

Typically, an understanding of the formal and informal structure will not result from interviews only with senior management. It will emerge gradually from interviews with people at various levels and in various functions and with various family members. The number and length of the interviews should be well managed, and will depend on the size of the organization and the difficulty of the situation. We try to conduct enough interviews in enough depth to enable us to understand the main features of the two structures.

A Look at Power

One aspect of the formal structure warrants special attention: the matter of who in the family and the business has the *legal power* to take various actions. Many issues regarding the succession and estate plan and its implementation center on power. Power can emanate from someone's expertise, skills, contribution to the business, or family role. However, legal rights confer even more power. Legal rights dictate everything from who can hire and fire the attorney to who can leave which assets to whom.

The most important legal rights include those of ownership, votes, vetoes, and financial claims. These rights define who has the power to sell the company or its assets, who must approve major decisions, and who shares in the profits of the business or in the proceeds of a sale of assets. As all attorneys and most business people know, these are not mere details. They are facts that the estate planning team must possess in order to help the family craft a workable plan—or even to understand the family and the business. These legal rights are also critical to the keep-or-sell decision.

In some cases, the family or even the testator may not understand where legal power resides. For example, conflict ran deep in a client company of ours in the building materials business. In this company, most of the next generation (who were all adults and cousins) wanted to keep the business in the family and start running it as the parent generation retired. The four sets of parents in this large family were, however, aware that some cousins (that is, their children) disagreed on the future course of the business. At least one cousin wanted to sell the business and set up shop for himself, or to split the company into two divisions, one of which he proposed to run. Seeing the potential for conflict among their children, two sets of parents did not want to pass the business on to them. In fact, to forestall conflict, the two brothers who ran the company wanted to sell it and distribute the proceeds equitably among the two generations. This set the two generations against one another and fomented factions within each generation.

In reviewing the ownership structure, we learned that the parent generation had, through a gifting program over the past few years, *already given* a majority of the voting stock to their children. This meant that, regardless of how the parents felt, they lacked the legal power to sell the business over the cousins' objections. The rules did not allow it. This would not, of course, preclude the parent generation—moms, dads, uncles, and aunts—from trying to persuade their children to support a sale. ("I built this business, and I want to sell it.") But legally, the cousins did not have to sell the company and, in fact, had the power to stop a sale.

We were surprised to find that neither generation realized this. They were so stuck in family-role behaviors that they were unaware that the rules had changed. The gifting program had, over several years, given a few percentage points of the voting shares per year to each son, daughter, nephew, and niece. The shift occurred so gradually—and role-driven beliefs were so persistent—that no one noticed that the votes had shifted. With those votes, the cousins had real power. They also had a new incentive to grow into ownership roles. When they realized that they were owners, some of the cousins started acting more like owners. In other words, the rules—the rights and responsibilities that came with the voting shares—helped them assume their new business roles. That is exactly how a business evolves, with the active participation of the next generation.

To establish where legal powers reside in a family business, the attorney must obtain, review, and brief the Roles and Rules facilitator about:

- All documents regarding ownership, such as articles of incorporation, organization by-laws, and partnership or trust agreements
- All documents pertaining to important past events, such as sales and acquisitions of major assets, mergers, buy-outs of partners, spin-offs, actions at law, or IRS or regulatory action
- Employment contracts, with special attention to profit sharing, stock options, equity stakes, and termination provisions (such as "golden parachutes"), as well as contracts with major customers and suppliers
- Mortgages and loan agreements, with special attention to balloon payments, prepayment penalties, and covenants regarding default and remedies in case of default
- Any letter or side agreements that may evidence a current or potential ownership stake, lien on assets, or right to approve or block a course of action, such as the sale of the business.

Legal power resides in legal documents, and someone's legal power may constitute a show-stopper in the succession and estate planning process. A testator or owner cannot be forced to do something against his or her will (the multiple meanings of "will" in the English language is no accident). Nothing, including Roles and Rules, can make people play roles or follow rules that they refuse to acknowledge. If a testator is determined to behave in ways others see as wrongheaded or even spiteful *and has the legal right to do so*, then family members must accept that reality. Thus, when difficult behavior arises, it's essential to know who has what legal rights.

Toward a New Structure

Many family businesses have little formal structure. Some have few defined business roles beyond president, foreman, worker, driver, and bookkeeper. Some abide only by basic business laws, such as contract law and the Uniform Commercial Code. Such businesses run almost entirely on family roles. There is nothing inherently wrong with that arrangement, unless the business grows too large to be managed that way. A small, single-site family business can run well with a strong owner at the helm. Opportunities for advancement for both family and non-family employees may be limited, and the business may fail to keep pace with industry developments. Yet the business may thrive for decades, with the need for Roles and Rules arising only around the succession and estate plan.

In fact, any system that lacks rules to ensure fair participation by all parties must run mainly on roles. Witness the difficulty of "bringing democracy" to Iraq, a former dictatorship now containing strong proponents of theocracy. Dictatorships and theocracies run on roles, not rules. Dictators cast themselves as the ultimate authorities. Theocrats claim to operate under divine guidance. No one gets a true vote and no one gets to participate, because the dictator or theocrat claims wisdom from above and the right to structure society and its institutions as he sees fit.

The effort to bring democracy to Iraq is an extreme, but very real, example of a Rules Crisis. A Rules Crisis occurs when people with roles-based power in a society, business, family, or other system stand to lose that power. If the power is not transferred to someone in a true leadership role, who plays it for those lower in the hierarchy and in keeping with true rules, chaos will ensue. That's why a family business usually needs a new structure, new Roles and Rules, if it is to be passed along to the next generation. The new structure is the outcome of a successful succession and a successfully addressed Rules Crisis.

Let's go back to the four brothers whom you briefly met in Chapter 1. You'll recall that they ran their marina informally, on the basis of their family roles. By not giving their children specific job responsibilities, performance evaluations, and mentoring in management, they failed to prepare them for leadership roles in a durable structure. By compensating their children based on their ages rather than their work, they perpetuated family roles instead of fostering new business roles. They provided no clear reporting structure, no career paths, no ways to earn more responsibility. We discovered all this as we conducted interviews and facilitated family meetings. We realized that chaos would ensue if the next generation merely tried to fill the brothers' management roles as they retired. This business needed new Roles and Rules, but where to begin?

Even before interviewing anyone, we set up a contract with this client as we do with all clients. This contract provides an overview of our approach and likely challenges and sets reasonable expectations. We define the key aspects of the engagement and ensure that the client understands and endorses our approach. Then we conduct a family meeting or two to allow the estate planning team and the client family to get to know one another. At these meetings we introduce the need to agree to some basic rules. These, as you will see in Chapter 6, are most often communication rules and meeting protocols, because usually in these situations a few family members tend to dominate every discussion and others are rarely heard.

In this case, at our first meeting with the whole family—the four brothers, their wives and children, and the children's spouses—we worked with them to develop communication rules. Of course, we knew these rules, such as listen without interrupting, respect all opinions, and refrain from personal attacks, but we went through the exercise of developing them with the family anyway. We do this to lead the family through an orderly process and to gain their buy-in to these rules.

Then we wrote up the rules and had each family member sign a statement saying that they would abide by the communication rules. (See Appendix C for sample communication rules we've developed with families.) Communication rules make for calmer, more fruitful family meetings, but there is another equally important benefit: Family members see first-hand how to develop and agree to rules. For many families, this is a revelation. They typically see ways of collaborating, making decisions, and doing business that they have never before experienced.

As Chapter 4 will show, the facilitator applying Roles and Rules succeeds by playing the role of leader and mentor that the family needs him to play. Each family has its own needs, but all families must see the facilitator acting in role and developing and applying rules. That way they learn, through experience, to play business roles and abide by business rules. They see kiss-down behavior, of a sort, in action. The facilitator cannot truly engage in kiss-down behavior because he stands outside the hierarchy and has neither a position nor seniority in the business. But he does model new behavior that enables the testator, owners, and successors to understand kiss-down behavior. They don't have to hear the facilitator talk about Roles and Rules, although that can be useful. They do have to see the facilitator playing a leadership role and employing rules in an even-handed way.

This is not a magical process. Some family members resist movement to rules. Some refuse to engage in the process. Remember, in a Rules Crisis people with roles-based power, typically the owner-testator or the spouse or both, often want to retain that power. In any event, the Rules Crisis arises when there is conflict over the roles that will exist after succession. In the case of the marina, we had to convince the brothers that the operation had grown too large to be managed informally. We had to convince them that they owed it to their children to start running the boatyard as a business. It took time, but we did convince them (although they refused to allow outside directors on the board, which we had recommended).

Business rules define and reinforce business roles. For instance, we helped the brothers define distinct areas of responsibility and a chain of command. We helped them develop hiring criteria, compensation plans, and performance evaluations. We helped them define meeting schedules and protocols. All of these constitute business rules. In developing and using these rules, the brothers and their children began to develop new roles. The need to delegate, conduct performance appraisals, participate in meetings, and so on helped to define and reinforce their managerial and professional roles. It's never enough to tell someone, "Okay, now you're a manager," and expect them to perform the role. They need policies and procedures—rules—that dovetail with the demands of the role.

Movement from roles to rules takes time, and there is no guaranteed outcome. However, with the right facilitator on board, the estate planning team and a client committed to keeping the business can greatly improve their chances of establishing a sound structure to pass along to the next generation. We examine the work of the facilitator in Chapter 4.

Bear in Mind

- Together Roles and Rules define an organization. Roles define the hierarchical, vertical, rank-related elements of the structure. Rules define the equalizing, horizontal elements of the structure and how people interact in the organization.
- Every organization contains a formal and an informal structure. The formal structure defines the official reporting relationships and operations. The informal structure describes the way people influence one another and work with one another in practice.
- To understand how an organization works, the Roles and Rules facilitator asks about what comes to people (input), what they do (work), and what they produce (output). If emotions arise in these discussions the interviewee is responding to something related to the roles in the organization.

- It's essential to learn at the outset who in the family and in the business has the legal power to take or prevent various actions. In a legal matter such as an estate plan, legal power can trump any other kind of power, and may therefore limit what the estate planning team and facilitator can accomplish.
- The Roles and Rules facilitator does not have a preconceived notion of the structure of the business or of how the business should evolve. Rather, he facilitates the evolutionary process.

CHAPTER 4

The Facilitator:
Bringing Law and Order to Town

The last thing that a family in conflict needs is an additional adversary. Yet that is exactly what many attorneys add to the mix, sometimes merely by their presence. If they also behave in an adversarial manner, they increase tension, foment confrontation, and hamper progress toward a workable estate plan. Many lawyers strike an adversarial posture almost reflexively because the U.S. legal system is adversarial by design. In our system, attorneys represent complainants and defendants and present arguments until a judge or jury pronounces one of them the winner and the other, by implication, the loser. The arguments are orderly and the judgment rests on the application of the law, but litigation is still a battle in which attorneys represent the combatants.

Although an adversarial approach can help an attorney's clients in court, it is a must-to-avoid in a difficult estate planning situation. But how? What's the alternative? How do you reduce conflict when family members, and perhaps your client, are fighting? How do you promote a just and fair outcome? How do you avoid immortalizing conflicts in the documents that constitute the estate plan? As an attorney playing an adversarial role, you can't. However by acting as a facilitator or by bringing in a facilitator, you can.

The type of facilitator needed depends on the level of tension in the family business. (We'll discuss indicators of the level of tension later in this chapter.) In relatively low-tension cases, the attorney crafting the estate plan may take the role of facilitator. In moderately tense situations, a suitable member of the planning team can act as the facilitator. This may be another attorney or an expert such as a trust officer, CPA, financial planner, or other business advisor. It may be a consultant or even a trusted friend of the family. In high-tension situations, a facilitator experienced in family dynamics or conflict resolution, perhaps with a background in psychology, would produce the best results. The last condition notwithstanding, the goal of the consultation is neither psychotherapy nor family harmony, but rather maximizing the chances of a smooth succession and minimizing the likelihood of later litigation.

In difficult estate planning situations, it is hard for one person to deal with both content and process. Content and process are two different things. The facilitator focuses on the process, while other members of the estate planning team—the attorney, insurance agent, trust officer, CPA, and financial planner—focus on the content related to their areas of expertise. The facilitator's first loyalty must be to the process, rather than to a person or faction within the family or to a specific outcome. That loyalty frees the facilitator from allegiance to a particular participant, faction, or outcome. That in turn frees the facilitator to bring out the family members' points of view and to help them develop a structure for the business and a succession plan that can modify or accommodate their various points of view.

The facilitator plays a role both for the business and for the family as a whole. This is not to say that the facilitator pays no attention to individual family members. She does. But that attention resembles the kind that a teacher gives to a student. A teacher gives a student attention when he needs it, but never lets the needs of a single student interfere with the learning process of the class.

In this chapter, we examine the role that facilitators play in the Roles and Rules approach to succession and estate planning, and how they can best play that role. We also show how to present our approach to the client and family in ways that generate their buy-in.

What It's Like, and How It's Different

Attorneys have recognized the high cost of conflict, especially in situations involving family law. In response, the legal profession has developed ways of settling disputes short of litigation, most notably arbitration, collaborative negotiation, and collaborative mediation. These methods resemble, but also differ from, our approach. Attorneys and other readers familiar with conflict resolution may benefit from the following comparisons:

- In *arbitration*, the parties and their attorneys present their arguments to an arbitrator, usually an attorney or a retired judge, and agree to abide by his decision (hence, the term "binding arbitration"). Arbitration is less formal and costly than litigation; however, it produces *a* solution, that is, the arbitrator's solution, rather than the parties' solution. Roles and Rules helps the parties develop *their* solution.

- In *collaborative negotiation*, the parties and their attorneys agree to cooperate and to exhaust collaborative procedures before resorting to litigation. Collaborative negotiation differs from arbitration in that the principals reserve the right to go to court and the attorneys are more in control of the process. While participants in Roles and Rules retain the legal right to go to court, litigation is strongly discouraged.
- In *collaborative mediation*, the attorneys oversee the process and allow the parties themselves to negotiate. The attorneys cannot represent the parties in court. Expert information and information about assets, income, and so on are openly shared. The parties focus on developing win-win solutions—playing to tie, if you will—not on winning a legal contest. In this context, the attorneys help the parties develop their own solution. They guide, but do not control, the process.

As we write this, many attorneys and clients are interested in the relatively new area of collaborative mediation, for several reasons: First, it produces a solution faster than litigation. Second, the solution will usually be satisfactory to both parties. Third, the parties have more control over the outcome than they would in either litigation or arbitration. That increased control reduces uncertainty. However, collaborative mediation assumes a healthy level of goodwill, and its success depends on peoples' willingness to share information and to seek a solution, rather than a victory. Hiding assets or clinging to a hidden agenda renders collaborative mediation impossible.

Goodwill may be lacking in a feuding family, yet a knowledgeable facilitator can encourage parties to share information, particularly hidden agendas, and to act in good faith. He can foster a willingness to change, for example by revealing fruitless patterns of behavior within the family. A facilitator can help an attorney craft rules, for instance as provisions in trust or partnership agreements, that will blunt or mitigate negative behavior, such as drug use or irresponsible spending. Even in hopeless situations, a facilitator can at least help the family accept a testator's wrongheaded decision or help warring parties agree to disagree. A facilitator can also recommend simply paying a difficult family member to go away, a tactic worth considering with impossible people.

Another potential, but very real, benefit provided by the facilitator using Roles and Rules is the personal and professional growth that family members can achieve. Transferring a business from one generation to the next represents a difficult developmental task, especially for troubled families. Those families need more than a legal transfer of assets. They need to assume new roles that help them execute increased or decreased responsibilities, and they need to adopt new rules that professionalize the business. Doing so can help them grow as people.

New Roles

You'll recall that the four brothers who ran the multimillion-dollar marina needed to assume specific responsibilities and adopt proven management practices. In doing these things, they transformed themselves from brothers running a boatyard to owners managing a business. They also started mentoring the children who wanted to be in the business.

Although we helped them define the roles and some broad business rules, Jim Reid, the facilitator we introduced to the brothers, was instrumental in this family's transition. Jim is a management consultant with a good amount of charisma. He's also a religious man and a believer in servant leadership, which is one good way of defining the role that leaders must play for their followers. So in his first meeting with the entire family after he was hired, Jim brought a large pan of water, a washcloth, and a few towels into the room. He then proceeded to wash the feet of the management team. When he was finished, Jim turned to the family and said, "If anybody wants to be a real leader in this company, they have to be willing to serve other people."

This was not something we would have suggested, nor would it have impressed some clients in a positive way. But the effect on this family, which happened to be Roman Catholic, was profound. It vividly demonstrated that anyone who wanted to play the role of manager had to play it for his or her people. This was the company where the next generation had been taking three-hour lunches, had no defined responsibilities, and had lobbied their fathers instead of working for what they wanted. These behaviors differed sharply from the hard work, dedication, and sacrifice the four brothers had put into the business in their youth. As a result, the younger generation hadn't earned the respect of the workers at the marina and were unprepared for increased responsibility. Thus, they benefited from a dramatic demonstration of servant leadership, as well as from the establishment of sound business practices.

Jim established hiring guidelines, compensation policies, and performance standards. He held regular meetings, supplemented by impromptu harborside conversations. And he enforced the rules. Jim demonstrated his commitment to principles of fair play and good business judgment and began to earn the brothers' respect, despite the occasional difficulties his approach presented to some of them. For instance, a son of one of the brothers wanted a sales job that was being created. However, the job description stated that one of the requirements was experience in yacht brokerage. The son didn't have that experience or any real sales experience. Jim, who was essentially the acting CEO, coached the brother in charge of that position not to hire this nephew. Neither the son nor his father were happy with this decision. They pointed out that in the past other children had been hired without fulfilling every qualification for a job. The son's father argued that he owned a major share of the marina, and had a right to have his son in the business. However, they had to live with the decision, for two reasons: First, they had agreed (in writing) to start running the business according to rules, and the rules stated that experience in yacht brokerage was a requirement for the job. Second, Jim's contract had been structured so that he could be fired only if *all four* brothers agreed to fire him.

This last provision proved to be extremely important. As noted earlier, without a contractual provision or other legal standing vis-à-vis the company, for example as a trustee or a director, a facilitator has no real power. Without real power, the facilitator may be subject to the roles-based whims of the owner, the owner's spouse or offspring, or any party with true legal power. Demonstrations of servant leadership and gaining the family's confidence are all well and good. But if at all possible, the facilitator should have actual power rooted in a contract, a trust or partnership agreement, or another legal document. By agreeing that all four of them had to agree to fire Jim Reid, each brother gave up some power. They did this after we explained that the facilitator would inevitably take steps that one or more of them would object to, but those steps would be necessary for the good of the business and the family. Therefore, the facilitator needed the power to take those steps.

Lack of actual power places the facilitator in the position of having to kiss up to the owners. You cannot play a role for someone you have to kiss up to for fear of being fired, demoted, or ignored. A facilitator must play his role for the family and for the business, not for an autocrat who has failed to prepare anyone to succeed him.

In another case, which involved real estate holdings, Bob Hanrahan, another facilitator who has worked with us, had the legal status of successor trustee. This situation involved an apartment building held in a trust for two brothers, whom we'll call Dick and Dan, and their slightly impaired sister, whom we'll call Cathy. The three siblings had accepted Bob as successor trustee, and the trust agreement stipulated that the successor trustee could, if he deemed it necessary, order the sale of the building in order to pay the living expenses of the sister. Bob never threatened them with this power or abused it in any way, but because Dick and Dan knew that Bob could go to court and get an order for the sale of the property for Cathy's benefit, he had tremendous influence.

One of the most important factors in a successful Roles and Rules consultation will be the quality of the relationships the facilitator forms with various parties, particularly with the identified client or the most powerful party, if that is another individual. The client and anyone with power must have enough respect for the facilitator to take his or her advice. The facilitator must also have a contract, the status of trustee, or at least the ability to quit the engagement, if he is to avoid coming under the sway of the client, another powerful individual, or the informal structure.

Roles are hierarchical and connote rank, and rank confers power. People in superior roles are supposed to play those roles for the people under them, but often they don't. The facilitator comes on board to teach them how to do that, mainly by example but also, let's say, through influence. The more actual, legal power the facilitator has, the greater his influence. Therefore, it is in the family's interests to relinquish some power to the facilitator, as long as the facilitator understands Roles and Rules the way Bob Hanrahan does—as a maieutic process.

The Maieutic Way

As a model of human behavior, Roles and Rules is not prescriptive but descriptive. The model describes how human identity develops and how human interactions occur. The model describes the nature of roles, and notes that interpersonal and psychological problems occur when people don't play their roles well for others. The model describes the nature of rules, but does not say that people should or shouldn't play baseball or poker or form partnerships or LLCs. It merely describes what happens when rules are in place or not in place. When rules are not in place, role-based behavior will prevail, usually to the detriment of people in subordinate roles. The model implies that the family should be allowed to develop their own Roles and Rules, rather than have them dictated to them. That way, people can realize (in both senses of the term) what they want their family and business to be.

Thus the facilitator should use Roles and Rules in a maieutic (*may you' tic*) manner. The term maieutic indicates a Socratic mode of inquiry that brings other people's ideas to fruition. Maieutic stems from the Greek word for midwifery, which Socrates, whose mother was a midwife, used to describe his method of delivering other people's concepts. A midwife has a certain relationship to the baby. It is not the midwife's baby, yet she must assist the delivery because the baby cannot deliver itself and a mother in labor is engaged in a painful, dangerous, disorienting task. Socrates played the role of midwife to his students' ideas, posing questions in what became known as the Socratic method. He didn't pose questions just to capture their interest. That was part of it, but the main goal was to lead them to know what they thought and, ultimately, to know who they were.

A facilitator will *usually* produce the best result by taking a maieutic approach. Certain leadership and instructional roles, such as military commander, do not call for a maieutic approach. The role of an army officer is not to deliver the soldier's concept of a soldier, but to deliver the army's concept of a soldier, to the field of battle. The soldier takes orders, thus fulfilling the army's role expectations. Army officers have no apparent interest in maieutic process, which would be out of place in the military. However, the military epitomizes the hierarchical, roles-based organization. The military's "rules" are strict role expectations that the soldier must meet if the army, itself a weapon of war, is to fulfill its mission of physically overwhelming the enemy.

Helping a family business move from family roles to business rules will often—but not always—be a maieutic process. Ideally, it should be. But every family business and estate plan requires a certain type of facilitator to effect the transition.

Types of Facilitators

In practice, sometimes we facilitate the succession and estate planning process and the transition ourselves. Most often, we facilitate the early part of the process—assessing the Roles and Rules in the business (that is, the structure) and helping the family define new ones—and then, when the conflicts or difficulties have abated, turn the transition over to another facilitator.

In assisting the transition, the facilitator's role takes different forms, because she must model the kind of leadership that the family requires. Few family businesses have experienced the kind of consistent, supportive, even-handed leadership that characterizes the best professionally managed organizations. (Granted, many professionally managed outfits lack such leadership.) Professional managers set clear goals and develop a plan to achieve them, give subordinates the authority and resources they require, hold them accountable, and reward them according to their performance. In our experience, few troubled family businesses readily accept this type of manager. The people who've been running the family business resist losing their power and fear being shown up by new management. In such situations, the family typically benefits by first experiencing a facilitator who plays a non-threatening, exploratory role. Then, later in the transition, the family can accept a more directive facilitator. In general, the type of facilitator a business requires depends on the level of tension in the business, which we'll discuss later in this chapter, and on the personalities and managerial abilities of family members.

Broadly, the types of facilitators include the Acting CEO, the Umpire, and the Maieutic Consultant, as illustrated in Figure 3-1. This diagram does not include the adversarial attorney, because an adversarial approach is incompatible with Roles and Rules. Also, we are not implying that a facilitator would stay in one of these modes at all times. These are broad types, which relate to Roles and Rules in a general way as depicted in the diagram.

Figure 3-1

Three Types of Facilitators

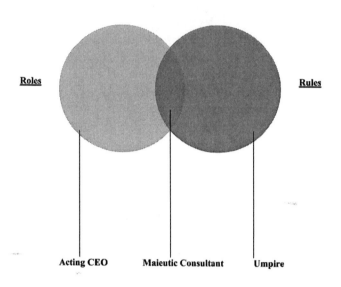

| Acting CEO | Maieutic Consultant | Umpire |

As the diagram indicates, the Acting CEO brings a more roles-oriented approach to the task of facilitating the transition, while the Umpire uses a more rules-oriented approach. The Maieutic Consultant (or MC) relies on Roles and Rules in facilitating the succession and estate planning process and the transition. The following subsections explain how the three types of facilitators operate in practice.

The Acting CEO

The Acting CEO plays a strong leadership role for the family. Like all good facilitators, he models the kind of leadership that the family and business can most readily identify with and benefit from. The family business in need of an Acting CEO requires a strong and directive, but fair and professional, leader. This type of facilitator operates best when the new Roles and Rules have been developed and a workable structure has been established for him to oversee and direct. The Acting CEO needs a first-rate business background and, ideally, management experience. This facilitator is more comfortable telling the family what the business needs, and telling people what to do, than he is exploring the issues, addressing family dynamics, and developing Roles and Rules. Therefore, the key Roles and Rules should be in place, although the people in the roles will not all be fully prepared for them and a number of rules will still need to be developed. The Acting CEO must understand Roles and Rules, but need not understand the model deeply.

The person playing this role should not be authoritarian. He must understand that he is the acting CEO, not the CEO. The goal is not to take over the business, but to show the family, particularly the successor to the current or recently retired CEO, how to take over the business. This facilitator needs strong mentoring skills. He must bring the successors into their management roles as smoothly as possible.

Jim Reid played the role of Acting CEO for the four brothers with the marina we've discussed. Jim is not authoritarian, but he enforces the rules: An owner's offspring without the job qualifications will not be hired. Yet Jim also went out of his way to model servant leadership for the family. Jim played the role of charismatic leader, who, being strong in his own identity, was able to use the role to direct others to play their roles. Using his business judgment and a hands-on approach, he supplied the catalyst the organization needed to move people from the old family-based roles that had been hindering the development of a new business structure into new, business-based roles.

Although the Acting CEO prefers a relatively roles-based approach, he abides by the rules. He sees that meetings start on time, costs are controlled, financial reports are reviewed, plans are generated and implemented, and results are measured. He shows the successors how to support their people with coaching, criticism (in private), praise (in public), performance reviews, fair compensation, and performance-based promotions. He himself also plays by the rules the family members agreed to, and thereby teaches them that no one is exempt from rules. Most of all, he shows everyone how to kiss down, how to play a role for people of lower rank, and how everyone participates and contributes their best by operating according to rules.

The Umpire

The Umpire prefers to work more from the rules side of Roles and Rules. Generally, the Umpire is most useful in family businesses where the key roles are filled, yet there's a real need for rules, which may or may not be in place. If they are in place, the Umpire mainly works as rules enforcer, but not in a heavy-handed or judgmental way. If the rules are not in place, he acts in an advisory role to help the family put them in place.

Unfortunately, people often ignore established rules—including rules they have agreed to in writing. To avoid having to play an authoritarian role, the Umpire must employ consequences rather than punishment. Consequences are clearly linked to the rule, and logically result from an unwillingness or inability to abide by the rule. In other words, consequences are rules-based. Ideally, the consequence should be part of the rule. So if someone ignores the rules of a meeting, they may not be invited to the next one. If someone violates their check-signing authority, they can lose that authority. Like rules, consequences apply to everyone.

If possible, the Umpire should be involved in formulating the rules, so that he can help the family develop, and agree to, consequences. But bear in mind that rules apply across the horizontal dimension of the organization, and do not necessarily apply in an identical manner at all levels. This fact often leads people of relatively high rank to conceive of their roles as placing them above the rules, a misunderstanding the facilitator must work to correct.

Rules, however, are not set in stone. If a rule doesn't work, consider changing it. As in a democracy, the manner in which a rule changes should itself be determined by rules. If someone from shipping and receiving helped develop and agreed to the original rule, then ideally someone from shipping and receiving should be involved in the rule change.

The Umpire oversees the rules side of the business, but in doing so he also plays a role. First, he personifies the respect that everyone must have for rules. Second, he practices fair, evenhanded leadership. Third, he coaches everyone regarding the rules—business policies and procedures and legal realities and requirements—as they learn their new roles. Finally, he plays his role impartially, the way a judge plays the role of "justice" in a courtroom. A judge doesn't make the law and doesn't take sides. Rather he ensures that the proceedings are conducted in accordance with the law, and that the law is applied logically and fairly to the case. The judge plays the role of judge for the litigants, for the jury, and for society, not for himself.

Similarly, the Umpire applies rules in the form of widely accepted management principles, policies, practices, and procedures to the family business. He does this, as should be clear, not by recommending them but by helping the family to develop, adopt, and adhere to them. An Umpire can be an attorney or an accountant, financial advisor, or management consultant, preferably with a basic understanding of Roles and Rules. The Umpire doesn't have to spend as much time in the family business as the Acting CEO, because modeling leadership is not as essential here. What is essential is that the family business implement and maintain the business rules that they agree to adopt.

We've worked with a facilitator named Ron Wolfe, a real estate specialist whom we think of as a "rules guy" and who usually operates as an Umpire. In situations involving large real estate holdings, he has (among other things) helped families maintain communication and meeting protocols and develop useful reports and metrics for properties under management.

"When there are multiple properties," Ron says, "the financial reports have to be easy to understand and useful for decision-making. One real estate trust I worked with kept one set of books for the capital items and another for operating items, but the two sets of books were never merged. Also, reports that could have been one page long went to twenty pages and listed every single transaction. Nobody was cooking the books, but you couldn't track what was happening and compare performance among properties easily."

Ron helped correct this and introduced consistent performance measures. He also enforced meeting protocols, adapting Roberts Rules of Order to the situation. These protocols helped previously uninvolved family members participate without being shouted down by more vociferous members. When the family saw how the protocols made meetings fairer and more efficient, they started operating in a more businesslike manner. The rules diminished the disruptive effect of their family roles while reinforcing and supporting their business roles, which is exactly what is supposed to happen.

So the Acting CEO, who represents the roles-based side of Roles and Rules, also adheres to and respects the rules. The Umpire, who enforces the rules, also plays a role for the family and the business as he teaches and enforces the rules. Thus, neither type of facilitator is limited to the world of roles or the world of rules.

The Maieutic Consultant

The *Maieutic Consultant* (MC) also keeps one foot in each world, understanding and operating by Roles and Rules as each situation dictates. However, among the three types of facilitators, the MC has the deepest knowledge of Roles and Rules, the most skill in applying the model, and the greatest flexibility in dealing with family business situations. The MC is equipped to enter the succession and estate planning process or the transition itself at any time. The MC is an essential player when the estate planning team has been stymied by lack of goodwill on the part of one or more family members or when high levels of tension threaten the process.

Helping the client to deliver the business to the next generation demands that the MC forgo a personal point of view, refrain from taking sides or playing favorites, and eschew any preordained outcome. This implies that the family or testator may indeed choose to break up or sell the business or that the family may never reconcile. Relationships in the family may indeed be irreparable. The parties with the power may refuse to relinquish that power or even to share it. They may be unwilling or unable to play the roles of parents for their children or senior managers for the business. Or a disgruntled family member who lacks power but who has value to the business may insist on leaving. The MC would view none of these outcomes as failure, because she recognizes that some people cannot or will not play their roles for others and abide by rules. Having no point of view or preconceived outcome frees the MC from formulas and recipes. She is positioned to elicit and deeply understand the points of view and the Roles and Rules at work in the business. She is also well prepared to help the family truly develop their own vision and a new structure that will take them and the business forward. If some family members hold conflicting visions, she can help them work toward the best possible solution.

For instance, Bob Hanrahan, who intuitively works in many ways like a trained Maieutic Consultant, dealt very effectively with the case of Dick, Dan, and Cathy that we mentioned earlier in this chapter. The two brothers and their sister had been left an apartment building by their mother, who had survived their father. The trust agreement controlling the building stipulated that Cathy's interests were to always come first. (Recall that Cathy was slightly impaired.)

As Bob describes the situation:

> The brothers were angry that the trust favored their sister, and they were correct in perceiving favoritism. Their mother had favored Cathy at their expense, but she had her reasons. Yet Dick and Dan were taking their anger out on their sister, putting her down, excluding her from family business and family events, and this created tension between the them and Cathy. I had been named successor trustee. I had the power to petition the court to sell the building to pay Cathy's living expenses—if necessary.
>
> One day, I met with Dick and Dan and gave them copies of the trust agreement with the key passages highlighted. I told them, "This document is your mother talking to you," and reminded them that they had agreed to make me successor trustee, which they had. I said, "We are all charged with the responsibility—you as family and me as trustee—to carry out your mother's wishes, whether or not we agree with them. Do you agree with that?" They looked at me kind of funny but said, "Yes."
>
> I then reviewed the agreement with them. Almost instantly, they started bringing up their issues about Cathy so I asked them, quite seriously, "Do you believe that Cathy is normal?" They thought about that and said, "No, she's never been normal," and I said, "Then do you think you should judge her by normal standards?" They said, "No," and that was a breakthrough. At that meeting, they accepted reality: Their mother had decided to provide for Cathy first and to a greater degree. That had been her wish and her goal, and there was no sense in making that difficult or in being angry, certainly not at Cathy.

After that, I gradually brought Cathy into the management of the apartment building. I showed her the books—the rent rolls and the expenses. I didn't do this because I thought she would become a great property manager, but to give her a new role, to bring her into the process, and to show her the source of her income. This worked out well. She now comes to me and says things like, "I never knew it cost so much to do this," and "We need to take care of that." She is growing and maturing, and her brothers are thrilled. In fact, they told me it's about time she got involved. So everybody has received this very positively.

As an MC, Bob didn't limit his focus to the role of Acting CEO or Umpire. He played both. He made it clear that he had the power to petition the court to sell the property, but he didn't threaten to do so. He represented their mother and in effect played the role that she had vacated—that of Cathy's caregiver and protector. He also represented the rules, invoking the trust agreement and the need to abide by its provisions. The brothers had to accept that the trust would operate as their mother wished, primarily to the benefit of their sister, whom they agreed was impaired. Also, given that their sister was the primary beneficiary of the trust, they welcomed her involvement, to the extent that she could be involved, in the management of the building.

Each type of facilitator has his place in the intergenerational transfer of a business or set of assets. Generally, the Acting CEO works best when there are people who require coaching and mentoring to grow into management roles; the Umpire works best when the leadership is in place and rules must be developed or enforced or both; the MC works best (and is required) in the most difficult situations, which are characterized by a lack of goodwill or a high degree of tension or both. The MC can also set up the Roles and Rules context in virtually any succession and estate planning situation.

Dynamic Tension

In some cases it might be best for one facilitator to work with the business through the entire transition, but that is not always possible or even desirable. Many businesses require a different type of facilitator at different stages of the transition. We ourselves most often work with a family first to bring down the level of tension, establish communication, generate goodwill, and improve the business structure, and then call in another facilitator to see the business through the transition. We work as Maieutic Consultants to help the family develop its vision of the business and define new Roles and Rules. After that, depending on the family and the business, an Acting CEO, an Umpire, or another MC, in consultation with us, helps the family operate in their new roles and with their new rules.

Even more important than the stage of the transition, however, is the level of tension experienced by the family and the business. An estate planner must assess and periodically reassess the level of tension by observing the client, family members, and people in the business for the following behaviors and characteristics:

1. Open animosity, arguments, or aggressive or passive-aggressive behavior, such as family members not speaking to one another
2. Client's lack of willingness to give the facilitator permission to interview family members, managers, or employees
3. Repeatedly getting stuck on the same issue or circular argument
4. People ignoring agreed-upon rules or commitments
5. Sibling rivalry, competition for affection, or parental favoritism toward one or more children
6. Misuse of authority, responsibility, or power
7. Long-standing complaints and resentments that have apparently not been addressed
8. Widely divergent levels of financial success, professional accomplishment, or social status among family members
9. Divergent levels of contribution to building the business or assets among family (and perhaps non-family) members
10. Family members hiring their own attorneys, CPAs, or other professionals or threatening or launching legal actions

Although assessing the level of tension as low, medium, or high is subjective, behaviors and characteristics are observable. The more of them you observe and the more intensely they manifest themselves, the greater the level of tension. For example, the presence of a few behaviors or characteristics, mildly exhibited, would indicate low tension. The presence of several, strongly exhibited, would indicate high tension, as would any occurrence of the more extreme behaviors, such as family members retaining their own counsel. In between would be medium-tension situations and varying degrees of difficulty.

These behaviors often point to psychological problems in the family. Yet neither the estate planner nor the facilitator is qualified to solve those problems, nor has he been hired to solve them. You apply Roles and Rules simply to keep those problems from undermining the estate plan and the transition. That implies that in moderate- to high-tension cases the facilitator should have a sound knowledge of Roles and Rules and its application. In the more difficult cases, the facilitator must help the family to develop and use Roles and Rules.

The facilitator in these cases also requires absolutely first-rate communication, mediation, negotiation, and conflict resolution skills—in addition to business and managerial skills.

In high-tension cases, the facilitator must be willing to assert genuine authority. We work hard to persuade reluctant clients to share their power and agree to rules that allocate power to the appropriate members of the team and the business. If the client will not relinquish some power, the case is probably hopeless. We share that realization with the client before we exit a seemingly hopeless case, at which point he or she will sometimes, but not always, see the potential ill effects of certain choices and relent. One of the real benefits of Roles and Rules is that it helps the estate planner understand the sources and flows of power in the situation, and thus the probability of success. When that probability is low, it is time to move on. For instance, when the difficult testator is the founder of the business *and* holds a controlling ownership interest *and* will not share or relinquish any real managerial power, then the chances of an orderly, fruitful succession are extremely low. You have to recognize such situations for what they are and either avoid them or adjust expectations accordingly.

Finally, advisors should be aware of the phenomenon of splitting, in which one or more family members unite with one or more other family members in opposition to and at the expense of others. This highly destructive group dynamic often results from exclusion, deception, or otherwise turning one person against another. For example, one family member may report something that another said in terms that seem outrageous.

To combat this a consultant must get everyone to agree to say what they think in meetings and to refrain from voicing negative remarks about others afterward. Opinions not voiced at meetings must be excluded from the process, while those voiced at meetings must be considered within the process. In this way the consultant legitimizes and rewards certain statements and behaviors, and negatively reinforces others by taking them off the table. This is essential because neither the facilitator nor anyone else in the group can understand an individual's thinking or the group's dynamics if people withhold their opinions or use them outside the process to foment factional behavior.

Team Play

We are often asked about the relationship between the facilitator and the estate planning team and the client. Who pays the facilitator? Who does the facilitator work for? How do you present the facilitator to the family?

As a matter of policy based on experience, we work for the people with the authority over and responsibility for the business. Thus the senior generation is most often our client. After we establish the alliance with the client, we have the client hire the facilitator, whose client is either our client or the family business. We retain the role of attorney for the senior generation and advisor to the family business *if* that has been our role. The facilitator consults with us and together we develop the succession and estate plan. We define the estate planning team to include the family as well as our professional team. That way, everyone in the family has a role and a point of view, and everyone understands that everyone's point of view counts. This is a significant element of the contract because it enables the facilitator to use Roles and Rules in the planning process. Ideally, anyone with a stake in the business or the assets should somehow be included in the process and if they are not, we need to know why and with what potential effects.

The client pays our fees as legal counsel (again, if that has been our role) and consultants. When applicable, the client also pays the facilitator, usually directly, in the facilitator's capacity as acting CEO, temporary board member, management consultant, or facilitator. We tell the client upfront that complex cases present family and structural issues that we have to address for the succession and estate plan to succeed—and that this work costs money. We have found that in difficult cases addressing the family issues comprises a significant portion of the work in comparison to developing the trust agreement and the tax plan. In some cases an attorney could actually earn additional fees from follow-on litigation and trust work by *not* helping the family to address its fundamental issues. However, that is hardly in the best interest of the client and the business. We tell clients with family issues that time and money spent dealing with those issues is time and money well spent. We also point out that litigation and family conflicts down the road may well undermine the business, not to mention family relationships, if the difficulties are not addressed at this time. In some cases, we talk with the client about the spiritual dimension of playing a role in a hierarchy, such as father or mother in a family or CEO in a business. In this context, we discuss the concept of altruistically playing a role for those lower in the hierarchy. We also emphasize the value and satisfaction of establishing a legacy as opposed to that of simply passing along assets and accounts.

We involve the client in choosing the facilitator who succeeds us. After we explain the need for and the role of the facilitator, the client interviews one or two of the people we work with and brings that person on board as an independent consultant. We match the facilitator to the type of business, the requirements of the situation, and the personalities of the key family members. Usually, but not always, the first facilitator hired is the right fit, but if he isn't we bring another on board as soon as possible. The facilitator doesn't have a lot of time to grow into the role.

We present the facilitator as a consultant who works with us to strengthen the structure of the business and to help everyone learn new Roles and Rules. We point out that it would be too expensive to hire an attorney in that capacity, and we stress the need for the facilitator's business expertise. If the facilitator has a background in psychology or mental health, we usually have not found a need to mention it. As noted, this is not therapy and few families appreciate any suggestion that they may need a shrink.

The facilitator has to sell himself to the family. We cite the facilitator's qualifications and experience, but the relationship depends somewhat on chemistry and on how the facilitator matches the needs and expectations of the client. For instance, a roles-oriented Acting CEO is just what the four brothers at the marina needed. They responded extremely positively to the charismatic personality of Jim Reid and to his religiously rooted foot-washing exercise, and Jim had the sensitivity to know that they would. The more rules-based Ron Wolfe wouldn't think of washing anyone's feet (except his own) and, indeed, would probably not be as good a fit with this client. Jim, on the other hand, would be thrown out of many conference rooms for showing up with a pan of water and a towel. In sum, a facilitator's personality, judgment, and actions determine his fit with a client.

Practice-Related Issues for Attorneys

Using Roles and Rules in estate planning raises several considerations for attorneys, which are detailed below. As you review these points, consider the fact that an estate planning situation characterized by family conflict holds a high probability of distress, waste, failure, or follow-on litigation relative to one free of such conflict. Therefore, the following considerations should be weighed against the probability of such negative outcomes:

- *Increased time for developing the estate plan and increased fees for the client.* It generally requires more professional involvement and a longer timeframe to employ Roles and Rules. Conducting interviews, analyzing family dynamics, and facilitating meetings all take time. Given this, these activities should be limited to cases where negative family dynamics threaten to undermine, or have undermined, the estate planning process and the client can afford the added expense. Again, the need for our method is typically altered or reduced when the business is being sold and the proceeds divided among family members.

- *Resistance on the part of family members.* Roles and Rules cannot be employed explicitly unless the senior generation endorses the process. Our approach differs from the usual approach to estate planning, and that will be obvious to the client and family. So, the attorney must explain the process, the need for it, and the expected benefits. Resistance from family members can often be addressed by rules that encourage or require their participation in the process at some level.

85

- *Strained family relationships as psychological issues come to the surface.* We set realistic client expectations and warn that things may get worse before they get better, particularly if problems have long been suppressed. Old habits and ways of interacting die hard, and it takes time to learn new skills. Therefore, some frustration may occur in the short term.
- *A change in the attorney's position vis-à-vis the process and the estate planning team.* If an attorney is unable or unwilling to play the role of facilitator, it is best to call in someone else to play that role. The attorney retains responsibility for all legal, tax, and other technical aspects of the estate plan, but *may* have to relinquish the leadership role in the planning process and the transition—and she must be comfortable with that.
- *Issues of client identification, client confidentiality, and conflict of interest.* While loyalty to the process rather than to a person or outcome is a useful posture, the goal of developing the best possible estate plan should be in the letter of engagement. Our approach implies doing more than just writing whatever provisions the client wants into the will or trust agreement. Also, considerations of client confidentiality may limit a lawyer's communication among family members. These issues should be resolved and any necessary permission secured before extending communication beyond the client.

Adopting Roles and Rules requires some adjustment for most estate attorneys. (Again, Appendix B discusses issues of client identification and professional standards for attorneys.) However, we have seen our clients and our practice enriched and broadened through this approach. Along the way we've found that being honest with clients, frankly discussing our approach and its potential costs and benefits, and clearly explaining the facilitator's role helps them decide whether or not to work with us.

Facilitating the Transition

The next two chapters discuss a specific case and reveal our working methods in detail. While it's possible for an attorney or another professional on the estate planning team, such as an accountant or trust officer, to facilitate this process, we've found that a dedicated facilitator produces the best outcome. In situations characterized by high tension or a marked lack of goodwill, the MC is essential to the team. By bringing deep knowledge and equal measures of Roles and Rules to the process, the MC creates the context for a well-founded plan and the smoothest possible transition. Playing the role of facilitator for the family represents a task in itself, and not everyone is equal to that task. We work repeatedly with skilled facilitators for a simple reason: They help family businesses evolve into professionally managed companies.

Bear in Mind

- Roles and Rules resembles other methods of conflict resolution designed to avoid litigation, such as arbitration, collaborative negotiation, and collaborative mediation, especially the latter.
- At its best, Roles and Rules is a maieutic process, that is, one that delivers the family's vision of the new business and its structure. Trying to impose a solution on a feuding family tends to be counterproductive, mainly because the power to effect change resides in the family, not in the estate planning team.
- Broadly, the three types of Roles and Rules facilitators are the Acting CEO, the Umpire, and the Maieutic Consultant. The Acting CEO operates more from the roles side of Roles and Rules, and the Umpire more from the rules side. The MC balances both sides and more explicitly employs Roles and Rules.
- Estate planners and facilitators must assess the level of tension in a family business rather than ignore it or hope it will go away. The greater the tension, the greater the need for a dedicated facilitator (and, in mid-to-high tension cases, for a Maieutic Consultant) and for Roles and Rules.
- Our approach raises several issues for attorneys and other estate planners, and these should be explicitly addressed. Chief among these are the nature of the process and the relationship between the client, the family, the facilitator, and the estate planning team, all of which should be clarified as soon as the need for Roles and Rules is established.

Part Two

A Case in Point

CHAPTER 5

The Past Need Not Be Prologue: Analyzing Family Roles

Most family businesses have a rich past, yet few families have closely examined, let alone analyzed, their histories. That's unfortunate, because people and events in the past largely determine the roles that family members play in the present. For that reason, scrutinizing the past can help people see the origins of their roles and the roots of their difficulties. Estate planning presents the ideal opportunity, as well as the motivation, for a family to examine the roles played by previous generations. Even in two-generation situations (founder's and children's) examining the past can illuminate the present.

The advisor can assist the family in this examination by acting as a facilitator and guide. Again, this is not family therapy. However, delving into the family and business history in a non-judgmental way helps the advisor build trust with the family and permits the family to extend "partial family membership" to the facilitator.

Roles are more deeply rooted in the past than rules. They are also less logical, malleable, and comprehensible. Those characteristics contribute to the power of roles, and seeing the origins of roles helps people to see that power. This examination of roles will rely on stories, anecdotes, character sketches, and oral history, and include content from interviews with family members and perhaps non-family members. This material enables the family and facilitator to examine and discuss the roles that people, living and dead, played in the family and business history. This in turn helps family members place themselves and the business in a richer context and, perhaps, reconcile themselves with the past and choose which things to carry forward and which to change. In this way, the past need not be prologue to an unchanging story, or, if it is to be, it will be by choice rather than through the mindless acting out family roles.

In this chapter, we examine the current situation and the history of a family business to identify the sources and effects of *roles*. The next chapter will focus on *rules*. This separation parallels the need to separate the Roles and Rules aspects of a family business so they can be understood, improved, and then combined into one sound structure.

Two Caveats

Before we proceed, two caveats are in order:

First, although this chapter focuses on roles, Roles *and* Rules are always at work in any organization. Though it's a bit artificial to treat Roles and Rules separately, it is not inaccurate. Roles explain people's identities, and Rules explain their interactions. Analyzing them separately lets us isolate the distinct nature and effects of each, which clarifies the situation and points to a path forward.

Second, analyzing family history is neither an effort to slot people into stereotypes, such as domineering father or weak sibling, nor an attempt to solve psychological problems. Rather, it is a way of identifying the effects of family roles on the business so people can remove the impediments to the succession plan and, perhaps, develop new, more useful business roles.

Looking Back to See Ahead

In this chapter we'll examine the history of the building supplies company mentioned in Chapter 3, which we'll call Acme Building and Home Supply. The following symptoms of Acme's problems surfaced in interviews with family members:

- We repeatedly heard that meetings were disorganized, and saw that people were arguing rather than getting work done.
- We realized that certain family members resented certain situations and one another.
- Some owners complained that they were being lobbied by opposing factions before every decision or vote.
- As a result of this conflict and tension, some family members wanted to sell the company, while others wanted to keep it in the family.

The latter point indicates an impending Rules Crisis and the need to make a conscious keep-or-sell decision.

Many estate planners try to address such problems without addressing family dynamics. They provide advice, guidance, or even "rules" of a kind. Yet it's not enough to give the family new rules in the form of business procedures or trust provisions. In contrast, a maieutic process helps the family to recognize what's going on in the business, and to realize they have the power to change it. As part of that maieutic process, we interview family members and develop a history of the business. Then we present that history to the family and ask questions (in a Socratic manner) that guide the family toward useful realizations.

Our goal in recounting the history of Acme Building and Home Supply here is to show in detail how this segment of such a consultation proceeds, how the facilitator conducts himself, and how family members respond. We also intend to show how roles are passed along in a multigenerational business and how they affect the business and family. And we will show how the owners of Acme, the Hartwells, responded to their history and improved their understanding of the roles they were playing and not playing. With that accomplished, we were better positioned to help the family to make the keep-or-sell decision and, if they decided to keep it, to help them define new business Roles and Rules.

We developed this family history from more than twenty-five interviews, which were often focused on the organizational structure. We realize that such extensive interviewing is seldom necessary and, even if necessary, may not be practical. In this case, Acme Building and Home Supply was a $60 million regional company with significant operations, and more than a dozen family members owned or worked in the business, or both. This justified extensive interviewing. Yet even a family history based on a few interviews can be quite valuable in analyzing roles.

Key Family and Business Roles

In this section, we present the *dramatis personae*, so to speak, the key family members and their business roles.

The Senior Generation

First, here are the members of the "parents' generation" of Hartwells (who are all over 65), their family roles, and their roles in Acme Building and Home Supply:

- The senior generation included four siblings: the company president, Peter (76), his vice president and brother Karl (74), and their sisters Pauline (72) and Kathy (68). Each of these senior-generation siblings had been left a 25 percent share in the business by their parents.

- The sisters, Pauline and Kathy, were not active in the business. Their parents had arranged for Peter to be the trustee for Pauline and for Karl to be the trustee for Kathy. Each brother handles his respective sister's interests in the business.
- Peter was a good money manager, so he handled the financial side of the business. He became president because he was the elder brother. He also became independently wealthy by investing in stocks as a sideline apart from the business.
- Younger brother Karl was an excellent operating manager, so he handled the day-to-day commercial and retail operations. Karl, however, had not invested on the side and lived mainly on his salary.
- Older sister Pauline is married to a successful senior executive, who has no role the business.
- Younger sister Kathy works as a relatively unknown sculptor and her husband, now deceased, had been a lab technician. Kathy and her three children are neither as educated nor as wealthy as the rest of the family, so she needs current income more than her three siblings do.

Up to the early 1990s, Peter, Karl, Pauline, and Kathy each owned 25 percent of the company stock. At that time, for tax purposes, they began distributing stock to the next generation. This created the situation described in Chapter 3, in which members of the senior generation who wanted to sell the company no longer owned enough voting shares to do so. (You may recall that they wanted to sell to forestall potential discord in the next generation.)

The Next Generation

Here are the key players in the next (cousins') generation:

- Peter, and his wife Linda have two children: Steve (48), a Ph.D. finance professor, and Sally (45), who holds a Ph.D. in history. Both children own shares in the business and are quite knowledgeable about it, but they have no day-to-day management role.
- Karl, whose wife is deceased, has three children: Cecil (48), Carol (46), and Charles (43). Cecil, who holds an MBA, is a savvy manager and marketing professional who has been an Acme senior manager and an officer of the company. Carol has been less involved with the business, but is very knowledgeable about it. Charles, a lawyer turned businessman, is Acme's corporate secretary. Compared with the other cousins, Karl's children dominate the management of the business.

- Pauline's children include Danny (44), Debbie (41) and Dusty (38). As "district manager," Danny oversees Acme's retail stores. After college he held management positions in several companies, then approached Peter about a position in the business. Peter hired Danny as an employee, not on the "officer track" that was provided for Karl's sons. Debbie and Dusty have little to do with the business and usually vote with Danny.
- Kathy's three children have no role in the business and tend to vote with Kathy, who votes with Karl.

As will become clear, the family is divided along a fault line that broadly defines two camps. One camp includes Peter and Pauline in the older generation along with their offspring; the other includes Karl and Kathy and their offspring.

The Conflicts in Summary

Until the mid-1990s, this closely held company rarely paid dividends. By then, however, Acme was generating significant cash, which could be either paid out as dividends or reinvested in expansion. Only in the past few years has the company grown large and profitable enough to pay substantial dividends, now about $3 million annually.

In our interviews and interactions with family members, we found three major areas of conflict:

#1. Senior Generation Conflict: In the senior generation, Peter and Pauline, on the one hand, and on the other, Karl and Kathy, tend to oppose one another. Peter feels protective of Pauline (and, by extension, of her son Danny), and he supports her positions and she his. Karl feels protective of Kathy, who is relatively poor, and he supports her positions and she his.

Note that this paring of elder brother and sister and younger brother and sister parallels the birth order, and the arrangement of Peter as trustee for Pauline's interests and Karl as trustee for Kathy's. On top of that the two brothers often individually oppose one another, as do the two sisters.

#2. Next Generation Conflict: In the cousins' generation, Peter's children—the Ph.D.s not working in the business but who are active owners—favor selling it, mainly because that's Peter's position. Pauline's children, Danny, Debbie, and Dusty, also want to sell the business, mainly to support their mother's position and Danny, who wants to go out on his own.

Meanwhile, Karl's children—Cecil, Carol, and Charles—want to keep the business and grow it aggressively. Kathy's children want to keep the business because they want their relatively poor mother to have steady dividend income.

#3. Intergenerational Conflict: Across the two generations, the children who
want to keep the business—Cecil, Charles, and Carol (Karl's children) plus
Kathy's children (not named here)—oppose the parents who want to sell it
(Peter and Pauline). By the same token, Steve and Sally (Peter's children)
and Danny, Debbie, and Dusty (Pauline's children) oppose the parents who
want to keep the business (Karl and Kathy).

Where We Came In

Peter and Karl had been managing the company, but both wanted to retire
soon. They had postponed retirement, mainly because they foresaw unpleasant
consequences for the next generation—that is, they saw, but did not understand,
the impending Rules Crisis. Karl's sons, Cecil and Charles, are moving into
management roles and staving off Pauline's son Danny's efforts to either gain a
senior officer position or sell the company.

Other troubles abounded. For us as advisors, however, the overall goal was
to help the family to understand its situation, control its conflicts, and make
sound decisions—particularly the keep-or-sell decision and any succession
decisions—in a lucid, useful manner. Incidentally, splitting the company into
two separate entities, one commercial and one retail, was another option, which
Danny sometimes raised. We worked with the Hartwells in a highly maieutic
way, which included many interviews as well as meetings of the type we recount
later in this chapter.

Here are the key things we heard in interviews with family members.

Peter, CEO, Chairman, and Older Brother:

Peter was well aware of the conflicts between Karl's sons, Cecil and Charles,
whom he saw as quite aggressive, and Pauline's son Danny. Karl's sons were smart,
educated, and knowledgeable about the business, but were not as hands-on as
Danny. They tended to dominate meetings with their strong personalities and
debating skills. Although Peter had supported Karl's sons' entry into the business,
he now saw them as ambitious and rude. He felt that he had to protect Danny
from their exploitation and humiliation, since as CEO he was in charge and his
sister Pauline expected it of him.

Peter knew that Pauline would rather sell the business than see her son
Danny suffer at Cecil's and Charles's hands. To Peter, the cousins' conflict was
forestalling his retirement because he couldn't agree to any succession plan that
left this situation unresolved. Seeing little chance of a resolution, Peter and Pauline
would vote to sell the company, and lobbied others to vote with them.

When we asked Peter how he handled this tension in his role as CEO and chair of the meetings, he said he "had to be forceful with Karl's children." His priorities as CEO seemed to be protecting Danny and Pauline and dealing with the company's finances. He could not identify any true managerial role he had with anyone. Rather he saw himself as a policeman. He said that in the old days he and Karl worked well together without having to talk much or argue, since he handled the finances and Karl handled operations. At this point, Peter saw no problem with the way he played his leadership role.

Karl, President, Chief Operating Officer, and Younger Brother:

Karl perceived his role in the business with a great deal of emotion. In interviews, he said he had "given his best" without recognition from his father or older brother. He felt his financial compensation had neither made up for the extra time he had put in out of devotion to his father, nor reflected his contribution over the years. Indeed, his contribution had never been quantified in dollars or formally assessed in reviews.

Karl saw the business as having been driven first by his father and then by his older brother. He felt that he and Peter had always mingled family roles and business roles. He also felt that he was a competent operating manager. He had, however, been reducing his managerial role as he neared retirement and at this point interacted mainly with his sons Cecil and Charles, who were assuming (and grabbing) more responsibility.

Pauline and Kathy (Peter and Karl's Sisters):

Although they held ownership shares equal to those of Peter and Karl, Pauline and Kathy had scant knowledge of the business. However, each of them discussed the tension they felt between themselves over dividend distributions. Kathy needed the money to live on, while Pauline, who married a successful executive, did not. Therefore, Kathy favored paying dividends while Pauline favored reinvesting in the business.

Pauline criticized her sister for her low earnings, "poor work ethic," and dependence on the dividends. She said, "Mother and father never meant for us to become dependent on the business. They wanted us to be self-reliant." Kathy told us (and Pauline) that Pauline, having married a highly paid executive, had accomplished little on her own and shouldn't talk about self-reliance.

Pauline viewed Karl's sons, Cecil and Charles, as people who wouldn't let others speak their minds at meetings. She saw them as a threat to her son Danny, and was determined to spare him from suffering at their hands.

The Cousins:

In interviewing the cousins, we realized that Peter was not running meetings with a fair hand and ensuring that all could participate. Overall, he appeared to be permissive while expecting everyone to behave well; then, when they failed to, he became frustrated and responded with tough and rigid posturing.

The interviews with the cousins revealed a deep rift along the lines of family roles. Karl's family felt that since Cecil and Charles knew the business better than the other cousins (including the very hands-on Danny, in their eyes), they should make the major decisions. Indeed, most of the other cousins had little knowledge of how to run the business; they were owners, but passive ones.

Cecil and Charles sincerely wanted to create prosperity for subsequent generations of Hartwells and felt they could grow the business through reinvestment and expansion. They wanted leadership roles because they believed they were the most experienced, educated, and skilled of the cousins. But they didn't know how to play leadership roles, nor had they been shown how. Nevertheless, they repeatedly encouraged the senior generation to let go and let them run the business, which Peter and Pauline opposed for reasons explained above.

Danny felt he possessed deep knowledge of the business and solid management skills, and that he'd contributed a lot over the years. Yet he also felt overwhelmed by Cecil and Charles. He wanted to sell the business and use his stake to start a new venture in construction materials. As noted, he also raised the option of splitting the business into two separate companies—one wholesale and one retail—so he could run his own retail chain. His mother Pauline and Uncle Peter supported Danny, but they preferred an outright sale rather than a split.

Roles People and Rules People

The two Hartwell camps break out into what we broadly view as Roles People and Rules People. The Roles camp includes Peter, Pauline, and Danny, who want to sell the business, divide the business, or otherwise avoid having to manage the business by rules. Before the Rules Crisis, CEO Peter ran the show based on his role of eldest brother. Now, however, a Rules camp has arisen in the form of Karl's sons, who want to run the company on the basis of the numbers with the aim of achieving growth. They aggressively assert their power, but on the basis of their qualifications as Ph.D.s and attorneys and with the stated goal of professionalizing the business. They have also developed reliable figures showing that Danny's decisions have not been particularly profitable.

The Situation

The foregoing situation prevailed until the need for a succession and estate plan arose upon the impending (if reluctant) retirement of the senior generation. Family roles had been the primary way of functioning for decades but as the cousins, particularly Karl's sons, became more involved and Peter and Karl continued to age, the business faced a Rules Crisis—a situation in which their roles held less power. For instance, the rules that applied to the voting shares applied to everyone, regardless of their role. If people wanted to sell, they could vote to sell; if they didn't want to sell, they could vote against it. One vote was equal to any other vote regardless of a voter's experience, knowledge, or position in the company. Similarly, the rules of the succession and estate plan would, if properly formulated, override family roles.

But role behavior dies hard. Peter's and Karl's retirement would create a void and there was no clear line of succession. Factions lobbied one another for votes regarding the keep-or-sell decision and on key policy issues, such as dividend distributions. Regarding the latter, people argued about paying dividends or retaining earnings from the standpoint of their family roles, rather than a business standpoint. For example, Pauline takes Kathy to task for needing the money, and Kathy argues that Pauline doesn't need the dividends because she married money.

The Hartwells presented complex relationships and a long multigenerational history, which we'll get into momentarily. However, even in a two-generation case, the family business history gives rise to—and explains—the impact of family roles in the business.

Recent History

Consider the senior generation roles: You have four siblings, born in boy-girl-boy-girl order (Peter-Pauline-Karl-Kathy). That generates older-brother/younger-brother roles, older-sister/younger-sister roles and, in this case, an older dyad and a younger dyad. Peter feels protective of Pauline, and Karl feels protective of Kathy. Their parents—R.L. (Richard Lawrence) and Elizabeth, who died in the 1970s—reinforced the brothers' and sisters' roles by naming Peter Pauline's trustee and Karl Kathy's trustee.

A fair amount of sexism and gender-biased attitudes prevailed in the family. We don't mean this as judgmentally as it may sound, but that is the case. (Sexism reflects a roles-based view of the world, that holds that men and women are not equal and which can be summed up, "Men are breadwinners, and women bear and rear children.") R.L. and Elizabeth, the grandparent generation, were products of their times when men generally handled business matters. In the United States, the main careers open to women, aside from housewife, were teacher, nurse, and beautician. Women seeking business careers usually entered retail, fashion, or publishing, and seldom reached senior positions. Very few women entered the construction materials trade, and the Hartwell women certainly weren't encouraged to do so.

How did these family and societal roles carry over to the family business? In five ways:

First, although Peter's real interest lay in the financial markets, Peter's father gave him the job of CEO; Karl felt this was unjust but had not spoken up about it. Over the years, under R.L.'s direction, younger brother Karl had done more than Peter to grow and manage the business. Peter played the stock market and became a proficient and wealthy investor. In fact, a number of cousins felt that, although he was the CEO, Peter lacked the knowledge and experience to run the company. Some suspected that Peter became chairman and CEO thanks to his role of older brother, while Karl's role of younger brother led to the lower-ranking role of president and COO. Neither brother had spoken about the situation except with their own families, and there never had been an open examination of the impact of their father's decision.

Second, Pauline and Kathy were bequeathed no real roles in the family business. Their brothers were appointed trustees of their ownership interests and the trust created, or more likely reinforced, the Peter/Pauline and Karl/Kathy dyads which carried into the business. The rules of the trust mandated that Peter protect Pauline's interests and Karl protect Kathy's. Those rules reflected their parents' roles-based world view. These were family scripts, and the family members played their roles more or less as directed. This points up the importance of crafting rules based on fairness rather than role expectations. (Given the circumstances, Pauline and Kathy might count themselves lucky that the Acme shares were evenly distributed among the four children.)

Third, these sibling dyads fueled conflict. For instance, Karl would say, "I'm concerned about Kathy's family. They don't have much money, and if we don't pay dividends, how will they live?" To which Peter, along with Pauline, would say, "She's the one who married a lab technician and became a sculptor. Besides, Mom and Dad always said we shouldn't become dependent on the business unless we work in it." To which Kathy would say, "Don't kid yourself, Pauline. You married a big shot, but you dropped out of college and never accomplished anything on your own. And Peter, Dad *gave you* the top job in a successful business." Which leaves everyone where they started, if not further behind.

Fourth, the family roles carried into the cousins' generation as well. For instance, the cousins lined up with their parents on the potential sale of the company.

Also, Peter and Karl both gave Karl's sons, Cecil and Charles, senior management roles and the chance to become company officers (which they did). But Pauline's son, Danny, an MBA and a solid manager, had been stuck as a district manager for years—as an employee. Danny received second-class treatment from his uncles for the crime of being their sister's son.

Fifth, family roles generated emotions that affected the business. Peter's and Karl's fears for the next generation led them to stay on long after they wanted to retire. (Both brothers were wealthy enough to retire years earlier.) In the cousins' generation, Karl's children (Cecil, Charles, and Carol) resented their father's second-class status relative to Peter. Meanwhile, Danny's feelings of being stifled led him to lobby to sell the business. He found no effective way to confront his cousins and resolve his issues, and the structure had no rules of conflict resolution or mediation. Peter felt frustrated and unable to play a mediator role or to lead, for example in meetings, without being a bully or protector. He did not know how to set agendas and ground rules for meetings or how to use managerial practices and procedures in the business. Also, Peter would have been happy to invest his share of the proceeds of a sale of the business in securities.

So, there was plenty of conflict to go around. It had, of course, lay dormant for decades. Every family business has its problems and most families learn to live with them—up to a point. That point arrives with the imminent transfer of the business from one generation to the next.

Which Roles Are Whose?

The pressure generated by the Rules Crisis forces family dynamics to the surface. These dynamics comprise the roles people are playing and not playing and the resulting factions, alliances, and conflicts.

Let's examine the business roles in the Acme case:

- The leadership role was for all intents and purposes missing. Peter was CEO, but was not playing that role and was perhaps not suited to it. Karl was a more knowledgeable manager, but stood in his older brother's shadow. It was too late in life for Karl to assume sole leadership of the company. Someone in the cousins' generation had to fill that role.
- No one was playing the role of mentor for the next generation. Indeed, the next generation had largely replicated divisions in the parent generation. For instance, among Karl's sons, older brother Cecil believed that he should be senior to his younger brother Charles. They and others needed to develop new business roles, but they hadn't been taught how.

- Certain owners, such as Pauline and Kathy, did not play the role of owners. True, Peter and Karl had always controlled their interests, but Pauline and Kathy were well into adulthood. Similarly, female cousins, such as Danny's sister Debbie, automatically voted with their brothers or fathers. If the passive owners wanted a voice in the company, and wanted to stop being lobbied, they needed to assume ownership roles.
- Pauline's son Danny resented Karl's sons, Cecil and Charles. Pauline lobbied Peter to "do more for Danny," but Peter and Karl have already installed Karl's (admittedly competent) sons as senior managers. These parent-son and uncle-nephew roles generated tension. Indeed, Danny's desire to sell the business and go out on his own grew directly out of family roles.

The company required a true CEO reporting to a true board of directors, and a firmer reporting structure. The transfer of the company to the next generation provided an opportunity to professionalize the business in this way. But that would mean moving into business roles and leaving behind deeply rooted family roles.

Ancient History

Here is the history of Acme Building and Home Supply as it emerged at a day-long retreat with the family:

> In the late 1800s, the great-grandfather of Peter, Pauline, Karl, and Kathy had a farm in Oklahoma, a wife, and ten children. Great-grandfather sent his second son, Winthrop (the senior generation's grandfather), to college and upon his graduation, loaned him $80 to go to California with his new wife, Frances, to start a new life because, as second son, he wouldn't inherit the farm.
>
> Shortly after Winthrop and Frances arrived in Los Angeles, they had children and wanted their own home. (They would have four children: Charles, Richard Lawrence, called R.L., Marie and Rose.) Winthrop started as a bookkeeper for the Southern Pacific Railroad, and quickly rose to senior accountant. But when anti-monopoly sentiment soured the railroad's fortunes, he lost his job.
>
> Winthrop had seen huge quantities of lumber traveling to Southern California by rail and believed Los Angeles would soon grow as San Francisco had after the Gold Rush. So he talked his way into a job as a foreman with a homebuilder.
>
> We asked the family, "What do you think of that?"

Peter said, "It's remarkable that he could move from accountant to construction foreman. But then, he's said to have had quite a personality."

"That's important," we said. "Many family business are started by a charismatic personality."

In seven years, Winthrop had his own homebuilding operation, which expanded rapidly as Los Angeles grew to over one million people by the late 1920s. With no investments in the stock market, the business survived the Great Depression, but then grew more slowly. Winthrop's oldest son, Charles, went to college and became a banker with Wells Fargo. R.L. earned his degree in night school and worked in the family business. After World War II, Charles joined the business as comptroller and soon became president. R.L. was general manager and handled day-to-day operations.

Several people said, "Hmmm," and we prompted them to elaborate.

Danny said, "Already you see two brothers, one who's in the trade and the other . . . ." He trailed off. Peter and Karl said nothing, perhaps, like Danny, sensing that the discussion could take an uncomfortable turn.

We asked, "Where do all these roles come from?"

"From Charles and R.L."

"And where did Charles and R.L. get their roles?"

Peter said, "From Winthrop. But Winthrop did things differently from his father by leaving the business to *both* sons. Charles and R.L. both inherited the business just like Karl and I did." Peter stopped, then said, "Maybe Winthrop wanted to be fair to both sons because his older brother inherited the farm."

"Right," we said. "Who made Winthrop the second son? Who made Charles the first son and R.L. the second? Who made Marie and Rose daughters?"

"They were born that way," Pauline said.

We asked Peter, "How did you get to be CEO?"

He laughed, "I was born that way."

"That's right! First son, second son, daughter—all these are roles we're born into." We had an idea: "You know, this is Los Angeles, the movie capital. You might think of these roles as coming from Central Casting. But you can be very creative in the way you play your roles. You don't have to play them the way your parents and uncles and aunts did."

We said, "Danny, before you were saying something"—we checked our notes—'you have two brothers, one of them is in the trade and the other . . .' and then you trailed off. Where were you going with that?"

Danny glanced at Peter. "I, ah, think it's a little like Uncle Peter and Uncle Karl. Uncle Peter is a financial wiz, like his Uncle Charles was, and Uncle Karl has always been the guy talking to the mills and contractors and floor crews like his father R.L."

Everyone nodded. Peter and Karl looked at one another.

"Could this have something to do with your family roles?"

There was wide agreement on that. In case after case, we have seen family history repeat itself—or, rather, we've seen people repeat family history. Yet most families seem only dimly aware of the power of family roles in business decisions.

"Look at your ancestors' spirit and ambition," we said. "You have a couple leaving home to make a new start. He loses his accounting job and gets a job as a foreman, but he's still seeking opportunity. He sees houses being built, and he wants to be part of that. Then his sons Charles and R.L. take over the business and grow it into a company that's putting up whole developments. These are seriously entrepreneurial, forward-thinking people."

Some eyes filled with tears, and people said they'd always thought of the founders as resourceful and charismatic, and revered them as the builders of the business. (Family members often idealize the family history at a time like this, which fosters a sense of closeness which can extend to the facilitator.)

"Let's look at what they did next," we said.

"They broke up the business," Karl said. "They sold it. Charles took his share and started a community bank with some partners, and R.L. started Acme Building Supply, which became Acme Building and Home Supply."

"Why did they sell the business?"

"They didn't get along well enough to run it together," Pauline said.

Peter said, "There were business reasons, too. I remember hearing that R.L. wouldn't report to a board of directors, and Charles wanted a board."

We said, "Pauline said they didn't get along. We heard in our interviews that things came easily to Charles and were more of a struggle for R.L. Charles had a football scholarship, then went into banking, but R.L. was more of a worker bee—solid, dependable, and smart, but not the type that Charles was. Does this resemble anything today?"

Everyone saw the parallels between Charles in banking and Peter in the stock market, and their both being financial types and having brothers who were operational types.

Peter said, "Karl and I have both made our contributions to the business. But I see how these roles, like older brother and younger brother, can move from generation to generation."

Karl agreed. "I think that's true. My children, and my wife before she died, often told me I should be CEO of the company." Karl looked at Peter, and they gave one another half-smiles that spoke volumes. "Frankly, I often agreed. But Peter and I each had our territory, and it's been good for the company."

We summarized: "So, Peter and Karl's relationship sort of parallels the one between Charles and R.L."

"Can we get back to one thing?" Cecil asked. "What about Charles and R.L. splitting up the company?"

We said, "Tell us about that."

Here, family members spoke about Charles' desire to bring in outside investors or take the company public to raise money to grow the business. He wanted a board of directors and a formal management structure, but R.L. did not. So they sold the business, then called Ventura Home Builders. Charles found partners and started a community bank in Pasadena, which was later sold to investors for millions. R.L. started Acme Building Supply, which later became Acme Building and Home Supply.

We said, "Is any of this history repeating itself?"

"It sure is," Peter's daughter Carol said. "Some of us are talking about selling the company because people can't get along or might not get along. Only thing is, Charles and R.L. agreed to sell, but now some people want to sell and some don't."

"Well," we said, "Charles and R.L. sold because they couldn't agree on the future of the business."

Several people told us later that this gave them goose bumps. They not only saw Peter and Karl replicating Charles and R.L.'s relationship, but also saw that they might sell a solid company because of their differences.

"Let's get the real question on the table," we said. "What's best for the business now?"

"To make it as professional and profitable as possible," Peter said. Then he said, "I guess I am like Charles, but I believe the best thing for the business is to have the best possible management. If Danny thinks he's qualified, he should be able to make his case. If Cecil or Charles would be the best CEO, they should make their cases. Maybe we should even think about hiring someone from outside. But we should stop making the oldest kid CEO."

Coming from Peter, this resembled Nixon's visit to China. He was a "roles guy" coming to understand rules. He respected Karl, but had played the role of CEO like a big brother. At this point, maybe he was "looking out for Danny" or maybe he felt he didn't have to worry about his children, who had Ph.D. careers. Or—what we believe—perhaps Peter saw that the good of the company might come first.

Then Kathy, who rarely spoke up in meetings, said, "Can we look at how the family history affected the women? Pauline and I have almost nothing to say about the company. I know I've let my brothers handle things, but that's just another family role thing. Charles and R.L. ran it without their sisters—who we've barely mentioned today—and that's the deal R.L. left us."

"I guess that's true," Karl said. "Maybe Peter and I shouldn't be making every decision for our sisters, but that's the way it's always been."

"We have to stop mindless repetition of the past," Pauline said.

"From now on, let's do it mindfully," Cecil wisecracked.

"Seriously," we said, "what do we know about these conflicts and the choices you face?"

This kicked off a discussion of how the family roles drove the current conflicts. It's too long to report in more detail here, but regarding the three major areas of conflict we cited earlier, the following occurred:

#1. Senior Generation Conflicts: The family saw that the Peter-and-Pauline camp and Karl-and-Kathy camp were rooted in the trusts created by R.L. and in family roles. They also saw that tensions between Peter and Karl stemmed from family roles and giving the older brother the top spot regardless of his interests or skills. People were surprised that they had never noticed the parallels between Charles and R.L. and Peter and Karl. In each case, the older brother was perceived as charismatic and financially oriented and the younger brother as a "worker bee" and operationally oriented, and their family roles carried into the business, with the father's blessing.

#2 Next Generation Conflict: The cousins realized that the urge to sell the business grew more out of family issues than business issues. Peter and Pauline wanted to sell because they assumed the cousins wouldn't get along well enough to run the business. (Pauline's and Danny's animus toward Karl's children didn't help.) The cousins saw that they needed to recognize the effects of family roles and decide to keep or sell based on business concerns and on their needs, not on their parents' needs.

#3 Intergenerational Conflict: Recognition of family dynamics in the senior (and in the Charles-R.L. generation) illuminated the source of certain attitudes and behavior. For instance, Peter and Karl realized they'd contributed to Danny's disaffection by denying him the kind of senior officer position given to Karl's sons. Danny realized that some of his resentment of his cousins, Peter's and Karl's children, may relate to feelings toward his (more powerful) uncles. While people had business reasons for their positions—Danny wanted his own show and Kathy wanted dividends from a secure source—the cousins saw that their parents had also fostered or reinforced these positions.

This summary covers only the major aspects of that day with the Hartwells. Along the way people experienced many small epiphanies regarding family roles and the need to limit their damaging effects on the business. They also saw the positive things the senior generation had done. For instance, unlike Charles, Peter remained in the business all his life. Unlike Charles and R.L., Peter and Karl found ways to get along, for the good of the family and the business. Unlike the sisters of Charles and R.L., Pauline and Kathy now (if belatedly) felt ready to become more involved in the business.

When the Hartwells saw how the Charles-R.L. fault line had extended to Peter and Karl, and how that fault line might extend into the next generation, they felt a need to put their history in the past and their roles in their place and to make the keep-or-sell decision fully conscious of why they were making it.

Maieutic Facilitation: No Conclusions

We have taken the time to portray this family history in some depth partly to show how the Maieutic Consultant works. The Maieutic Consultant conveys the history of the business to the family, but not conclusions. Instead, the MC asks questions that lead family members to draw their own conclusions. To do this the facilitator must be familiar with the history, which builds credibility with the family, and must understand the family dynamics that emerged from that history.

Again there's the difference between a Maieutic Consultant and a consultant: A Maieutic Consultant leads the client and family to their own inferences and conclusions, while a consultant formulates his conclusions and recommendations, presents them, and tries to create buy-in. Allowing family members to voice their own ideas, interpretations, feelings, and desires helps them develop their own insights. Those insights are more valuable than those of an outside expert because they are *their* insights.

In this work, the Maieutic Consultant must proceed with skill and sensitivity. How? First, by creating an atmosphere of calm, exploratory interchange and respect for all views and feelings. Second, by asking questions about the roles dimension and rules dimension as distinct domains and helping the client put them together in their minds. Third, by dealing with difficulties realistically, non-judgmentally, and even-handedly. And finally, by framing the discussion in terms of Roles and Rules and addressing family dynamics as part of a business consultation rather than a therapy session. Of course, no matter how skillfully an advisor facilitates such discussions, not everyone will see his own shortcomings, refrain from blame, and apologize or forgive.

For instance, a meltdown could have occurred when Peter and Karl saw the similarities between themselves and Charles and R.L. But these men had come to terms with one another and enjoyed a good level of success and closeness. That helped them view themselves and their past with some objectivity and relevance to current needs. Also, we had prepared the ground in prior interviews by asking about the Roles and Rules aspects of the reporting structure. We also mentioned the possibility that difficult emotions and areas of conflict might arise, and that only respect and understanding would keep the discussion on track.

We would like to report that, at the end of the session, all family members held hands and sang Kumbaya in three-part harmony. They did not, nor did we ask them to. Indeed, a fair amount of work still needed to be done, which we take up in Chapter 5.

Bear in Mind

- When there is evidence in initial interviews that family roles are undermining the business structure, the business history can illuminate those roles and their effects.
- The facilitator must develop the history with family members with the aim of limiting the negative impact of family roles on business roles. This places any emotional responses in the proper context, a business context, and aligns the facilitator with the family along the common goal of a sound succession plan.
- Family members may be re-enacting family roles without realizing that roles come from "central casting" and are "assigned" largely by birth order, family tradition, and societal norms.
- When family members realize the source and effects of their roles, they may see that unacknowledged, unaddressed role expectations can impede their ability to learn to play business roles in keeping with business rules.
- Insight alone will not bring about change. Families also need guidance regarding their business roles and the rules they will need to help them work well within a healthy business structure.

CHAPTER 6

A Strong Foundation:
Generating the Right Rules

With an understanding of the family roles affecting the business, the advisor and family can turn to the task of establishing sound rules of succession. The goal, again, is a new business structure comprising business Roles and Rules. This structure will enable the transfer of power to the next generation. Note that, perhaps on the basis of what they learned by examining the effects of family roles on the business, the testator and family may decide to sell rather than keep the business. In that case, the work on family roles has not been wasted because it will help them to craft workable rules for the sale of the business and distribution of the proceeds.

Again, the ultimate rule is that everyone dies. That fact, together with society's rules of taxation, transfer, and distribution of a decedent's assets, fosters the Rules Crisis. Recall, too, that you need rules—as well as new roles—to address that crisis and forge the future of the business. That's a real break with the past, in which the business ran on family roles, and it can be a painful break.

In this chapter, we continue our examination of Acme Building and Home Supply with a focus on the *rules* aspect of the consultation. This parallels our treatment of roles in the previous chapter. Note, however, that we will cover what we call legal rules, as distinct from business rules, separately in Chapter 7. By legal rules we mean provisions in wills, trusts, contracts, and business structures that ensure liquidity, preserve capital, and minimize taxes, *and* that address family-role difficulties. These difficulties may include sibling rivalry, rogue children, and personal problems, such as addiction or compulsive spending, among other issues. The legal rules are relatively technical tools and thus warrant separate coverage.

Rules as Tools

In some cases, solid rules may already be in place and family members may be ignoring them or be unaware of them. For example, in the case of Acme Building and Home Supply, Peter and Pauline in the older generation wanted to sell the business, as did Danny in the cousins' generation. By force of his personality and family role, Peter may have been able to persuade his brother Karl or sister Kathy and perhaps his children to vote for a sale. But at that point enough voting shares had, through the gifting program, passed to the younger generation to put "the rules" on the side of those who wanted to keep the company in the family.

So, even in cases with existing rules, the advisor or Maieutic Consultant often must help the family develop, accept, implement, and operate by rules. Each family has unique needs based on family members' personalities, relationships, skills, finances, and retirement schedules. Rules can help address these needs. They can also help people understand the demands of business roles, and then decide whether to accept a specific role in the business. The right rules help people play their business roles by promoting fair, objective, rational decision making, and fostering a kiss-down organization. In these ways, rules can minimize the effects of family roles on the business.

Of course, the family must be ready, willing, and able to live with rules—or be able to reach such a state in a reasonable timeframe. Absent that, they should seriously consider or reconsider the keep-or-sell decision. A family unable to live with rules will find it difficult to impossible to see the business through the transition to the next generation. As a result, the family may experience discord, the business may suffer losses, and the family finances may be put at risk. The keep-or-sell decision must therefore be made with an objective evaluation of the family's readiness, willingness, and ability to live by business rules.

That said, no set of rules can guarantee a happy outcome. People who are determined to persist in their family roles, even to the detriment of the business, will usually find a way to do so. Even well-crafted, agreed-upon rules and the example of a superb facilitator can't help some people. As we've noted, Roles and Rules does not work in every case. It simply works more reliably for us than any other method we have seen or tried.

As you'll see in this chapter, this type of consultation differs sharply from one in which an advisor sits down and simply explains the legal rules to the testator and family. In difficult family situations, explaining the legal rules is never enough, which is why we take a maieutic approach. The family needs tools, and rules are the tools the family will use to craft their new business roles. Rules are the fulcrums and levers that lift people out of their old, family roles. They are the mallets and chisels with which they shape new roles. They are the levels and yardsticks that ensure fair, rational, businesslike decision making. And family members may need to learn how to use these tools through an "apprenticeship" with an advisor well-versed in Roles and Rules.

Back to the Structure: Business Roles Are Half of It

You'll recall that an organization's structure consists of Roles and Rules, with roles supplying the vertical, hierarchical elements and rules the horizontal, equalizing elements. In a troubled family business, the right organizational structure must be established or reinforced so that people will make decisions and choose behaviors based on business considerations rather than family role considerations. Without the right structure, business roles exist mainly in name and are either unfilled or poorly played.

For instance, in any dysfunctional hierarchy, the chief leadership role is vacant, divided, or poorly played. In succession, that role is about to pass to the next generation, or perhaps to a professional manager from outside the family. That successor must be chosen on the basis of what's best for the business and be prepared to play the chief leadership role properly. Leadership roles below that of chief executive officer will also have to be defined and filled. These depend on the needs of the business and, when the roles already exist, on the people in the roles.

These management roles must be organized into business functions, such as accounting, finance, sales, marketing, production, and distribution. All necessary roles must be defined or (redefined) and filled with a capable person. That may be the person currently in the job, who may have to change to meet the role's new requirements, usually with training, coaching, consulting, and mentoring. Often, competent people already occupy some business roles and need only a change in leadership to start functioning well. This is especially true of non-family members whose motivation and performance suffer amid bad family dynamics. These employees usually spring to life when they see the business being run like a business rather than a segment of Family Feud.

Identifying the business roles and filling them with people equal to their jobs is half the battle—and half the structure. The other half is the rules that define the roles and guide people's on-the-job interactions.

Where We Are in the Process

At this point in the consultation, the planning team understands the formal and informal organization structures and who has the power. The team

111

understands the origins of the family roles as well as their effect on the business. The team also understands the business roles and how people are playing or not playing them.

Consider the benefits of this understanding: For instance, in the Acme case, we realized that sibling rivalry, brother-sister dyads, and sexism were driving certain decisions (to sell the business, to favor Karl's sons over Pauline's son) and behaviors (Peter protecting Pauline and Danny, Karl protecting Kathy and her family, Pauline and Danny resenting Cecil and Charles, factional lobbying). Without that knowledge we'd be in the dark. Worse, so would the Hartwells, who had spent a lifetime being driven by these forces. Without that knowledge, we would be enlisted as supporting players or spectators in the Hartwell family drama. Peter and Karl would push their keep-versus-sell agendas at us. Family members would demand that we take sides, or accuse us of doing so. Pauline and Danny would tell us how unfair it all is. Cecil and Charles would tell us how much they know about the business and so on. We would be whipsawed between factions, told what to do by "the client" (Peter *and* Karl, mind you), and remain forever confused regarding what's fair, who's "right," and how we can help this family save a $60 million business. The knowledge provided by Roles and Rules helps the planning team see past the arguments, positions, and emotions.

At this point in a consultation, the facilitator should have shared the family history with the testator and family members, as demonstrated in the previous chapter. Thus, family members (to greater and lesser degrees) now understand their true situation. If this understanding has not been established through a discussion of the family history, it now must be established, perhaps in more direct ways. This can be difficult for several reasons: First, family issues are painful for most people to confront and discuss; second, people rarely enjoy hearing about their real or perceived shortcomings; third, certain dynamics and personalities—especially "strong" personalities, which may include the testator—try to assert control of the discussion; and fourth, discussing family issues productively requires skills that most family members (and estate planners) lack.

To the fullest possible extent, this discussion should be maieutic. The facilitator should *lead* the family to understand their issues and dynamics and lead them to solutions. This can be difficult with stubborn testators. Helping those who have power to relinquish it may entail clarifying the choices they face by means of direct questions: Do they want to sacrifice the business in order to settle a score? Do they want to consider the whole family or put one family member—or themselves—first? Do they want to set a conflict in stone or take steps to settle it now? Have they considered all the effects of placing the wrong people in key positions? What legacy do they really want to leave? (We cover these kinds of questions in greater depth in Chapter 8.)

At times, the attorney or facilitator must ask the testator to take responsibility for his or her choices. You cannot force a person do to so. Testators have the legal right (if not the moral right) to do whatever they want with their estates. If they choose, they may leave a multimillion dollar portfolio to the local pet cemetery. That's the rule. But then there's the role. To play their roles well, they should be honest and open about their decisions. They should do so for the emotional well-being of their families and to minimize anger, resentment, and legal action after the fact. Honesty and openness on the part of a testator can help the children and other heirs and would-be heirs to understand and perhaps even to accept seemingly wrong-headed decisions.

Running on Rules

When moving on to develop rules, we've found it useful to frame the effort in terms of developing the organization structure, if we haven't already done so for the family. If we have done so, we simply remind them of this framework—the business exists to take certain inputs, convert them to outputs, and deliver them to internal or external customers. People in various jobs (business roles) perform this work according to certain policies and procedures (business rules). Those Roles and Rules make up the structure of the organization.

Given this, the key questions become:

- What business roles are missing or being performed poorly?
- What rules are already being consistently applied and followed?
- What rules must be created, improved, defined more clearly, or followed more consistently?

Remember, the goal in this part of the process is to define the business rules—and the business roles—for the new structure. With that goal and these questions in mind, let's pick up where we left off with the Hartwell family.

Moving Forward

As a result of the work we did with the Hartwells on their family history and roles:

- Peter saw that automatically making the eldest son CEO was probably not the best way to proceed. He also suspected that trying to protect Pauline and Danny, while under the influence of sibling rivalry with his brother Karl, may have twisted his business behavior at times.

- Cecil and Charles (Karl's children) accepted the idea that *perhaps* Danny should have more of a senior management role in the business, although they were not prepared to report to him.
- Those who wanted to sell the business—Peter and Pauline (and sometimes Danny)—saw that there may be other solutions.
- Those who wanted to keep the business in the family realized that doing so profitably meant dealing with issues raised by their family history and roles.
- Danny realized that his family role—and his response to that role—was at least partly responsible for his position in the business. He also saw that it might be in his interests to start doing business on the basis of rules rather than relying on family roles.
- Passive owners, such as Pauline and Kathy and some cousins, wanted to play more of an ownership role. They also realized that subtle sexism had contributed to their passivity.
- Family members realized that lobbying one another for votes was not creating the best business atmosphere or decisions.

Moreover, the family witnessed the facilitator using rules in the sessions described in the previous chapter. They saw him conduct meetings according to rules, and saw how to go about developing rules. So, the family has been exposed to rules and to how they are formulated and how they work. (We reserved the material on rules until now, to keep Chapter 4 focused on roles.) In fact, the family's exposure to rules begins with rules that govern meetings and communication. Since that is where we usually introduce rules to a family, that is where we'll start this more detailed discussion of rules.

Start with Communication Rules

In interviews with the Hartwells, we repeatedly heard that meetings were disorganized and poorly conducted. This indicated that the chair of the meetings was not playing his role properly and that meeting rules weren't being followed or enforced. Indeed, as noted, Peter expected everyone to behave well, and when they didn't he became frustrated. Peter held role expectations and believed that those expectations and his role-based power would result in orderly meetings. His older-brother/uncle concept of his role and his need to protect Pauline and Danny also skewed his behavior (as well as Pauline's and Danny's) during meetings.

As estate attorneys know, situations like this are common. A dominant figure or faction controls the meeting. Or no one controls the meeting. Or the agenda favors or slights certain viewpoints. Or there is no agenda. As a result, we usually help the family develop communication rules and meeting protocols to establish a businesslike atmosphere and ensure that all viewpoints are heard. Of course, a strong figure will often say, "We don't need any communication stuff. I know how to run a meeting." At that point you, as facilitator, can acquiesce (which would undermine your role as facilitator of the process) or you can enter an argument (which you will either lose, thus undermining your role, or win, thus alienating the person being confronted).

Or you can figuratively usher everyone out of the room labeled "Roles" and into the room labeled "Rules." Family meetings provide an ideal opportunity to do exactly that, and to introduce rules gently. For this, we use a set of communication rules similar to those that we've developed over the years (reproduced in Appendix C). We do not dictate the communication rules. Instead, we list "develop communication rules" as the first item on the meeting agenda after the introductions. Then we lead the family members, including the unwilling, to develop rules similar to those in Appendix C.

This activity should take no more than 15 minutes. Keep things moving briskly, and make notes on a flip chart or board. Ask questions such as:

1. What do you think might contribute to orderly discussions?
2. How do you think we can avoid arguments?
3. How can we make sure that everyone's view is heard?
4. How do we make sure that nobody dominates the discussion? What sort of time limits do we need?
5. What kind of language might help us calmly discuss emotionally charged subjects?
6. What would be the best ways to discuss disagreements?
7. How can we resolve disagreements? How should we deal with disagreements that we can't resolve in a single meeting?

Notice that these are open-ended, rather than yes-or-no, questions. But be careful: You want to generate ideas not discussion, so, again, set a quick pace. Using an entire evening to come up with communication rules will not demonstrate the best use of time and money. When you hear a good idea, write it down and move on. You are showing people how to run a meeting and play the role of leader. So be sure to elicit and respect all views and gently squelch anyone's attempts to denigrate anyone else's view. When you've generated the ideas, pick the best ones, perhaps by vote, and you have the communication rules. If possible, create a document for them to sign at that meeting. If that's impractical, bring it to the next meeting and distribute it for them to sign.

Yes, that's right, have each meeting participant sign a copy, and sign it yourself. The act of signing an agreement makes people take it more seriously. In subsequent meetings, we have actually pulled out the signed agreement when someone has flagrantly violated it. That reminder of their better natures usually helps them get back on track. Also, when you, as facilitator, sign the agreement you model the kind of leadership they need. When you agree to the rules, you demonstrate the nature of true rules, which apply to everyone.

We sometimes use Roberts Rules of Order, in a modified form, to introduce "parliamentary procedure" and the notion that the speaker "has the floor" and so on. Most people have heard of Roberts Rules, and the voice of authority that they lend to the proceedings helps us to establish what they were designed to establish: order.

After you have the communication rules in place and the family has seen how well they work during a meeting or two (because you are running the meeting by those rules), ask if they've noticed a difference in the tone and productivity of their meetings. They will have. Ask for specifics. You will get them. They'll say things like, "Having an agenda really helps," "Now we all get a chance to be heard," "There's no yelling at each other," and, "Kathy never used to talk at meetings and now she does." If asking for this feedback seems touchy-feely or "obvious" to you, ask for it anyway. Communication rules work, but the family has to be aware that they are working. So emphasize that they are working by having them think and talk about it. This may be the first exposure that some, or perhaps all, of them have had to true rules—guidelines that everyone agrees to, abides by, and benefits from.

We have found that many family members have literally never witnessed a properly conducted business meeting. When they do, it's a revelation. They marvel at the effect of simple tools, such as hard-copy agendas, communication rules, and meeting minutes. They say, "Oh, so this is how it's supposed to be done." And they are right. That is how it's supposed to be done. Business should be conducted in a businesslike manner. We've often said to a family, "Your meetings now run in a businesslike manner because they are operating by rules. Our goal—and your goal—is have your entire business operating that way as the next generation comes on board."

Move on to Business Roles and Rules

Over the past century, the roles required in a business have become very well-defined. The modern executive team traces its roots to John D. Rockefeller, who over a century ago recruited talented, loyal men to manage various functions at his Standard Oil conglomerate. While not every business may require a full-scale executive team, every business does require people to perform specific functions.

In a family business facing succession, before defining the business rules you must define the new business roles. Who is the highest authority? In a business—and this point is key—power emanates from the owners. A proprietorship has one owner, a partnership has two or more owners, and a corporation usually has multiple owners. We won't detail legal business structures here, because they have been covered well in other books and are probably familiar to most readers. But power flows from the owner or owners through the formal reporting structure according to the management principle of delegation and the following related concepts (in *italics*):

- The owners *set goals* and formulate a *plan* to reach those goals
- They then *delegate* to managers the *responsibility* for implementing the plan and meeting the goals.
- They also delegate to managers the *authority* over human and other resources, such as money and equipment, and the tasks that are necessary to implement the plan and achieve those goals. Managers then delegate that responsibility and authority to supervisors who ultimately delegate them to employees.
- Superiors in this *chain of command* define and implement methods of *control* and hold the people below them *accountable* for getting the job done, just as the owners hold management accountable for reaching the company's goals.

Detailed coverage of management principles is beyond the scope of this book. However, this book is as much about power as it is about anything, and misuse of power is rampant in business. Much of that misuse involves violations of the principle of delegation as well as ignorance regarding goal setting, planning, controls, responsibility, authority, and accountability. Common mistakes include failure to set goals and plan, failure to delegate clear and reasonable goals, failure to define the tasks necessary to achieving the goals, and failure to provide the resources or the authority needed to perform those tasks.

Business rules—policies and procedures—preclude or correct such failures. Policies and procedures specify the responsibilities and the scope of authority of positions (roles) in the business. For instance, the salespeople, not the accountants, go out and sell the company's products to customers. Those salespeople report to the sales manager, not to the chief financial officer. Salespeople must follow certain procedures in opening a new customer account. That way, accounting will know about the sale and bill the customer for the correct amount. Myriad "rules" define and channel the power, resources, and activities of the business toward productive, profitable ends. When these rules are in place and are respected, you have sound management.

A good course in management will prepare reasonably intelligent people for management positions *if* they are willing and able to absorb the knowledge and act upon the principles and practices. Unfortunately, many people instead view management as simply "telling people what to do." They lack the skills of goal setting, planning, controlling, communicating, and evaluating and improving subordinates' performance. People who grow up in a business tend to model the management methods of their parents, uncles, aunts, or siblings. Lack of management skills complicates, and may undermine, development of a sound structure. Therefore, if those skills are lacking in people slated for management positions, they should be required to acquire them as quickly as possible.

The Next Phase

At this point the family has seen communication rules in action, and has probably seen the benefit in the form of fairer, more orderly meetings. The family has also seen the facilitator playing a role for them. The family understands the need to define new roles and new rules for the business.

Two questions guide the process of defining new Roles and Rules:

- What business *roles* are missing or being performed poorly?
- What *rules* must be created, clarified, strengthened, followed, or enforced more consistently?

What Roles Are Missing?

As noted earlier, in any dysfunctional hierarchy the leadership role is either absent or being poorly played. It may also be poorly defined, for instance split between two people, which can make it difficult even for competent managers to play. It's up to the estate planning team to analyze the root of the difficulty.

For example, in the Acme case, Peter was CEO and his brother Karl was COO. Their sibling rivalry aside, Peter was not playing the role of CEO effectively. He managed on the basis of family roles and role expectations. He made Karl's sons, Cecil and Charles, officers of the company, but made Pauline's son, Danny, a manager and employee. These were basically roles-based decisions. In meetings he expected people to behave themselves (in the absence of rules) and became frustrated when they did not. Meanwhile, Karl took care of day-to-day matters while resenting his brother's higher position and superior power. They didn't communicate nearly as often as they had when they were younger. Thus, the leadership power was split along the family fault lines. It was a family-based rather than a business-based setup.

Rules enable leaders to play their roles well. For instance, if rules were in place regarding various positions' requirements, then Peter and Karl would not be able to appoint Cecil and Charles officers so readily. There would have been requirements, known to everyone, that Cecil and Charles *and* Danny could attempt to meet. Rules would have leveled the playing field and made things fairer, and mitigated the "power to appoint" that Peter had assumed.

In enabling leaders to play their roles well, rules promote a kiss-down organization. Granted, it takes caring and commitment for a manager to play a role for his subordinates, but the right rules clarify what it means to do that. Rules such as those against sexually harassing employees or asking them to work without pay are givens; they exist to protect people who have less power in the hierarchical relationship. Rules also level the playing field by ensuring that all employees have equal opportunities to contribute, to develop their skills, and to earn raises, promotions, and other rewards. Rules that encourage kissing-down require and facilitate coaching, mentoring, and similar managerial behaviors aimed at developing employees' potential. By their very nature, rules discourage favoritism, turf battles, and unearned rewards. Of course, no rules can force a manager to play his role well. The willingness and ability to play a role reside in the person rather than in the rules. But rules can encourage kiss-down behavior and discourage kiss-up behavior. They can also weed out people who want the power, perks, and status that go with the role of manager but who have no real interest in the actual work of being a manager.

This underscores the importance of job descriptions in a family business, particularly one about to undergo management succession. If it's taken seriously, a well thought-out job description can help owners and hiring authorities select the right person for managerial and non-supervisory positions. Job descriptions have gotten a bad rap in some quarters. Whatever their shortcomings—they can't define every duty, they over-define duties, nobody ever reads them, and so on—their absence creates more difficulties than their presence. Many of the shortcomings may lie in the civil-service style of writing used in many companies' job descriptions. ("Incumbent maintains all customer files and periodically purges said files.") Also, many jobs cut across functions and require a level of initiative that's tough to capture on paper.

Nonetheless, a clearly written job description defines a functional role in the business, the knowledge and skills needed to play the role, and the role's goals, duties, and reporting relationships. It presents a set of guidelines for hiring people for the position and, more importantly, for judging their performance. In our experience, it is common for managers and employees to be hampered by the lack of such guidelines. Some managers who dislike formal job descriptions fear people saying, "That's not in my job description." Indeed, if people often deal with things not in their job description then perhaps their roles should be redefined. If on the other hand they believe something is not part of their job description when it is, then the document can clear up that misunderstanding.

A job description represents an intersection of Roles and Rules. The document defines the role, and the rules that inform the role. The baseball analogy would be that the pitcher—not the first baseman or third baseman—throws the ball across the plate to the batter.

In answering the question, "What business roles are missing or being poorly played?" we have found the following tactics to be helpful:

- During the input-output interviews, note situations in which people are not receiving their input in a useful form or timeframe.
- In those interviews, note the answers to the questions we presented in Chapter 3: Who directs your work? What helps you and hinders you in getting your job done? How are decisions communicated to you? Who conducts your performance reviews?
- Ascertain the criteria for raises and promotions. Are there such criteria? Do people know what they are?
- Find out who is and is not playing mentoring roles for specific people, particularly key people in the next generation.
- Identify disparities between the formal and informal reporting structures as well as multiple or fuzzy reporting lines. Be aware of people with undue influence. Try to ascertain the sources of influence or power beyond an individual's position, which may include seniority, skills, expertise, or family role.
- Ask about or observe the ways in which meetings are conducted and decisions are made.
- Note any fault lines and factions, sibling rivalries, and protective or hostile behaviors based on family roles carried into the business.

These tactics help you assess the business roles in the organization, and whether people are playing them properly. There are many ways to play a business role badly, but in a family business most of them involve a lack of business rules. Ah, but what rules?

What Rules Are Needed?

The most basic rules to address are those regarding ownership, because ownership is the source of power in the business. Who owns what portion of the business? Who can make decisions? Who needs to vote or sign off on various decisions? What happens if they don't? Are there certain milestones or dates at which ownership shares move to new parties? Are there conditions, perhaps in loan, merger, or acquisition agreements, under which ownership of assets can move to another party, such as a lender or partner? All of these questions must be answered with existing or to-be-determined "rules."

For Roles and Rules to work, those with the power must be sold on—or at least agree to—the approach. This means that those with power will have to give up some of it and agree to play by rules. All the explication of family history and roles in the world may fail to convince a testator to agree to reasonable rules. Some testators crave power. Others cannot see the damage they inflict with their misuse of power. A few simply don't care or actually want to damage the family or the business. In our experience, however, they are more often people who are simply incapable of playing their role for the family and the business. They cannot use their power to exclude an incompetent or disordered child from the business. They cannot "give more" to one child than to another, even when sharing equally will hurt the business. They cannot agree to hire an external manager or board member, even when one is clearly needed. They can neither let go of power nor properly use it. Such people have trouble agreeing to rules. For now, however, let's assume that the testator and others with power have bought into Roles and Rules and recognize the need for new rules.

As with communication rules, it is best to develop business rules *with* the family, even if you already know (or think you know) which ones they require. Usually, developing the rules with the family will generate better rules—better in the sense that the rules meet their specific needs and in the sense that the family can more easily buy in.

The facilitator serves several functions in developing the rules. First, he is still playing a role for the family—that of a role model of leader and, at times, perhaps rules enforcer. Second, he helps the family distinguish between true rules, which apply to everyone, and role expectations, which are handed down and apply erratically. Third, he helps them craft consequences that flow directly from the violation of the rule, in contrast to punishment. Fourth, he keeps the process on track, which is necessary because a family could easily spend an entire day developing rules and then forget the whole thing. Finally, this facilitator helps install the next facilitator—the acting CEO or umpire—or stays on to coach management in applying the rules.

Rules in Action

Business rules can be viewed as falling into categories related to certain management and business functions. While we encourage you to develop your own categories if you wish, these are the six into which we divide business rules:

- *Ownership:* These rules define who owns the business and who can make major decisions, such as a decision to sell the business or hire or fire the

CEO and other senior managers; these rules also define the composition and powers of the board of directors, if there is one.

- *Executive Team and Reporting Lines:* These rules define the basic organizational structure, for example, the number of operating divisions and layers of management, and the main reporting lines.
- *Finance and Accounting:* These rules involve business planning and budgeting, setting revenue targets, controlling expenses, and authorizing purchases, loans, and so on.
- *Human Resources:* These rules involve day-to-day management and the responsibilities of managers to their subordinates, including the form and frequency of performance appraisals, hiring and termination policies, and guidelines regarding salaries, benefits, training, promotions, raises, and managerial and employee conduct.
- *Operations:* These rules guide managers and employees at the level of their input and output. For instance, this category would include procedures for accepting deliveries, handling materials, storing inventory, running and maintaining machinery, submitting proposals to prospects and clients, using approved vendors, compiling and distributing reports, and so on.
- *Government & Industry Specific:* This category includes the larger realm of legal and regulatory rules that apply to all businesses and to specific types of business. For example, all businesses must file tax returns and observe child labor laws, but some are also subject to specific environmental or product safety regulations.

Remember that although rules apply to everyone, certain rules apply in different ways at different levels. (Everyone is paid for their work, but people at different levels can be paid different amounts.) Even so, rules bring order to on-the-job interactions, and do so by establishing transparency and fairness.

Transparency and fairness work to the benefit both employees and managers. Take, for example, a rule that managers must give written goals and performance reviews to their employees once a year. For employees, that rule reduces uncertainty about their goals and performance and rationalizes the process of earning raises and promotions. For managers, the rule sets a schedule and ensures that they will, at least once a year, set goals, evaluate performance, and play their mentor roles for their employees.

Rules for Acme Home and Building Supply

After we developed and shared the family history and roles with the Hartwells, we worked with them to develop rules in each major category:

Ownership:

As noted, we found that those who wanted to sell the company (mainly Peter, Pauline, and Danny) did not have the voting shares necessary to do so without significant legal action. When we made this clear, Peter and to a lesser extent Pauline, accepted the fact that the company would stay in the family, although Danny continued to have problems with this, particularly if it were not being split into two separate business units.

We were concerned by the exclusion of the women, mainly Pauline and Kathy, who had largely ceded their ownership roles to Peter and Karl respectively. While this arrangement had been fostered by the trust agreement structured by their father, R.L., there was no need or legal reason for it to continue. Indeed, it turned out that Pauline and Kathy were ready, willing, and able to start playing more active roles as owners. While Pauline had always been more vociferous than Kathy and closer to Peter, she now calmed down and started acquiescing less toward Peter. Kathy, however, was the big surprise: When she saw the effects of family roles, understood the basis of Peter's and Karl's power, and witnessed orderly meetings, she became more confident and began to express her views.

Equally important, we helped create six committees of various family members, some of whom served on more than one committee:

- Ownership and executive committee (board of directors)
- Finance committee to create the business plan as well as policies and procedures for budgeting, accounting, expense control, and investments
- Human resources committee to develop job descriptions and HR policies and procedures
- Operations committee to oversee the development of policies and procedures for the company's functional areas
- Conflict resolution committee that follows a designated process for settling differences
- Succession committee to plan and facilitate the transfer of the business to the next generation.

The first five of these were standing committees, while the last one would dissolve when Peter and Karl retired and the transfer was completed.

Forming these committees achieved several objectives:

- First, it gave family members official roles in developing the new structure. They understood that they were to play these rule-making roles for the business, not for themselves.

- Second, it created an orderly process for structuring the new organization. These committees had to meet every 45 days, with written agendas and with their "homework" complete. This not only brought everyone into the process but also, given the amount of work involved, saved the client time and money.
- Third, it helped people grow into their business roles faster than any other form of consulting would have. Committee members did research on the Web and in libraries and bookstores to gain the knowledge they lacked. They relished their roles on the committees and in charting the future of the business. They wanted to be informed and, frankly, wanted to look good at the meetings. Some of them were also preparing themselves for leadership roles they would play in the company.
- Finally, these committees got the work done. We sat in on their meetings and soon realized that they were "running with it." Of course, they needed guidance, particularly in the beginning, but they knew that they had to have a business plan, budgets, reports, policies, and procedures by certain deadlines and, to their credit, they took it seriously and got the work done.

Again, this case involved a business with significant revenues, profits, and operations, and more than a dozen owners. The company had also been managed mainly by the seats of Peter's and Karl's pants. Thus six committees and this intense effort were justified, which may not have been the case with a smaller or more orderly business.

With our guidance, these committees developed the following business rules in each area:

Executive Team & Reporting Lines:

Essentially—or at least provisionally—the company would remain in the family and be structured more formally into two divisions, but not into separate businesses. Cecil, Charles, and Danny would be considered to fill the CEO and COO positions to be vacated by Peter and Karl over the next nine to fifteen months. These men would also be candidates for the new posts of vice president of commercial operations and vice president of retail operations. However, other internal candidates could declare themselves. The ownership committee also reserved the right to hire an experienced manager from outside the family or company for any of these positions on an interim or permanent basis. We saw this as a long shot, but also felt it was wise to keep all options open and let no internal candidate even think about taking a position for granted.

It soon became clear that Pauline's son Danny believed he stood no chance of becoming CEO and, unfortunately, was dead set against reporting to Cecil, Charles, or anyone else in Peter's or Karl's family other than Peter or Karl. He basically wanted to be out on his own, either using his share of the proceeds of the sale of the business or heading up one of two units after a split of the business into retail and commercial divisions.

Much of the rest of the reporting structure remained in place, with purchasing managers, store managers, and maintenance, yard, delivery, and store crews doing their current jobs, but under more formal management.

Financial Management:

The main change in financial management was for more regular, more useful financial reports to be distributed to the owners and relevant managers. Revenues, expenses, investments, and performance measures were to be clearer, more detailed, and more available to family members.

The entire system was to become more transparent and more tightly managed. For instance, at the macro level a few people were charged with creating a five-year business plan, complete with quarterly financial projections. At a more micro level, formal purchase approval limits were established for all managers.

Peter initially resisted these changes. We virtually predicted this (among ourselves) because Peter could easily interpret the changes as an affront to his financial management, which he considered his strong suit. In a significant move, the committee considered his objections but overruled them. As we also predicted among ourselves, Danny resisted these changes too, because he had become used to Peter protecting him.

Human Resources Management:

Almost every family business in transition needs to develop clearer, firmer guidelines for managing people. As noted, Acme needed job descriptions, compensation guidelines, performance appraisal forms and schedules, and hiring and termination policies. Because they had previously worked with an excellent benefits consultant, and considered good benefits important, they had very little work to do in that area.

Operational Management:

In most areas of the business, Acme merely had to document the ways in which they were performing input-output tasks. Yet in doing so they discovered many redundancies, glitches, and delays. For instance, the paperwork required of small contractors picking up orders was needlessly complex and generated many complaints. They addressed this situation. They also streamlined their system of deliveries from their two warehouses to their retail stores and to construction sites.

Serious scrutiny of any operation that has grown up "organically" will lead to measures that will save time, labor, and money. Many family businesses undertake such an effort, but many others just accept the way they do things until someone points out a better way or the inefficiencies drive customers away.

Governmental, Industry Specific & Miscellaneous:

Thanks to Charles's role as the company's legal chief (corporate secretary) and Peter's insistence on complete and timely compliance with all tax laws, there was very little to do in the area of government and industry regulation. A simple review of these matters, easily completed because the records were well-organized and up-to-date, confirmed this.

Not a Weekend Project

The work described in this section took about six months to complete. Most family members were able to allocate time to these efforts, which were formidable in a company with multiple locations and a few hundred employees. In such a situation, the family is not only creating a new structure, but may actually be structuring the company for the first time. This work may be completely new to many or most family members, and that's one more reason that the facilitator must keep the effort on track and moving forward.

Break the Roles—Not the Rules

We said at the outset that Roles and Rules is not a formula or a recipe. By now it should be clear why: If it were, we could simply present to the client the roles and the rules that a business needs in order to run well, and recommend or insist that the family adopt them. However, those business roles and rules have been presented in thousands of books, articles, and courses. The problem is that family roles override business roles and rules: The CEO acts like Dad instead of a CEO, and so on.

The process of breaking the hold of family roles depends on recognizing their existence and effects. That happens when people are led to see, preferably in a maieutic manner, where their roles came from and how they are playing out in the business. The work we described in Chapter 5 prepares the family to accept the need and desirability of business Roles and Rules by showing them how family roles affect the business. When family members see where they are and how they got there, they can discern a path forward. They move along that path through positive group dynamics, peer pressure, and their desire to grow the business. They will say things such as, "Hey, you're playing your uncle role now, not your CEO role," and "We all agreed to the rule that both Joe and Jane sign off on those kinds of decisions," and others will concur.

Absent the sale of the business, it is in this way that the Rules Crisis is resolved. It is in this way that people change their behavior and attitudes. It is in this way that they move into their new business roles. And it is in this way that the estate planning team and the family separate roles from rules and then combine new Roles and Rules into a new, more effective structure.

In Chapter 8, we examine this process in more detail. But first, in Chapter 7 we examine specific legal succession and estate planning tools in the context of Roles and Rules.

Bear in Mind

- Knowledge of family roles enables the estate planning team to avoid becoming enmeshed in the family drama. That knowledge also helps the family to accept new business Roles and Rules.
- Business rules shape business roles at both management and employee levels, with job descriptions that define positions at those levels and policies and procedures that define interactions among those positions.
- The facilitator can gently introduce the family to rules by helping them develop communication rules. These amount to ground rules that make for fair and reasonable discussions in which everyone's view can be heard.
- The team and the family should then move on to define all business roles, at leadership, middle management, and employee levels, that have been missing, undefined, divided, or poorly played. Every position should be filled with the candidate who best fits the qualifications in the job description, or someone who can quickly gain those qualifications.
- It's essential to involve family members (and any key managers outside the family) in developing the business Roles and Rules to the greatest possible extent.

Part Three

Roles and Rules, Goals and Tools

CHAPTER 7

Legal and Financial
Tools and Techniques

Up to now, in this book we have focused mainly on the estate planning *process*, rather than on the legal documents that constitute the estate plan. In this chapter, however, we turn to the use of legal documents in the context of Roles and Rules. We do this, first, because we believe that families and estate planners should consider certain legal tools more often and, second, because the documents and legal tools comprise the "legal rules" of the estate plan. To attorneys and other practitioners, much of the information in this chapter may seem basic, because it is geared to general readers. Yet some of this content will interest practitioners because it shows how the legal tools and documents can accommodate and reinforce Roles and Rules.

At this point in the process, the planning team understands the family roles and their effect on the business, and has shared this understanding with the testator and key family members. The team has worked with the family to develop a set of business Roles and Rules to be passed on to the next generation. These business Roles and Rules should be reinforced through the use of the legal rules in the form of legally enforceable documents comprising the succession and estate plan. Here we discuss ways of doing that and explain key legal tools and documents for general readers. Again, to attorneys and other practitioners, much of the information in this chapter may seem basic, but the themes will be useful when drafting the succession and estate plan documents.

Three Overarching Goals

In general, the usual "legal rules" in succession and estate planning aim for three valuable goals:

- *Orderly Succession and Transfer of Assets:* Succession and transfer must occur with smooth continuity in management and orderly financial arrangements. These can be effected through trusts, business entities, or both. For a trust key considerations include the form of the trust, specific trust provisions, and choice of trustee. For a business entity they include the legal form, such as corporation, limited liability company (LLC), or partnership; the management, board of directors, and advisors of the business; and specific provisions in the LLC agreements or other documents. For both a trust and a business entity the governing jurisdiction may also be a consideration.
- *Asset Protection:* In situations where potential legal developments or litigation could expose wealth to unknown future creditors, certain other planning options are worth considering. These are not ways of sheltering assets or income from taxes. Instead, they are meant to legally and ethically place assets beyond the reach of unknown future creditors. The tools for this include generation skipping trusts, domestic and foreign irrevocable asset protection trusts, corporations, limited partnerships, and LLCs. Incidentally, the bankruptcy reform of 2005 increased the need for asset protection in both senior and subsequent generations. Indeed, given our litigious environment, we feel that estate planners, testators, and families often give too little consideration to asset protection.
- *Advantageous Compliance with Tax, Trust, and Business Law:* Any estate plan involving significant assets should aim to avoid probate, minimize estate and gift taxes, maintain privacy, and arrange for liquid funds to pay any estate taxes while preserving assets. (Readers unfamiliar with estate tax law may wish to consult Appendix D before reading this chapter or at various points while reading it.)

While either a trust or a business entity, or a business entity held by a trust, can embody the typical legal "rules" for an orderly transfer, we have found that with specific modifications certain entities, particularly generation skipping trusts and LLCs as discussed in this chapter, can accommodate Roles and Rules more effectively. Of course, the vehicles chosen to embody the "rules" and even the need for Roles and Rules will be affected by the nature and disposition of the assets. (We raised the keep-or-sell decision in Chapter 2 and will address it again in Chapter 8.) Before examining specific vehicles, we will discuss several basic issues concerning assets.

Types of Assets

A family's assets might include: a) a business, farm, or ranch, b) income-producing residential or commercial real estate, c) partial ownership interests in a business, farm, ranch, or in residential or commercial real estate, e) income-producing securities, or d) non-income-producing assets (houses, raw land, cars, boats, planes, collectibles, or securities), or e) some combination of these. Various assets require various levels of management, The greater the level of active management required, the greater the need for Roles and Rules. Yet we've found that Roles and Rules can mitigate the effects of bad family dynamics even when assets require less active management, as in the case of stock portfolios. The methodology works well in cases requiring new or modified family governance structures in which people learn to operate in new roles and to play by new rules upon the imminent or recent passage of assets from one generation to the next.

Even so, some assets are more liquid and divisible than others. Also, the reasons for dividing assets or keeping them whole will vary. A family may want to keep a real estate or stock portfolio whole in order to receive better service from, or achieve stronger bargaining power with, a management company, money manager, or lender. A family may want to keep a vacation home for sentimental reasons. Meanwhile, one or more family members may desperately need cash, which may obviate the need for long-term planning for the assets being liquidated. As noted in Chapter 2, if the assets are to be sold and the proceeds divided, the family benefits greatly from clear rules for valuing the assets, accepting a price and terms, and distributing the proceeds.

Many testators want to keep their plans for distributing assets secret and may, for various reasons, be encouraged by their advisors to do so. This often leads to resentment, anger, and lawsuits charging, for example, undue influence because someone correctly or incorrectly perceives that another party was left more. It's usually better for beneficiaries to know the provisions of the will or trust beforehand. In fact, we've found that, although most planners would not initially suggest this approach and may even discourage such a suggestion, it can be useful in many situations for the testator to suggest, in the environment of a carefully structured discussion, that the children help to decide how to divide the assets or the proceeds from a sale. This should, however, be done with the clear understanding that the final decision is that of the testator. That way, the children participate in making the rules governing the distribution of the assets among themselves. This may heighten the chance that the heirs will buy into the results in advance and, at the very least, give the defense attorneys another argument against any potential allegations of undue influence in the way the documents are written.

Testators' Issues and Wishes

We recognize that testators may not want to raise issues of distribution while they are alive, and that heirs may find it hard to develop a workable distribution. We also recognize that, without written waivers, attorneys face ethical issues of client confidentiality and multiple representation. Recognizing these facts, we still point out that, if handled judiciously and in a carefully structured discussion, it is often better to raise the issue of the distribution while the parent is alive rather than bury it and face higher emotional and financial costs later. For instance, we have seen testators ask the children to decide on the division of assets, with the provision that if they cannot decide then the testator will. Some, but not all, of these situations have worked out very favorably. Yet more often testators enjoy exercising their power to decide who gets what and will reject any suggestion of sharing information with the following generations. This power is legal and legitimate, but some testators ignore the potential for negative consequences, and others don't care. In any event, most testators leave their assets in some form to their surviving spouse, who then may or may not enlist family members in specifying the division among the next generation. That brings the issues up all over again.

The Law is Not Enough

The typical laws and documents regarding trusts, partnerships, corporations, and other operating entities do not usually specify all the rules required for an emotionally smooth transfer of assets. For instance, the fiduciary rules most likely incorporated into trust documents do not provide enough guidance to trustees dealing with poor family dynamics and often need to be expanded (see Appendix E for an example). Similarly, in cases that require it, we expand the rules in operating entity documents, such as an LLC agreement, to include special provisions as noted later in this chapter (see Appendix F for an example). When employing the Roles and Rules approach, the rules used to keep poor family dynamics from undermining a succession and estate plan must be explicit.

Four final caveats before we leave this general discussion:

1. In cases of poor family dynamics, it is often best to sell the assets and divide the proceeds, even if some parties object; that way, family members can go their own ways rather than battle over ownership or management issues.

2. We usually recommend that an independent party, such as an attorney, accountant, or other advisor, manage the sale and distribution of the assets in cases of poor family dynamics.

3. When assets are to be divided among heirs in a non-prorated way, we recommend that the valuation method be specified in the trust agreement and, if appropriate, agreed to in advance by the heirs. One standard method is to specify that a reliable appraiser conduct the valuation; if that value is not acceptable, the second party can have the asset appraised; if the parties still cannot agree on the value, the two appraisers can choose a third who's opinion can be final after consultation with the other two appraisers. Or the majority of the three appraisers can set the value.

4. When an asset, such as a business, vacation home, or art collection, will be given to one family unit to the exclusion of others, it is best that equivalent payments (which can be effected through life insurance policies, among other means) be made to the other family units—or that the decision not to make such payments be explained before the testator dies.

Valuation of a family business can be particularly thorny, especially when a child or other beneficiaries work or have worked in it for some time. Some value usually should be placed on their contribution or their "sweat equity," yet setting that in a way that everyone accepts can be difficult. The more explicitly and objectively that value is established *before* the estate plan is prepared and thereafter implemented, the better. Valuing assets years before a testator's death can be hard because asset values fluctuate and an actual sale provides the only true measure. So, the more acceptable the valuation method is to the beneficiaries, the better. Also, the more involved the key beneficiaries are in valuation and division decisions, the lower the probability of their turning to the courts later.

Then there are taxes, traditionally the chief concern of estate planners and a major concern in our approach as well. Much of our work actually aims to minimize taxes and preserve family wealth, since conflict in the family itself may hinder the possible use of certain tax minimization strategies. Given this and the effect of tax policy on trusts, readers unfamiliar with estate, gift, and generation skipping taxes may want to consult Appendix D for a brief overview of U.S. estate and gift taxes as of this writing.

Wills, Trusts, and LLCs

These are a few very general comments on wills, trusts, and LLCs and on the implications of Roles and Rules; these are directed more toward the general reader than to attorneys.

Basic Concepts in Wills

A will sets forth the manner in which the testator wants his assets distributed or disposed of after his or her death. A will can employ Roles and Rules, either in the language of the will or by specifying the creation of one or more trusts upon the death of the testator. The advantage of a trust is avoidance of probate and, because the provisions of the trust need not become public, privacy. With a will, the transition may be a bit more cumbersome because of the likelihood of the probate process, but this varies from state to state. When an estate includes a business, farm, or ranch, an LLC can be more useful in coordinating the management and the transfer of assets in combination with Roles and Rules, although a trust can also work.

(In California, where we do most of our legal work, living trusts are preferable to wills, because you avoid a cumbersome and costly probate process. Probate fees can be twice the cost of administering the estate through a trust in California. In many other states, such as those using the Uniform Probate Code, there's little difference between using a will and a trust, and in most of those states planners may make greater use of wills.)

Basics Concepts in Trusts

A trust holds a property interest assigned by one party (trustor or settlor) to the trust for the benefit of another party (beneficiary). The trustor appoints a responsible party (trustee) to administer and control the trust in accordance with the provisions of the trust agreement. An individual, a couple, or a group can constitute any one or two of the parties to a trust agreement—trustor, beneficiary, or trustee—or even all three parties. In practice, a trust functions much like a legal contract between the parties but with the added influence of tax and trust laws and the fiduciary rules.

The terms successor trustee and contingent beneficiary also warrant definition. The successor trustee takes the place of the initial trustee after the initial trustee dies, resigns, or becomes incapacitated. (Often the trustor names himself as the initial trustee and the spouse as successor trustee.) Successor trustees are designated in the provisions of the trust or nominated by another designated process. A contingent beneficiary is a party designated to receive assets when the original beneficiary dies, becomes incapacitated, or otherwise loses the right to receive the assets in question.

Trusts are important in implementing Roles and Rules for several reasons:

- *U.S. law recognizes a separation between the ownership and the use of assets.* This allows one party to legally control an asset while another party uses it or collects income from it. For example, a testator, say a mother, may stipulate that her child may collect income from an asset, but that the trust will hold ownership of the asset until ownership passes to her grandson, after the death of her child, when the grandson reaches a certain age, or under some other provision. This can keep the asset out of the hands of an irresponsible child, preserving it for the grandchildren while giving the child income from or the use of the asset. Such a trust can also be designed to protect the trust assets from any creditors of a child or another heir, even if the creditor is a current creditor of the child or another heir.

- *Trusts provide tremendous flexibility in controlling and distributing assets.* A trust can be structured so that upon the death of the testator and the surviving spouse, separate trusts, each with its own provisions, will be set up for each of their children. This lets the couple tailor the trust provisions to their wishes and the needs of each child. It also allows them to stipulate different management provisions for different assets, depending upon the extent to which the testator wants each beneficiary involved in managing or controlling the assets.

- *Because a trust is essentially a contract, it puts the force of law behind any "rules" that the testator and family require.* The provisions of a trust can direct the trustee to take virtually any legally permitted action regarding the assets in the trust (subject to tax laws, fiduciary rules, and public policy). For example, a trust agreement can empower the trustee to sell an asset or withhold its use if the beneficiary fails to fulfill certain requirements. In this way, a trust can establish or reinforce Roles and Rules to modify beneficiaries' behavior and provide consequences if they fail to perform in certain ways.

(On that last point, a few plays and movies of varying entertainment value have been based on the premise that a man or woman must marry by a certain age in order to benefit from a trust. In case you are considering such a provision, it would probably be unenforceable under trust law because public policy discourages forced marriages.)

Note that if the estate tax laws change after publication of this book, which is quite likely, certain tax considerations in designing a trust may disappear. Yet even if the estate taxes are eliminated, considerations such as asset protection, ownership and control, and provisions for implementing Roles and Rules will remain. Also, if the estate tax were eliminated, trusts may remain an effective "Plan B" should the tax return, which can hardly be ruled out.

For all these reasons, trusts are a key means of defining and enforcing "rules" in a succession and estate plan. However, as noted, LLCs are also valuable and, in certain situations, they may (typically in combination with trusts) be preferable.

Basic Concepts in LLCs

Limited liability companies (LLCs) have become popular in the United States because they provide many of the benefits of a corporation, such as limited liability for debts and damages arising within the business, while being taxed like a proprietorship or partnership. (In a proprietorship or partnership, income flows to the owner(s) and is taxed at the applicable personal income tax rates.) LLCs are chartered at the state level and therefore laws and fees regarding LLCs vary from state to state.

LLCs recognize that under U.S. law people are allowed to form contracts for virtually any legal purpose; thus, an LLC is essentially a contract among the parties to the business entity. This flexibility makes LLCs useful in managing the transfer of a family business. An LLC typically has a board of directors, which may be known by other names but embody the same concept, and officers or managers. The LLC operating agreement can include articles regarding the frequency of board meetings, methods for selecting board members, and similar items.

As with a trust, this provides flexibility. But the advantage of an LLC is that, as a business entity, it provides a means of organizing a business, which is not the main purpose of a trust, which is fundamentally based on fiduciary law. This means that management rules can easily be written into the LLC's operating agreement, which helps to hard-wire them into the new structure. This can also help an estate planning team address the inherent conflicts between a trust and a business, as described in Chapter 2.

Again, however, laws relating to LLCs tend to operate state by state, and these laws are highly subject to change, both in terms of the relevant statues and case law. So it's particularly important to have competent legal advice regarding these, and all, business entities.

Also, attorneys and other advisors may want to consider the fact that the use of business entities for "non-tax reasons" may be viewed more favorably by the IRS and state-level tax authorities than the use of entities driven only by tax considerations. So, while this matter has not as of this writing been settled in courts interpreting any federal or state tax codes, we believe that considerations of family dynamics in the context of Roles and Rules may represent a truly valid, business-based motivation for using certain entities.

We'll return to LLCs after we examine trusts in more detail. The key point is that the estate planner must help the family choose and create the best legal vehicle, given the testator's and family's goals and the Roles and Rules dimensions of the situation.

Types of Trusts: A Basic Overview

The concept and practice of using trusts originated in English common law some seven hundred to nine hundred years ago. In modern times, trusts have been developed for various purposes in light of family needs, tax legislation, and legal developments. As you read this basic overview remember that, as with all aspects of succession and estate planning, you must consult your own legal advisor before making any decisions. Broadly, the two key types of trusts are:

- Revocable Trust
- Irrevocable Trust

The following two sections provide a brief overview of these trusts.

Revocable Trust

A revocable trust provides for management of the trustor's assets during and, usually, after his or her lifetime. A revocable trust can be set up to become an irrevocable trust (explained below) upon the death of the trustor. In fact, a revocable trust is usually designed at least in part to become irrevocable upon the death of the trustor. This type of trust keeps assets out of probate (a consideration in some states, such as California, but not in others), and thus out of the public record, which enhances privacy. A revocable trust provides no tax advantages or asset protection for the trustor. Although the trustor is responsible for any taxes, they may be paid by the trustee, who must also pay any of the testator's creditors who come forward.

A revocable trust provides for a successor trustee, while preserving the trustor's right to change the trust provisions while he or she is alive. This provides the security of a trustee and professional management of the assets in the trust per the fiduciary rules, but lets the trustor retain control and the right to change his or her mind. The latter can be a powerful force for better or worse, so carefully consider the personalities and the situation when using a revocable trust and selecting a trustee. (Note that the testator can also readily change a will.) The classic case of a testator changing the beneficiaries of a trust (or a will) upon a whim or undue influence is familiar to most of us from books, plays, and films—and to some of us from court cases.

For an infirm testator, the trustee will manage the assets for the trustor's benefit in accord with the terms established usually before the trustor became infirm. This may help to protect the infirm testator from undue influence. However, sometimes a person can go to court, if a trust has not already been established, and have a conservator set up a revocable trust even though the trustor is incapacitated.

Although conservatorship may be voluntary, in involuntary conservatorship a court determines that a person is incapable of managing his or her financial affairs, and appoints someone to manage them. (Like all trusts, a revocable trust generally keeps the assets out of court processes, such as conservatorship, which most testators want to avoid.)

Again, a revocable trust can be designed to become irrevocable and morph into one of the types of irrevocable trusts discussed below.

Irrevocable Trust

An irrevocable trust has various purposes and takes different forms based on its use, but, as the name indicates, generally cannot be changed once it is set up. That said, many states have laws that permit exceptions, and the courts can often alter the terms of an irrevocable trust based on legal principles such as changed circumstances, which can include changes in the law and even in tax law. In such cases, a court may alter the terms of an irrevocable trust if it can be shown that if the trustor had known about the circumstances, he would have set it up differently. Also, in some states an irrevocable trust can be changed if all parties agree to the changes.

Irrevocable trusts are useful for asset protection for the beneficiary and for determining a) the amount of control someone will have over assets in the trust, b) the benefits they will realize from those assets, c) the application of Roles and Rules, or d) all of the foregoing. An irrevocable trust is also useful for providing incentives for beneficiaries to take actions the trustor sees as positive, such as completing school or submitting to periodic drug testing.

Types of Irrevocable Trusts

The legal profession has developed various types of irrevocable trusts for various uses in response to clients' and families' needs and financial issues, and in response to tax laws and the need for asset protection. For our purposes, the key types of irrevocable trusts include:

- Exemption Trust
- Irrevocable Life Insurance Trust (ILIT)
- Qualified Terminable Interest Property Trust (QTIP)
- Generation Skipping Trust (GST)

Exemption Trust:

Exemption trusts are one of several forms of irrevocable trusts that hold assets up to the amount of the estate tax exemption or generation skipping tax exemption (see Appendix D). The various names for this type of trust—bypass trust, residual trust, family trust, and B-trust or C-trust—arise more from legal terminology than actual distinctions in their function.

In other words, they all have the same function. An exemption trust enables a testator and family to use the estate and gift tax exemption of a deceased testator to keep assets out of the taxable estate of, usually, a spouse but even other heirs. The assets can go to any beneficiary, not just the spouse. The testator can place any amount of assets in the trust, but must pay the estate or gift tax on the value above the exemption amount that goes to any beneficiary (but not necessarily on amounts that go to the spouse, who is entitled to an estate and gift tax deduction, known as the marital deduction).

These trusts are generally set up for a surviving spouse. With an exemption trust, when the first spouse dies you have $2.0 million—the amount of assets that is exempt (as of this writing) from an individual's estate tax—in the trust. (This stands apart from the marital deduction.) On the death of the surviving spouse, the assets in the exemption trust *are not included* in the estate of that surviving spouse for estate tax purposes. However, any assets given to the surviving spouse which qualify for the marital deduction in the estate of the first spouse to die would be included in the surviving spouse's estate for estate tax purposes. This is the case whether the assets were given to the surviving spouse outright or in a marital or QTIP trust. For tax purposes, the value of the exemption trust is usually determined by the applicable exemptions (not already used for gifts) then in effect.

This trust, which usually goes into effect upon the testator's death, is among the most popular tools for minimizing estate taxes upon subsequent deaths. If the testator's spouse is alive, the spouse is usually the beneficiary, but any person can be the beneficiary of this type of trust. Also, an exemption trust can be structured similarly to a generation skipping trust (discussed below). As with the generation skipping trust, the spouse or other persons may be beneficiaries and, after their deaths, the assets can go to other beneficiaries with the payment of estate taxes.

Note on Power of Appointment:

A trust can provide various powers to accommodate testators' and families' needs and desires. For instance, the testator can give the surviving spouse a limited power of appointment (defined below) and thus the right to reallocate the assets of the trust on her death to almost anyone. Or he can limit the power of appointment to the bloodline or to a charity.

Power of appointment is defined by the Internal Revenue Code and by contract law. For tax purposes, which generally guide the meaning of the powers, a limited power of appointment permits the surviving spouse or anyone else to give the assets to anybody except his or her own estate, creditors, or creditors of his or her estate when all life beneficiaries are deceased. In contrast, a general power of appointment permits the surviving spouse or anyone else also to give the assets to his or her estate (that is, to himself or herself), creditors, or creditors of his or her estate.

That's a key distinction for tax purposes: With a limited power of appointment, the assets in an exemption trust *are not included* in the estate of the person holding the limited power. With a general power of appointment, the assets in the trust *are included* in that person's estate and are potentially available to future creditors. Thus, a general power of appointment is not desirable for these exemption trusts and, in practice, seldom used (except when the assets of a non-exemption trust may be benefited by being included in the estate of the beneficiary).

Irrevocable Life Insurance Trusts:

Irrevocable life insurance trusts (ILITs) are used to hold life insurance policies and the proceeds of life insurance, or other gifted assets. They can be very effective for leveraging a gift. (Again, see Appendix D.) For example, a trustor—or the insured, who is usually the same person—can make cash gifts to the trust, and the trustee, who cannot be the insured, can use that money to pay the premiums on the insurance owned by the trust. Then, on the death of the insured, the ILIT will hold the proceeds of the insurance, which are generally much larger than the value of the premiums paid.

The ILIT trustee can then use the proceeds to buy an ownership share in the family business or to compensate other heirs to help equalize gifts within the family. This effectively moves the funds from the insurance trust to the estate (assuming that is the intention), while preserving the tax and asset protection of the assets remaining in the trust, if the ILIT is drafted correctly. Then the estate can use the funds for liquidity needs, such as paying estate taxes or allocating those funds to beneficiaries who need cash and don't want to be in the business or own other assets. When the ILIT owns a share of the family business after using the insurance proceeds to buy that share from the estate, the ILIT's provisions (including Roles and Rules provisions) must be coordinated with those of any other ownership structures. Also, it may be possible to merge this type of trust into other trusts with the same terms to keep the number of trusts manageable.

Qualified Terminable Interest Property Trust:

The qualified terminable interest property (QTIP) trust, also known as the marital deduction trust, allows the trustor, upon his death, to transfer assets to his spouse free of estate taxes by using the marital deduction. Given this purpose, the QTIP would probably not be used if Congress eliminates the estate and generation skipping taxes, since the exemption trust will then provide the same benefits and the martial deduction will no longer be necessary to reduce the estate taxes. The QTIP trust allows all of the income and, if desired, a limited portion of the trust assets to pass to the surviving spouse while qualifying for the marital deduction (note that such gifts to a spouse can be unlimited). This would be the same tax treatment if the asset were gifted directly to the spouse. However, unlike a direct gift to the spouse, the trust provides for management and control of the assets after the trustor's death. It also allows for the testator's directions regarding the distribution of those assets upon the death of the surviving spouse.

In other words, the QTIP is a way to give assets to the surviving spouse without giving the surviving spouse control of those assets, unless the testator wants to. Thus the QTIP trust gives the testator the security of knowing that when the surviving spouse dies, the assets in that trust can go to one or more of his or her designated beneficiaries, who may or may not be heirs of the surviving spouse. The QTIP trust allows the estate to qualify for the marital deduction for the value of the assets in the trust that are available to the surviving spouse; however, the value of the QTIP trust is counted in the surviving spouse's estate and is subject to the estate tax upon his or her death if the marital deduction was used.

The QTIP can be extremely useful in situations of poor family dynamics. It can provide for independent or neutral management of the assets—in the form of a neutral trustee—when the surviving spouse would not be the appropriate party to manage them. (A neutral trustee has no family relationship with the testator and therefore would usually be unbiased and likely to follow the trust agreement as written as well as in spirit.) It also tells the trustee how to dispose of the assets upon the surviving spouse's death. For instance, if the testator has a child from a prior marriage or one of the couple's children is estranged from the surviving spouse, the child may be better served by the neutral trustee than by the surviving spouse.

Note on Irrevocable Trusts:

As previously mentioned, these trusts can be designed to do almost anything, within the bounds of the tax laws, fiduciary rules, and public policy. They mainly ensure that the testamentary objectives of the testators vis-à-vis any of the subsequent beneficiaries, including the spouses, are met. For example, the testator may not want to give the surviving spouse power over the exemption, by-pass, or QTIP trust, because he wants the power and the assets to go to his children or other designated beneficiaries when the surviving spouse dies (and not, say, to the surviving spouse's children). These are real considerations, particularly in light of U.S. divorce and remarriage rates and the number of lawsuits being filed by subsequent beneficiaries because of actions of previous trustees or beneficiaries.

Generation Skipping Trust:

The generation skipping trust is another form of irrevocable trust, but the term is a bit of misnomer and confusing to some people. The assets in a generation skipping trust do not skip over the next generation in terms of use. (Remember trust law separates ownership from use and control.) We've seen testators mention that they're going to use a generation skipping trust and watched children protest that they "need the money." But you can have the child in control of the trust as trustee *and* the child can receive income from the asset and use the asset while it is owned by the trust. However, when the child dies, the assets in the trust *will skip being included in that child's estate, to the extent of the exemptions originally used.* That's why it's called a generation skipping trust (GST).

Indeed, a GST for a child may be divided into exempt and non-exempt portions, yet have the same distribution terms. That can provide more control; however, the non-exempt portion will be included in the estate of the child or other trust beneficiary for estate tax purposes. This allows for control of the assets and provides asset protection from the beneficiary's or child's creditors. Of course, estate tax planning for the inclusion of the non-exempt trust in the beneficiary's or child's estate will have to be done to ensure that there is enough liquidity to pay any estate taxes due upon the beneficiary's or child's death.

The generation skipping exempt trust is similar to the exemption trust. It's based on the same concept, and essentially the same rules apply. A GST that is exempt is irrevocable and thus establishes orderly distribution of the assets to the children or grandchildren, while allowing for the option of independent or neutral asset management and the oversight of a trustee. In addition, when properly structured, both the exempt and non-exempt GST offer asset protection to the beneficiary because he has control and use of the assets within certain limitations, and can receive income from them *but does not own the assets.* An exempt GST (and in some cases a non-exempt GST) also helps keep assets out of the taxable estate by helping trustors and families use gift exemptions. As explained in Appendix D, as of 2001 the gift tax and the estate tax are separate, and the exemptions to the estate and generation skipping taxes are increasing. (The gift tax is usually paid by the giver, not by the recipient, unless other provisions are made.)

The GST and Roles and Rules

Leaving aside tax issues, both the exempt and non-exempt versions of the GST can be useful when a child or other heir doesn't want or need ownership in the business, cannot be entrusted with assets or control, or has creditors or an untrustworthy spouse. On those counts it can be useful for a similarly disposed child or other heir who is in the business, because the trustee controls the actual assets albeit within the framework of the fiduciary laws and the terms of the trust itself. Also, a GST may, when appropriate, provide for situations in which the trustee oversees a child in the business, so that the child is treated and rewarded fairly. In such cases, a GST may achieve the goals of both the testator and the beneficiary and thereby help reinforce the Roles and Rules approach.

Because ownership is separate from use, a testator can leave an asset to his child in a GST and the child can receive all or part of the income from, say, rental of a house or dividends from stock, without owning the asset. That also goes for distributions from any family business owned by the trust, such as an interest in an LLC or limited partnership. The trust can provide for professional or independent management or management by the child or other beneficiary—whomever the testator wants in control. The person in control can be a property or fund manager retained by the trustor or whomever the testator wants to run the business.

In addition, if a child is sued the asset cannot be awarded to the plaintiff or creditor because the child does not own it. When the child dies, the asset may not be included in his or her estate and, depending on the value of the child's other assets and prevailing tax laws, estate taxes may be saved. However, the extent to which this is the case depends on the values and the generation skipping transfer tax exemptions and how those exemptions were allocated.

Other Trusts

The names, number, type, characteristics, and legal issues of trusts are constantly changing. We have covered those we see as the most important above and offer brief comments on a few other types of trusts below:

- Living trusts are essentially the same as revocable trusts. A living trust holds assets for the testator and specifies that upon his or her death they will be moved to one or more specific trusts of various types, or directly to the designated heirs without probate. In contrast, with a will the testator continues to hold the property in his or her name, rather than as trustee of a living trust and, depending on state law, the assets may be subject to probate before they pass to the heirs.
- Grantor trusts are ignored for income tax purposes, but they can be effective for estate and gift tax purposes in that on the death of the grantor/testator, the trust assets will not be included in the grantor's/testator's estate. Grantor trusts can also be designed to include Roles and Rules type provisions.

- Irrevocable living children's or grandchildren's trusts are simply irrevocable trusts set up for children or grandchildren.

In any type of trust, the trustee requires careful guidance on how to administer the trust, and, when a family business is involved, guidance on how, in effect if not in fact, to act as an owner in the business. In the presence of poor family dynamics, this guidance should provide clear rules that go beyond the requirements of the present fiduciary rules in state law and in most trust agreements by including additional rules for trust administration developed within the Roles and Rules theme. (See Appendix E, for an example.)

Two Other Key Considerations

Before turning to LLCs, we want to raise two issues of importance in any estate plan: asset protection, which has been touched on above, and liquidity. We won't cover these relatively technical areas in depth here, but merely provide a few guidelines.

Make Asset Protection a Priority

Virtually any family with significant wealth should consider asset protection strategies. Here, the term asset protection refers to methods of keeping assets out of the hands of future unknown creditors, whether they arise as a result of litigation, bankruptcy, divorce, or normal business. (Again, asset protection entities are not tax shelters and do not necessarily reduce income or estate taxes.)

In today's litigious environment, asset protection is simply prudent. Anyone can become involved in an accident in which their homeowner's or business insurance does not fully cover liability for injury or death. It's impossible to identify every potential liability. For example, the previous attorney of a client of ours arranged for the testator to directly gift some real estate to his daughter. Then, when the testator became our client, we also arranged for him to gift his daughter with some real estate. However, we did so through an irrevocable exempt GST with the daughter as trustee, receiving all income from the real estate. A few years later, the daughter's husband went bankrupt. The creditors were awarded the real estate gifted directly to her under the previous attorney's arrangement because it had become marital property and therefore subject to the husband's creditors under California law; however, the creditors could not be awarded the real estate gifted in the irrevocable exempt GST. Generation skipping trusts that are non-exempt can also protect assets.

Insurance is another common, straightforward way to protect a family from liabilities arising from lawsuits, and should always be considered. Insurance policies for asset protection are usually handled a bit differently from those for estate and gift tax planning. As discussed above, an insurance policy for estate and gift tax purposes is generally owned by an irrevocable life insurance trust (ILIT). In contrast, insurance for protecting assets from future liabilities is owned by the parties who are potentially liable to creditors. As mentioned above, if estate tax, creditors, or Roles and Rules issues are a consideration, it is key that the life insurance policy *not* be owned by the testator. If it were, the proceeds would go into the estate and be subject both to estate taxes and exposure to the testator's creditors.

Any family with substantial assets should discuss asset protection options with their advisors. The applicable law varies from state to state, which means it's essential to consult an expert advisor, such as a member of the American College of Trust and Estate Counsel (ACTEC), who can be located at www.actec.org/.

Ensure Sufficient Liquidity

An estate plan must ensure that there are 1) funds for the business owner to retire on, 2) funds to pay any estate taxes that will become due, and 3) funds for other needs, such as buying out family members who need cash or have no role in the business. Insurance is a key tool for meeting all of those goals in some fashion. As discussed above, ownership of the life insurance should be in an irrevocable life insurance trust (ILIT) not only to save potential estate taxes, but also for asset protection and to maximize control of the proceeds. We look to incorporate Roles and Rules provisions when designing these trusts, because upon the insured's death the proceeds may be used to buy the asset, which will then be managed within the trust. In other words, whenever family assets may be involved, it's wise to ensure that Roles and Rules will apply as intended, even when the type of trust or the status of the assets changes.

Families and their planners have various options for ensuring liquidity, which are too numerous, complex, and subject to change to cover here. One simple option is to sell assets at the time of death to pay the taxes. Another option is that under certain circumstances payment of the taxes for a business can be delayed for up to fifteen years, with only interest due for five years, then principal and interest for the next ten years, all possibly being paid with cash flow generated by the business. Of course, the advice of an expert advisor is essential in arranging and planning for sufficient liquidity upon the testator's death.

Using Business Entities to Achieve Estate Planning Goals

We have found certain business entities, particularly LLCs, to be excellent vehicles for building Roles and Rules into the business structure as it is transferred to a spouse or the next generation. We tend to use LLCs as the business entity and use trusts to hold that entity interest, which is essentially a membership interest in the LLC.

As noted earlier, the regulations and laws that govern business entities are not sufficient to convey the rules required for a smooth succession amid family conflicts. Therefore, we expand the rules in the standard operating documents to include special provisions regarding how key decisions will be made and how business will be conducted. In Appendix F, you'll find a set of these provisions (with small changes) in what we informally call "the Roles and Rules article" from an actual LLC agreement for a client of ours who must remain anonymous. These provisions in the appendix are written in legal language, so we'll briefly discuss them here.

Roles and Rules in an LLC

You can do things in an LLC operating agreement that you cannot, to our knowledge, do in a corporation without potentially complex buy-sell, voting, or other types of agreements. That's because an LLC rests on the principle that parties are free to form contracts in any way they choose for any legal purpose, while a corporation is a "legal person" defined in a certain way by the law and subject to certain regulations and tax laws.

When family dynamics call for a Roles and Rules article in the LLC agreement, we customize it to the needs of the business and family. Yet these articles have certain provisions in common. For example, the agreement usually:

- Defines terms very specifically so that roles, such as board member, company officer, consultant, external board member, family unit, ownership interest, and so on, are clear
- Establishes a board of directors and company officers *and* the qualifications for such positions, and defines the terms of their service, the scope of their duties, and even how their performance can be evaluated
- Sets forth the procedures by which family members, or each family unit, must nominate and appoint or elect board members and company officers
- Specifies a schedule or frequency of board meetings, composition of a quorum, who can vote on various issues, and percentage of votes or voting shares (such as a majority, two-thirds, or 80 percent) required for certain decisions
- Defines permissible and prohibited actions for board members and company officers, such as loans to or from the company or pursuit of outside investments, as well as actions, such as felony convictions and

DUI convictions, that can disqualify a person from serving as a board member or company officer

- Includes provisions for the appointment of outside consultants who will help in the decision-making process, and the duties of such persons
- Defines the rights and roles of family members not actually involved in the day-to-day operations of the business

The Roles and Rules article for an LLC in Appendix F is only an example. The provisions can be written in any way that clearly defines the Roles and Rules, and positions and procedures, that family members and other parties must follow to keep family roles from hampering business operations or the succession process. The goal is not necessarily family harmony (although we won't stop anyone from pursuing it). The goal is to keep negative family-roles-based behavior from undermining the planning process, the transfer or management of assets, or the operation of the business. We've found that, when it occurs, family harmony usually emerges as a side-effect of people dealing with their emotions in a mature, rational manner and growing into their business roles.

The Nuts and Bolts of LLCs: A Case in Point

The sample Roles and Rules article in Appendix F was developed for the families of the four brothers who owned the marina (whom you met in Chapter 1). Given that the document is written in legal language, we explain its main features here. We knew, for example, that appointments to the board of directors would generate conflicts among the family units as well as sibling rivalry within the units since only one board seat was allocated to each family unit. Therefore, the article states that each family unit gets to name one person to the board. There's also the matter of how the family units appoint someone to the board of directors, so the article sets out a standard way of doing that.

To control sibling rivalry, secure agreement to the rules, and ensure that qualified people are appointed to the board, we can include a provision in the article that, for instance, each family unit will appoint a potential board member subject to the approval of the Board Approval Committee. (See sample illustration in Appendix F, paragraph 6.01(A).) This Board Approval Committee—made up entirely of non-family members—must approve the members of the board of directors nominated by each family unit. In addition, all the family units agreed in advance to a set of board qualification standards or job qualifications required by anyone appointed to the board. By including only non-family members on the Board Approval Committee and securing agreement to board qualification standards in advance, we helped to ensure that nominees will meet the educational and experience requirements agreed to by the heirs. We also helped to minimize sibling rivalry, in that siblings who did not qualify did not try to be appointed and could not be appointed. If a candidate does not meet the requirements, the nomination goes back to the family unit, which must nominate someone else.

These steps define how a family unit nominates board members, while controlling conflict and setting up ways of dealing with it. Moreover, we took the family through this process in practice sessions without the input of the senior brother of that family unit because family members, specifically two of the sons, had been fighting over a seat on the board. This dry run helped the next generation see another way of settling matters and in fact they did work it out. It also got the parents to abstain from selecting board members; instead, each family unit nominated prospective board members. By removing themselves from the appointment process, the parents avoided even the appearance of playing favorites, which had in the past fostered sibling rivalry. Having them step away and setting up objective qualifications and the method of nomination brought this about.

In situations of family conflict, we strongly recommend that planners and families consider writing such provisions into their trust and LLC agreements and agreements for other business entities *and* practice the procedures in advance. If a business is structured as a corporation, all this can be a bit more difficult but can still be done through written policies and procedures, changes in by-laws, voting trusts (which define who has specific voting rights, for instance, regarding members of the broad of directors), and buy-sell agreements. These may not carry the same weight or work as smoothly as provisions in a trust or LLC agreement and certainly will be more expensive legally to develop. Yet if people see the need for them, help develop them, and agree to abide by them, there's a good chance they'll work. Certainly, having procedures in written agreements is far better than having them issued unilaterally by the testator or not having them at all.

A Few Words of Caution

As noted, the testator, family, and advisor should be as specific as possible in crafting the trust documents and the business structure to reflect their intentions. Given the variability in the statutes and cases governing trusts and business entities, this may involve selecting the right state—that is, a state that permits such specifics *and* that has a record of following the intent of the testator as expressed in the documents.

For example, as of this writing, in Delaware trustees do not have to become involved with the business as an asset of the trust because provisions in the Delaware law allow a testator to name a "direction advisor" unrelated to the trustee. This advisor can direct the trustee to retain the business or other assets that are not or may not be proper for trust law purposes when the testator wants to retain those assets in the trust. The trustee does not concern himself with such directions. The direction advisor can also be a direction committee or other team that includes some or all of the beneficiaries. The Delaware law also in effect eliminates diversification requirements (explained in Chapter 2) so that assets that the testator wants to keep in the trust can be kept in it.

That feature of the Delaware law pretty much absolves the trustee of liability for the effects of those decisions and in particular for the effects of continuing to hold the business in the trust notwithstanding the risk of business failure and, consequently, losses to the trust. Indeed, in a high-stakes Delaware case, the court held that the trustee was not liable for business losses because it followed the terms of the trust and the dictates of the direction advisor. That would not necessarily have happened in California or many other states, where the concept of equity for the beneficiaries or general fiduciary duties might have been favored over the testator's intent as expressed in the documents.

Even so, regardless of the jurisdiction, you cannot assume that the trust agreement and business structure can accommodate all of the possibilities and contingencies you contemplate. You must plan for them and design your preferred responses into the documents. This means attempting to maximize the opportunities for, and probabilities of, good outcomes while minimizing those of bad outcomes. It may also mean defining the process of how to change the documents themselves.

Tools and Rules

Clearly, trusts and business entities can be used in many ways to achieve a testator's goals, secure a family's finances, and transfer a business or other assets with minimal tax effects and maximum control. However, amid poor family dynamics the relevant documents must include provisions that enable family members to move into their business roles by following business rules. Again, we emphasize that these documents must be prepared with the advice of a competent attorney or team of qualified advisors.

But even with solid documents, challenges lie ahead. Developing the documents themselves and completing the succession and estate planning process—and the transfer of assets—demands certain skills and attention to certain issues we have not yet covered. We cover those skills and issues in the next and final chapter, and provide insights that will help testators, family members, business people, and practitioners through the planning process and the transition itself.

Bear in Mind

- The commonly used legal "rules" and tools in succession and estate planning aim to achieve three main goals: orderly succession and transfer of assets, asset protection, and advantageous compliance with tax, trust, and business law.
- The legal "rules" regarding trusts and business entities are not enough to ensure a smooth transfer of assets and successful succession amid difficult family dynamics. Therefore, agreements in such situations need special provisions crafted with an eye toward Roles and Rules.
- Trust law separates ownership from use and control. Trusts thus enable testators and beneficiaries to get assets out of their estates and thereby lower their exposure to estate, gift, and generation skipping taxes.
- Asset protection, which places specific assets out of reach of future creditors, is especially important (and often overlooked) in our litigious society. Asset protection strategies usually employ certain trusts and business entities that isolate assets from liabilities arising from situations not directly related to the assets. They also protect owners of assets from liabilities arising as a result of ownership of those assets.
- Because trusts and business entities such as LLCs are basically contracts, they are extremely flexible documents that can include provisions that encourage, discourage, modify, and provide consequences for certain behaviors. They can also specify meeting frequency, job qualifications, permissible sales and purchases of assets, permissible investments, and other decision rules, policies, and procedures.

CHAPTER 8

Leading the Family—and the Family Business—Forward

In this book we have explained Roles and Rules, in general and as applied to succession and estate planning. We have also explained the Rules Crisis, issues of structure, and the role of the facilitator. And we have studied a family business in a Rules Crisis, and looked at ways to use legal rules and business structures in the context of Roles and Rules.

In this chapter, we provide more detailed guidelines for using our approach, as well as specific questions to ask regarding business continuation, legacy issues, and successors' preparedness. While we direct this chapter primarily toward advisors, we are also addressing testators and families facing difficult planning processes or transitions.

This chapter assumes that the advisor, testator, and family are anticipating or dealing with the Rules Crisis and will therefore benefit by applying Roles and Rules to the succession and estate planning situation. To assist them in that application, this chapter marshals the preceding material into something of a practicum or field guide to Rules and Rules and maieutic consultation.

How Testators and Families Think

When testators, families, and advisors perceive current or future problems, they usually ignore them or assume that "things will work themselves out." In other words, they engage in denial. Even when they do acknowledge problems and decide to tackle them, they usually define them in ways that limit the "solutions" to those that won't work. That is, they define the problems in purely business terms or in personal terms. As a result, the description and diagnosis of the problem are inaccurate, detrimental, or both.

For instance, people define the problem in business terms when they believe that simply appointing "the right person" to a business role, such as president, will straighten things out. Often the testator and family honestly believe that a son or daughter is qualified because "they've been watching Dad run the company all their lives." But that doesn't necessarily prepare offspring to lead the business. For their part, advisors may try to prepare successors by explaining sound managerial practices, but that won't work when family roles dominate the business.

People define the problem in personal terms when emotions lead them to conclude that the testator or a family member doesn't care about the family or wants to destroy the business. Family members may feel that if they could just talk to the person in question or if they would only listen, things would improve. Well, they wouldn't. Indeed, neither giving people management guidelines nor talking to them in the usual ways will address the Rules Crisis.

Most clients can understand that a Rules Crisis occurs when a business running on family roles must start running more on business rules. This casts addressing the Rules Crisis as a natural developmental or evolutionary task rather than as someone's fault. It also challenges the testator and family to face that task, regardless of what they call it. It challenges them to move from Roles to Rules and to transform the family business into a "real" business. If, for whatever reason, the family is unwilling and unable to deal with this task, the testator or family should, as noted in Chapter 2, probably sell the business. This is not to assume that they will sell the business nor to insist that they sell it, but to recommend that they seriously consider doing so.

Shifting into Emotionally Neutral

All of this said, the description of the situation should be emotionally neutral. The family may or may not be ready, willing, and able to deal with the Rules Crisis. If they are not, they are not bad people or somehow inadequate. They are simply not ready, willing, and able to invest the time and effort required to deal with it. That's not a poor reflection on the family, despite the use of the terms crisis and developmental task. Rather, it's akin to deciding not to attend graduate school or not to take in a foster child.

We might admire someone who completes graduate school or who takes in a foster child, but we don't see deciding not to as evidence of character flaws. Moving from family roles to business rules requires effort, knowledge, and skill. But deciding not to take up that challenge is fine. But it's not fine to decide to transfer the business to the next generation without dealing with that challenge.

If and when they do decide to deal with the Rules Crisis, families and advisors need the binocular perspective of Roles and Rules. Alone, neither the rules-based perspective of the attorney nor the roles-based perspective of a therapeutically oriented consultant will meet the case.

Dealing with the Rules Crisis

This section summarizes our broad recommendations for addressing the Rules Crisis, whereas subsequent sections will provide more specific guidelines, analysis, and suggested questions. Broadly, we recommend that the advisor and the testator and family perform the following tasks to deal with the Rules Crisis (which can arise in some form whenever assets requiring active management, including real estate and financial portfolios, are involved):

- The advisor should help the testator and family to understand the Rules Crisis and see it as a developmental task. To do this the testator and family should:

  - Understand the evolution of the family business and its current status: How did the business grow to its current size? How did the management team come about? Are successors prepared to assume control of the business? Do they feel prepared?
  - Understand the structure of the business, that is, the Roles and Rules in the business: What is the official authority structure and the actual influence structure? Do authority *and* influence emanate mainly from roles or from rules? What are the incongruities between the two structures? Do people feel as though they are operating on family roles or on business rules?

- The testator, with input from the family as appropriate, must decide whether the business will be kept or sold. By "kept" we mean that the business will be passed on to the next generation. Family members will be managers or owners, or both, and will make decisions about the business. By "sold" we mean that family members will have no control or decision-making power in the business, and their financial benefits will not be tied to the business.
- The advisor guides the family through the keep-or-sell decision and helps the family separate emotional and financial issues. For instance, a testator might see that his love of a business could prompt him to keep it when he should sell it. Financial issues to consider include the size, profitability, and prospects of the business. If these are insignificant, then

the stakes in the decision are relatively low. If, however, the business is (for the family) large, profitable, and positioned for growth, the stakes can be very high indeed.

- Depending on the keep-or-sell decision, which we discuss in depth below:

  o If the business is to be kept, the advisor must prepare the family for the Rules Crisis that lay ahead. This amounts to "professionalizing" the business by establishing, adopting, and, when necessary, enforcing, business Roles and Rules. The parties must focus on the roles *and* the rules.

  o If the business is to be sold, the advisor must work with the family to craft rules that will enable the family to sell the business and divide the proceeds in accord with the testator's desires and, hopefully, the good of all. The parties need to focus mainly on the rules.

- Finally, the advisors must guide the family through the sale or the transfer of power and, eventually, the administration of the estate. As noted in Chapter 4, a family business often needs someone to help them apply the rules. Most families benefit from, and many require, the guidance of an acting CEO, rules enforcer, or Maieutic Consultant before and during the Rules Crisis.

The only cases in which the Rules Crisis does not become a "crisis" are those in which the founder has taken the step of incorporating business rules into the operation during his or her tenure, usually well before retirement. If this is done properly, it generates a structure composed of Roles and Rules in which everyone, including the founder and family members, has been accountable for their performance in well-defined positions, and where successors were prepared through training, experience, and mentoring to assume leadership positions. This is rarely the case in situations characterized by poor dynamics.

Questions for the Keep-or-Sell Decision

The stakes are so high and the downside risks so large that the keep-or-sell decision must be taken seriously and made explicitly. Yet many families simply assume that the business will remain in the family without considering the potential consequences.

The overarching questions are: How viable a structure has the testator and family created to pass on to the next generation? If a viable structure is not in place, what will it take to create one? As you'll recall, any organizational structure is composed of Roles and Rules. Given this, we have found the following questions to be valuable guides in considering the keep-or-sell decision:

Roles Questions:

- What has the senior generation done to assess the current structure and create a viable structure to pass along?
- Has a family council or succession committee been formed to help prepare the next generation for their new roles? Have there been family meetings about succession?
- Is there an advisory board that includes one or, preferably, two or more non-family members? Has the senior generation sought outside expertise and independent advisors whose advice they use?
- What kind of mentoring has the senior generation performed for the next generation?
- Has the senior generation assessed and educated the next generation regarding issues of money and self-reliance? What has been done to teach next-generation shareholders and beneficiaries about their rights and responsibilities?
- What discussions have taken place regarding the business and ownership roles that the next generation will play? Have they begun to play those roles?
- How are non-family managers and employees in the business treated? What can be expected of them when the business passes to the next generation? Has their future been considered? Has the transition been discussed with them?
- Has the elder generation explicitly prepared itself to step out of its management roles at a specific date?

Rules Questions:

- Has the business been "professionalized" by means of a written mission statement, policies, and procedures?
- Does the business follow standard accounting practices? Does management compile and review monthly, quarterly, and annual financial statements?
- Is financial information shared appropriately? Do all stakeholders know the true financial position and performance of the business or assets?
- Are there written job descriptions, and formal hiring, training, and compensation guidelines? Is there a formal procedure and system for conducting performance reviews? If so, is it being implemented?

- Is performance rewarded with money and increased responsibilities? Are raises and increased responsibilities given for performance and contribution to the business, or on some other basis?
- How does management make large and small decisions? Are large decisions made deliberately and with input from relevant parties? Are small decisions delegated to the lowest levels at which they can be effectively made?
- Do all owners, managers, employees, and other stakeholders know where they stand, or are some of them unaware of decisions and developments that affect them?
- In other words, are business rules in place? Does everyone know and understand the rules? Does everyone acknowledge and submit to the rules?

If the senior generation has done little to create a structure that can survive them or to prepare successors, that implies that the next generation has not been adequately prepared and thus argues in favor of a sale. The testator may say that he prefers to pass the business to his heirs, but his actions do not bear that out. It's sometimes possible to lead the testator to understand this and to accept it, and that is best done in a maieutic manner.

Conversing with the Client

As we noted in Chapter 2, although the keep-or-sell question should be answered early, it's often best not to pose it starkly at the very outset. Asking the question before the testator and family understand the tasks they face may prompt them to stick with their preconceived decision. It's often useful first to engage the testator in a conversation about the business and his or her desires and intentions. This not only informs the advisor, but can make the testator aware of factors he hadn't considered.

This is a conversation with a purpose. It aims to move the testator to think beyond standard tax and discount planning and preconceived ideas about the disposition of assets. In some cases it's a wakeup call for the family business. Questions like those we present below help an advisor to work in a maieutic manner. The questions focus on how the testator feels about the business, how well he has prepared successors, how Roles and Rules operate in the business, how decisions are made, and so on.

Such questions can prompt the client to consider both the keep-or-sell decision and the estate planning process in a new light. For example, suppose the founder answers "No" to questions about the preparedness of the next generation to manage the business. Suppose he finds such questions offensive. Suppose interviews reveal that the next generation is not prepared or has no interest in running the business. One hopes the logical conclusion would be to sell the business.

Here are examples of questions to ask testators (and perhaps the spouse, children, and other potential beneficiaries), grouped by general category:

Business Continuation

- To what extent do you want the business to continue? Why?
- In what way do you want the business to continue? What does it mean to you that the business continues?
- How much are you invested in your children having something that resembles your relationship to the business? To what extent do you feel they should "carry on in your shoes"? How does this feeling vary as you consider each beneficiary?
- Do you believe that if the business is kept in the family that its revenues and earnings will grow and the business will increase in value? Why or why not?
- To what extent would you prefer that the business stay in the family? To what extent would you prefer that it be sold? How important to you are your spouse's and heirs' feelings about keeping or selling the business?

Legacy Issues

- To what extent do you want to provide for the financial security of your beneficiaries? Does your intention vary for various beneficiaries, for example for your spouse versus your children or for some children versus others? If so, why?
- To what extent do you want to pass on the business in order to leave something behind? How important is passing on the business in terms of leaving a legacy to your heirs? How important is it in terms of your "living on" after you die?
- To what extent are you motivated to pass the business on to your heirs in order to provide useful employment for them or to give them something to do?
- What do you really see as the best thing for your children, as a group and as individuals? Do you feel it's best to sell the business and give them capital either outright or in trust, or for them to run the business?

Preparedness for Succession

- Describe the levels of interest that your spouse or children have, as individuals, in assuming control of the business.
- How do you rate their skills, judgment, and ability to run the business, again as individuals?
- How much time and effort have *you* invested in preparing one or more of your children to assume leadership of the business?
- How much have *they* invested in preparing to assume leadership?
- How much time, effort, energy, and money are you willing to invest to prepare one or more of your children to assume leadership?
- What is your assessment of the next generation's readiness to take responsibility for the business or assets, given family dynamics and the potential for conflicts?
- Considering your total current life situation—including your age, health, marital status, living situation, desires, aspirations, and plans—how soon, and to what extent, do you wish to retire *and* withdraw from the a) management and b) ownership of the business?

These questions can be used in a conversational manner or worded to be answered on a Likert scale, which allows respondents to rate their preference or the importance of a factor. Such questions might be, "On a scale of one to five, how important is it to you that the business stay in the family?" or ". . . how prepared do you think your successors are to take over the business?" In the answer choices, "1" would be "Not at All Important" or "Not at All Prepared," and "5" would be "Extremely Important" or "Very Well Prepared." Standardized responses enable you to compare people's attitudes more objectively, although there is, of course, still a very subjective element to the answers.

What's the Answer?

If the testator's answers reflect the following, the decision to sell the business would probably be preferable:

- Lack of desire or preparedness on the part of the next generation to assume ownership and management of the business
- Lack of a sound business structure—that is, one composed of rules as well as business roles—or lack of willingness to develop such a structure
- Desire of the testator to "live on" in the business *without* having considered the beneficiaries' interest in running it or having prepared them to do so

- Lack of realism in the testator's assessments of the heirs' interests, desires, and skills (Note that the testator may overestimate *or* underestimate someone's interest, desire, and skill.)
- Unsubstantiated or unrealistic assessments of the value of the business as an operating entity or as an asset to be sold

The most basic question is, What do the testator and beneficiaries want to do? If the testator wants the business to continue, selling it may, ironically, be the best way to ensure that it does. In other words, in some cases the business may stand the best chance of continuing as a business if it is sold. In such circumstances, selling it *may* also be the best way to provide for the heirs' financial security. After all, if they are not prepared to run the business, it's probably best to cash out while the value is presumably high and to distribute or invest the proceeds. In some situations, however, the testator may not want to consider this alternative, even when it is likely to be best. If the attorney sees that the business may indeed be sold when the testator dies, then the attorney might do well to suggest that certain provisions regarding the sales process, distribution of assets, and related issues be written into the estate planning documents as contingent provisions in case of a sale.

Facing the Rules Crisis

As noted earlier, testators, families, and advisors are usually unaware that the family faces a Rules Crisis if they are going to keep the business. It's not just that they don't understand the Rules Crisis in the terms we employ. It's that they don't accurately gauge the challenges they face in transferring the business to the next generation. As a result, they find themselves unprepared for these challenges and the ensuing problems.

To solve a problem, one must first acknowledge that there is a problem and then understand the problem itself. Absent that, people fall back on emotional, roles-based behaviors, such as blame, demonizing, denial, helplessness, silence, avoidance of decisions, and failure to move on. We've noted the effects of these behaviors on the business and family, and on attorneys, trust officers, and other advisors. Extinguishing these behaviors requires an intervention geared to calming the situation, explaining the problem, and moving people toward change. The need for an intervention can occur at the planning, transition, or post-transition stage, but the earlier it takes place, the better.

Early Intervention: A Pound of Prevention

If an ounce of prevention is worth a pound of cure, early intervention in estate planning problems equals a pound of prevention. Why? Because if things deteriorate far enough, the problems can become virtually insoluble. So avoiding or arresting deterioration is tremendously advantageous.

Although succession planning ranks among the most important management skills in a family businesses, it's typically given short shrift. Business owners know that the survival of the business and beneficiaries' incomes depend on it. Books, articles, courses, and conferences emphasize the importance of succession planning and provide how-to information on the subject. Yet it's not something most testators enjoy facing, and thus they tend to put it off or do a boilerplate job of it. In the absence of true succession planning, which ideally begins at least five years before the founder's retirement or death, intervention often becomes necessary. The need for intervention arises when roles-based behavior threatens the stability of the business or implementation of the plan. Another indicator is the presence of tension as described in Chapter 4.

The next three subsections discuss our interactions with the testator and family in more depth, but we emphasize that the earlier an advisor intervenes, the better. Unfortunately, that may be hard to do if the Rules Crisis is perceived as too far off to be of real concern. While early intervention is generally better, the approach to the consultation and the tasks involved remain fundamentally the same.

Explaining the Problem

At any stage, we try to help the testator and family to focus on the problem, essentially by describing the situation and the stakes involved. To do this we typically:

- Show the pie chart we presented in Chapter 2 (Figure 2-1) and ask the testator and family members about their priorities; our goal here is get their attention and to introduce the factors at work in succession and estate planning
- Quote the statistics on the survival rates of family businesses, and explain that the future of the business and the family's finances depend on "getting this right"
- Describe the nature of the Rules Crisis and explain it as a universal phenomenon, one that all family businesses face, but mention that some families deal with it better than others
- Explain that if the family is going to deal with succession, they must choose which level of participation they want from their advisors, from three broadly defined levels:

- *Level 1:* The advisors provide a succession and estate plan based on the usual goals and rules of transferring assets with minimal tax liability, and proper liquidity, asset protection, and legal transfer.
- *Level 2:* The advisors provide the above services, *plus* rules in the form of special provisions and tailored business structures that incorporate Roles and Rules, as described in Chapter 7, *and* a facilitator to guide the business and the family through the transition, as described in Chapter 4.
- *Level 3:* The advisors provide the above services *plus* an attorney in addition to a facilitator in a more hands-on role. The facilitator and attorney work with the testator and family to implement the roles and the rules needed to help the family make the transition to managing the business as a business.

In presenting the Roles and Rules approach—that is, Level 2 or 3 services—we find it useful to give the client a memo outlining the risks and potential difficulties, and to provide examples with which they can identify. We've found that sometimes after clients have heard us describe the risks and difficulties and opted for a standard approach they then encounter problems and say, "We didn't know it could get *this* bad." When people see something in writing upfront, they tend to take it seriously. Indeed, such a memo constitutes notification similar to that provided by physicians to patients in the form of a video, information sheet, or consent form, which are all now routine before a procedure. Of course, we are usually willing and able to help the family when they discover their problems later. But even with the Roles and Rules approach, we warn testators and families that matters may worsen before they improve. This often occurs when long-standing issues are finally addressed.

Admittedly, we can paint a somewhat grim picture; however, when there are millions of dollars of assets at stake amid poor family dynamics, it only makes sense—in the interests of all parties—to apprise clients of risks and potential difficulties, to offer them ways of addressing them, and to give them the opportunity to accept or refuse relevant services. It's really a matter of advising clients and establishing their intention in clear, specific terms. In this way, the advisor is not "selling a solution" but rather presenting alternative services from which the client chooses, with the advisor's guidance.

We also apprise clients of the uncertainty they and their assets and families are exposed to if the estate is thrown into the courts for any reason. Probate and trust law varies by state, and the courts vary in the way they handle these cases. Both create uncertainty regarding the outcome not only of actions at law, but even regarding testators' wishes as expressed in trust agreements. In sum, we try to help clients understand their needs and make a fully informed choice.

Crisis Intervention

If early intervention has not occurred and the family has not been prepared, there is still a way to help them by using a modified Roles and Rules approach. If a family is confused, paralyzed, or chaotic after the testator dies, we meet with them as soon as possible and explain that there are rules governing this situation. We've found that family members often have no real understanding of their rights and responsibilities. Even many trustees don't fully understand their responsibilities under the trust agreement and the law. This is understandable if people haven't been prepared, and dealing with the result is among our duties.

In chaotic situations, we explain that it is not "open season," that people have certain rights and responsibilities, and that there's no call for confusion, paralysis, or chaos. The lawyer will explain the probate code, fiduciary rules, and rules set forth in the trust document itself. He'll provide articles that explain the role of the trustee in layman's language and educate the trustee and family on the subject. Upon hearing about the rules and their responsibilities, family members usually have little to say or fall silent. Sometimes they will have questions, but typically they leave and develop their own interpretations, some of which must be modified as administration of the estate continues. In cases of a business or family in chaos, we often need a facilitator to "bring the law to town" as described in Chapter 4.

The complexity of these cases depends on the difficulty of the family dynamics, the family members' expectations, the intractability of people's positions, and the extent to which family members have been exempt, or view themselves as exempt, from rules. As this book has shown, dealing with these conditions is a task unto itself, and anyone who assists in that task provides a valuable service.

From Chaos to Problem Solving

People who are emoting, fighting, or pushing their positions cannot solve problems. Therefore, we try to help people move into problem-solving mode. Broadly, a problem-solving process involves five stages in which people:

1. Become aware that they may have a problem or face a crisis
2. Acknowledge that they have a problem
3. Understand their problem and their needs
4. Develop alternative solutions to the problem
5. Commit to and implement the solution that best meets their needs

The table below summarizes what advisors can do to assist the testator and family facing a Rules Crisis at each stage of this process:

To Help the Testator & Family Business:	The Advisor Can:
Become aware that they may have a problem or face a crisis	Explain the Rules Crisis, and the situation, statistics, and stakes, and explain that the legal rules do not preclude this crisis; use articles and other readings, PowerPoint exhibits, videos, and actual cases to explain and dramatize the crisis; mention that subsequent alternatives include potentially larger legal fees, family conflict, and risks to the business
Acknowledge that they have a problem	Ask questions that uncover conflicting attitudes and aims; point out behaviors that may undermine the business
Understand their problem and their needs	Assess the structure of the Roles and Rules in the business, and the effects of family roles, and share the results with the testator and family
Develop alternative potential solutions to the problem	Revisit the keep-or-sell decision and propose a Level 2 or 3 involvement by the facilitator and attorney, or begin at least some level of facilitator involvement
Commit to and implement a solution	Work with the testator, family, and business to move the family to adopt business rules (and roles)

You might think of the role of the facilitator or the advisor as that of helping people move through this process, a process of change. People don't resist change in order to be difficult or to undermine themselves. They resist change because they feel that their roles are threatened. They fear, resent, and resist the loss of power, influence, security, importance, independence, or recognition associated with their roles. That is hardly irrational. After all, when you introduce rules into any roles-based situation, people's roles *are* threatened. Without clear rules that apply to all, people have little choice but to cling to their roles.

The best, or at least optimal, solution is to guide them to choose to develop new roles in the context of the legal and business rules. Or, again, they can sell the business or assets and divide the proceeds.

Taking a Truly Maieutic Approach

We explained the maieutic approach in Chapter 4, so we need not cover it in depth here. It's a Socratic approach in which people are led to express their own conclusions in a rational, iterative manner. However, four points are worth emphasizing:

- Family dynamics in estate planning are too complex and personal, and the outcome too uncertain, for any practitioner or advisor to "know what's best" and to dictate a course of action. Hence, the need for a maieutic approach.

- Many consultants recommend keeping family roles or "baggage" or "issues" separate from the business. They also recommend policies, procedures, and best practices by which the family can run the business like a business. The CEO and family members typically listen to and even agree with this advice, then find it impossible to follow. Clearly, families need something more than recommendations.

- The something more that families need is a facilitator who can model the role of leader until a family member or someone else can assume that role. The advisor thus helps people define and adopt policies, procedures, and other business rules. This generates buy-in, and gives the testator and family a greater stake in the success of these measures than they could have in mere recommendations.

- A maieutic approach and Roles and Rules helps practitioners maintain objectivity, perspective, and humility amid unsettling family dynamics. This recognizes that a family can't be changed by an outside agent, a will, or a trust agreement. It recognizes the legal rights of sane adults to dispose of their assets as they see fit, and it positions the practitioner to help family members to accept that fact, which can be painful. It also recognizes that sometimes the only solution is to sell the business or buy out parties who cannot or will not play by rules.

We recognize that a maieutic approach represents a significant investment in time, money, effort, and expertise. It should therefore be used only when the risks and consequences of a negative outcome warrant it, and when the client and family are willing to pay for and participate in it. Even so, nothing can guarantee a specific outcome when human nature is involved.

Testators who pass their businesses on to successors whom they haven't prepared undermine their goal of perpetuating the business. These testators want to establish a legacy, or perhaps a monument, aside from money, something that holds meaning for their families and lives on after them. Yet if the successors are not ready, willing, and able to manage the business, then all of that—including money—is put at risk.

Given the fiduciary rules and the case law, testators who attempt to manage the business from the grave through a trustee and trust agreement, or by means of entity-based solutions, generally cannot succeed for long. Suppose the business experiences several unprofitable quarters. If the trustee fails to safeguard the interests of the beneficiaries, for instance by selling their stake in the business, then in most states the beneficiaries could sue the trustee for not executing his fiduciary responsibilities and securing their continued income. Yet selling the stake could put the trustee in conflict with the managers of the business. It could also ignite factional warfare between family members who want to (and can afford to) ride out unprofitable periods and those who cannot. In a very real sense, it's an impossible situation.

Unfortunately, in succession and estate planning and execution, impossible situations sometimes develop and must somehow be accepted.

Acceptance Isn't Easy

In her groundbreaking book *On Death and Dying*, Elisabeth Kübler Ross identified five stages of dying: denial, anger, bargaining, despair, and acceptance. In the final stage, acceptance, the loss is internalized and perceived as part of life's process. Although those stages apply to the dying individual, they can also be applied to the survivors. Acceptance on the part of the survivors is especially important—and difficult—when a testator has blatantly favored one child over others, or has cut off, cut out, or disowned one or more children or other beneficiaries. Unless the survivors are resigned to the situation, clearly understand it, or employ extremely effective coping mechanisms, the outcome can ruin the business.

Even with a good plan, not everyone will necessarily be happy. Remember, the goal of the estate plan is not to make everyone happy; rather, it is to comply advantageously with tax, trust, and business law, protect assets from unknown future creditors and claims, and achieve orderly succession and transfer of the assets. Amid difficult family dynamics, it is highly unlikely that all parties will be happy with the plan. While Roles and Rules cannot ensure happiness, it can prepare people for the way the trust agreement will work, for the way the trustee or managers of the business will work with them, and for their new roles in the business. This does help to minimize the risk of future conflicts.

Of course, neither the estate nor the succession process will administer itself. Nor does every family employ Roles and Rules or benefit from it as we would wish. Nor do they always behave as they agreed to and as we anticipated. Indeed, as the old joke in the scientific community goes, under the most carefully controlled conditions of heat, light, nutrition, oxygenation, and stimulation, the organism will do whatever the hell it wants to do. This is even truer of people.

Last Words for Estate Planners

Roles and Rules does not guarantee any particular outcome, nor it is meant to. In fact, it's surest benefit may well accrue to estate planners. There is much to recommend an approach that will enable estate planners to identify negative or hopeless family dynamics early in the process. The forces unleashed by the testator's death, which may include recriminations, lawsuits, countersuits, and malpractice charges, may render the engagement far from worthwhile. Some situations are familial time-bombs set to explode upon the testator's death and when they cannot be defused, they are to be avoided. That's a fact that advisors must occasionally accept.

We've seen a number of cases in which the chances of a workable estate plan are minimal, and they've been characterized by:

- Testators who cling to their family-roles-based behavior regardless of negative consequences; these include those who refuse to share or relinquish power while refusing to prepare a successor
- Testators or beneficiaries who won't acknowledge that certain rules apply to them and therefore ignore sound management practices, dishonor contracts, or deny legal realities
- Animosity between spouses, which often comes to the fore as the dominant spouse starts to lose his or her faculties; another potential source of irreconcilable difficulties arises from spouses or children from previous marriages with real or alleged claims to the estate
- Animosity on the part of one or both parents toward a child or children, or on the part of a child toward one or both parents, or among children
- Refusal or failure of children to participate in problem solving
- Determination on the part of any family member to judge any estate plan as unfair and contestable

As noted above under Crisis Intervention, in such situations advisors must meet with the family as soon as possible and outline what must be done in the specific situation, emphasizing that this is a legal situation and that everyone must operate in a rules environment.

The Challenge of Complexity

Nothing does away with the complexity of human relationships and behavior, and succession and estate planning amid difficult family dynamics is inherently complex. That's why it's so helpful to have a model, such as Roles and Rules, that brings an understanding of human relationships and behavior into the work. That understanding provides a framework that enables you to consider the complexities involved and to accommodate them. It helps you avoid or neutralize negative forces while capitalizing on positive ones. It recognizes that family dynamics are just one more consideration, like tax minimization and asset protection, that must be acknowledged and addressed in the planning process and in the transfer of assets.

The ultimate measure of a good estate plan is the way in which events transpire after the testator's death. With a good plan, all affected parties have been prepared for what will happen. People understand their business roles, the rules for ownership and management, and the steps in the administration of the trust. They have realistic expectations about the business and their finances after the death of the testator, and they are prepared for their new roles and may even have assumed them.

Thus, although the testator's death represents a loss that brings grief as well as change, the necessary and desired business, financial, and administrative transition can proceed in an orderly manner. Moreover, the business is positioned to be sold in an orderly manner or to evolve to its next stage, with the owners and managers ready to effect that evolution and lead the business to continued prosperity.

Bear in Mind

- If a family does not want to deal with a Rules Crisis and prefers to sell the business instead of facing that task, that's fine. What's not so fine is deciding to keep the business without dealing with the Rules Crisis as the developmental task that it is.
- To deal well with a Rules Crisis:

    - The testator and family must understand its nature and inevitability, and decide to keep or sell the business in light of it.
    - The advisor should help the testator and family to deal with the Rules Crisis, and help the family make the keep-or-sell decision as objectively as possible.
    - The planning team must guide the family through the sale of the business or the transfer of the business to the next generation.

- An advisor may lead a client to make the keep-or-sell decision in the best way by posing questions designed to lead the client maieutically to that decision.
- Chaos often arises when a testator dies and survivors don't understand the Rules Crisis. In such cases, the family must be helped to see that it is not "open season" and that certain rights and responsibilities are dictated by the probate code, fiduciary rules, trust agreement, and trust law.
- Given the challenges of estate planning amid difficult family dynamics, there can be no guarantee of a good outcome; however, testators, families, and advisors can take steps to minimize the chances of bad outcomes and maximize the chances of good ones.

Appendixes

APPENDIX A

Derivation of Roles and Rules and Its Application to Succession in Business

by

Richard P. Goldwater, M.D.

This appendix explains the derivation of Roles and Rules as a model of the mind or "psyche" and shows its conceptual application to business structure and succession. This appendix includes the following four parts:

- *Part 1: Dualism and Monism* explains that dualism and monism are distinct, equally foundational and important, and at the same time, vitally opposed ways of knowing. "Roles" and "rules" describe how dualism and monism manifest themselves in everyday life, both psychologically and socially. Roles are dualistic because one plays a role for another above or below one in a hierarchy. Roles therefore imply rank. Rules apply to all regardless of rank. The reporting structure of any business is made up of roles and rules in its vertical and horizontal dimensions.
- *Part 2: Dyad and Monad* presents dualism and monism in sequence. Dualism and monism taken together at the same time may show a grid or perhaps a pie chart, while dyad to monad shows a developmental flow chart. A psychological example of the dyad to monad sequence is the parent-child dyad that produces a developing, individual child. We shall describe the will to survive and the profit motive as monads.

- *Part 3: A Periodic Table of the Psyche* presents a chart of psychological and social attributes and their relationship. (It is a "periodic" table in the sense that it presents attributes of the mind or psyche as a series of repeating stages.)
- *Part 4: A Periodic Table of a Business* applies the psychosocial chart to the business corporation. This chart demonstrates that human social structures, of which one is the business corporation, resemble and in a sense replicate the psyche and its "two ways of knowing."

For the record, "mind" and "psyche" are usually synonyms. "Psyche" represents "the mind" as a whole, as made up of identity, emotion, thought, and the will to act. "Mind" is sometimes taken to mean something more limited, such as thinking or cognition.

To recap, the first part explains the premise that there are two ways of knowing. The second part demonstrates philosophically what follows from that premise, and the third shows how those two ways of knowing combine to make up the structure of the psyche. The fourth part shows how those two ways of knowing combine to form a business structure, and how that structure can be passed along to successors.

I offer these ideas as heuristics and guidelines to prompt readers to explore new avenues of thought and to understand and solve problems in human development and interaction. These are not "rules," nor can they be proven in the usual sense of the term. Rather they are a means—and a model, if you will—of understanding people and their behavior.

My goal is to demonstrate the eventual unification of dualism and monism, these mortal and immortal antagonists. I say mortal because adherents of various dualistic and monistic doctrines have killed and are killing each other over the difference. I say immortal because these ideas have been around forever. To accomplish this "consummation devoutly to be wished," I must rigorously treat each as equally important and inherent to human nature. I believe that this document may accomplish my goal.

Please know that this material is inherently technical in that it employs terms that may be, or seem, unfamiliar and defines a few terms in ways that differ slightly from their usual meaning. It is also, frankly, somewhat challenging in that it develops a systematic approach to how we think (and feel, and thus "know"). In other words, this line of inquiry employs the mind to understand the mind, a problem familiar to anyone who has even a passing acquaintance with philosophy or psychology. While the mind is ultimately the only tool we have with which to understand the mind, that fact does present inherent complexities and challenges, which I do my best to simplify here without shortchanging readers.

Part 1: Dualism and Monism
1.1 How You Know What You Know

Roles and Rules™ represents epistemology in action. Epistemology is the branch of philosophy concerned with the nature and validity of knowledge. In epistemology, what counts is not what you know but *how* you know what you know. In this section I present the premise that two equally fundamental, consistent, and important ways of knowing—dualism and monism—underlie all that we know:

- Dualism is the philosophy that there are two explanatory principles, and that therefore there are two kinds of things to explain. Examples of these two kinds of things include good and evil, and mind and body. Dualism establishes distinct categories. *Roles are dualistic* because they presume the categorical distinction of the actor of the role from the other for whom or for what reason the actor plays the role. The "actor" is the subject of the role, or is subject to the role, and the "other" is the object of the role. We shall see shortly that dualism and therefore roles are necessarily hierarchical.

- In monism, there is one explanatory principle, and therefore there are no categories. Instead, there are only interactions, which may occur among objects, numbers, or people. *Rules are monistic* because they apply uniformly to interactions among every number, unit, and particle. The rules of addition and subtraction apply to all numbers; the rules of baseball apply to all the players in the game. It is monistic to say that rules of mathematics and science can explain whatever may exist.

Can this distinction—dualism and monism—really explain all we can know? Yes. As I hope to demonstrate in these pages, all perception and understanding is an amalgam of these two ways of knowing. The mind works this way, and the brain is wired this way. For instance, visual perception both categorizes a thing and registers how it moves and interacts. The retina at the back of the eye is a direct extension of the brain. There are two types of receptors on the retina—one for color (cones) and one for black and white (rods). The cones receive the most focused light, so that the brain may identify and classify things, while the rods are sensitive to movement, but cannot resolve detail.

Over the centuries, many thinkers have argued that time and space or good and evil are *a priori* categories, which means that they underlie all thought. However, the numbers two and one must be more fundamental and precisely descriptive than any categories designated by words. By dualism, we mean an absolute or irreducible two-ness, and not simply the integer 2 to which one may either add or subtract other integers. Absolute two-ness is represented not as an integer, but as dyads of categories and specifics. These cannot substitute for each other, add together, or otherwise combine. For example, the category, "fruit" cannot be a piece of fruit, and no piece of fruit is so perfect as to be the same as its category. A category is an ideal and perfect whole, while a specific is just an instance of that category. Discontinuity necessarily exists between category and specific because one is qualitatively above the other. Category and specific have a hierarchical relation that numbers do not. Numbers exist along a continuum. The integer three is not of higher rank and therefore is not "better than" than the integer two. Three dollars are better than two, but two mosquito bites are better than three.

The perception of hierarchy introduces the idea of rank, which makes possible the perception of social class and status. The existence of corporate, church, and military hierarchies is made possible because dualistic, categorical perception is possible. So—and this point is key—what defines dualism is not the perception of opposing categories, like good and evil or mind and body, but the perception of categories, period. Categories necessarily imply that there may be specifics. The category fruit implies that there may be specific things that are fruits. Categories thus imply dualism and hierarchy.

What about apples and oranges? Those words refer to different categories, right? You cannot mix apples and oranges. Where is the hierarchy there? It is implied in the distinction of apples from oranges as specific members of different categories of fruit. They are members of different hierarchies; each is a specific member of its own category. You can add apples and oranges as pieces of fruit, or you can ignore their fruit identity and add them as objects, as two different "things." But as specifics of different categories, they cannot be combined.

Here's another key point that follows from our apples-and-oranges comparison: hierarchy precludes free interaction among members of different classes. When something outranks something else, as things do in a hierarchy, it means one can affect the other more than the reverse. That means they cannot interact freely. A category can affect a specific more than the reverse. Military officers command privates, not the reverse. (Meanwhile, numbers freely interact according to the rules of math.) A corollary of this point is that because rules do not apply equally to different ranks as they would to numbers, different rules may exist at different ranks. So, military officers may be entitled to better food as well as to more pay than enlisted personnel.

Rules guide interaction. Laws, a form of rules, operate across social classes, permitting interaction among individuals, for instance on a nation's roads or in business contracts. Drivers of luxury cars must follow the same rules as drivers of jalopies; all parties to a business contract are bound by the contract. Yet free interaction permits and supports the development of individuality. The rules of baseball allow each player to develop his own style of play and allow each game to unfold individually. The rules of grammatical syntax enable people to interact verbally in creative and comprehensible ways.

On an entry level, one considers dualism as a dyad of category and specific, and monism as a uniform set of rules. However, that dualism and monism are categorically distinct means that *the distinction of dualism from monism is itself dualistic. Dualism ultimately refers therefore not to opposing categories per se, but to the distinction of categories and specifics, on the one hand, and, on the other, of rules and numbers.* This would seem to elevate dualism above monism, which would defeat any attempt to perceive them as "equally foundational" ways of knowing. I'll resolve this problem in Part 2.

Again, our goal is to treat dualism and monism, category and rule, and hierarchy and interaction as equally important, so they may, later in these pages, be unified in a conception of how the world as we know it exists.

1.2 Roles and Rules

Roles and *rules* are informal psychological and social labels for dualism and monism. A role is dualistic because it implies the distinct other for whom one acts more than for oneself. Other may mean another person or other people, or it may be an ideal such as patriotism. In the theater or at the cinema, the other is the audience.

Roles like parent, child, friend, and teacher are social categories. We can say that because a role outranks whoever acts in it just as a category outranks a specific. A role outranks whoever acts in it because the role defines which actions suit the role (just as the category "apple" defines the properties of specific apples). For instance, the role of parent defines certain actions taken on behalf of the child; the role of Hamlet defines actions taken on behalf of the audience and the other actors in the play. As categories, roles imply a duality of role and actor-in-the-role. So, we say that *a role is to an actor in the role as a category is to a specific.*

Just as roles outrank those who play them, some roles outrank other roles, as they do in a military or corporate hierarchy. Roles distinguish parent and child, general and private, physician and orderly. The higher the rank, the more general is its scope. In the military, the highest rank *is* general. A general and a private cannot interact as equals because they are members of different categories and ranks. When my elder son was about 15 months old, he called his mother "Mommy" and his father "Daddy-mommy." I was a kind of mommy, and a lower ranked one at that, akin to "lieutenant mommy."

Unlike roles, *rules* apply equally to everyone in the rules-based situation. Rules apply to interactions, for instance among vehicles on the roads, players in a game, and citizens in a democracy. Rules apply to everyone equally regardless of rank. No one in a company is allowed to commit fraud, and everyone in a family must knock on the bathroom door. In a company, people relate according to their roles and ranks, but at a company softball game, everyone plays by the same rules of the game.

1.3 Emotions Are Categories

Emotions place experiences into categories and classes of felt meaning, such as happy or sad. Understanding that emotions function as categories explains a lot about them. Indeed, they seem to force perceptions into categories without any need for logic or analysis, depending on the individual. Emotions may seem arbitrary, especially to others. One may say, "I know how I feel," or, "That's my feeling on this, whether you like it or not." The other person may feel completely differently about the same perceived thing.

Emotions are inseparable from the roles we play for others and that others play for us. Our emotions begin in the roles others play for us, starting from mother and father and moving on to teacher, coach, pastor, and employer. As we progress toward adulthood, our emotional lives grow more in the roles we play for others, rather than in the roles others play for us. We become friends, lovers, spouses, parents, workers, professionals, and so on, and perform for others the actions associated with those roles.

Stereotypes generate emotions in that they identify the roles that others play in our minds. As a categorizing mechanism, emotions create or respond to stereotypes of people as beautiful or ugly, jock or geek, country clubber or working stiff. Emotions also recognize and respond to signs of social class and rank. Royalty, movie star, and parent are social ranks that evoke the idealizing emotions of rank-worship, such as loyalty, deference, and so on.

Emotion and logic function as antagonists in many public debates, as is the case in arguments based on anecdotal evidence versus those based on statistical studies. For instance, although data show that seatbelts save many more lives than they cost, some people will not wear them. They prefer the *feeling* of freedom or control although the numbers logically indicate that seatbelts make one safer.

Emotions, roles, and hierarchies manifest dualism in everyday life. Logic, rules, and free interaction manifest monism in everyday life. Emotion and logic are equal elements of knowing. Neither can be eliminated, despite religious exhortations that eschew logic, and despite scientific methods that ignore emotion or that reduce emotion to a kind of primitive cognition. Emotion without logic would make one an hysteric, while logic without emotion would make one a computer. Emotion and logic ought to function together as do the right and left halves of a brain. The two brain hemispheres have different functions and often compete with or inhibit one another, yet we experience ourselves as whole people. However, emotional subjectivity sees only itself, while scientific, logical objectivity sees only the world. Roles and Rules puts dualism and monism together in a conception of structure.

1.4 The Meaning of Emotionality

Let us look at emotions on their own terms. Many people think of emotions as impulses, as drives toward expression or behavior. However, emotion refers not to how one moves, but to how one *is* moved. In fact, we describe something that elicits deep emotion as moving. Some things make us feel happy, and other things make us feel sad. Emotion is thus a felt response to input. We watch a catastrophe or drama on television, and we are affected. It moves us.

Emotion is a perceptual response that sorts experience into categories of feeling. TV programmers know this and therefore provide horror, food, religious, sports, action, romance, and comedy channels. We can literally almost dial an emotion. Publishers of genre fiction, such as romances or horror stories, also know this. How an emotion "feels" is what it "means" to us, whether that meaning is romantic or horrifying or what have you. That meaning may be something one is dimly or expressly reminded of, such as loss, desire, or anger, or it may be social or collective meaning, such as patriotism. It is in this way that emotions are categorical.

1.5 Logic and Rules

It is not necessarily logical that anything outranks anything else. Under the rules of logic, things may either lead to or follow from each other (as in cause and effect), but they do not logically outrank each other.

Logic doesn't necessarily tell us whether an interaction flows one way or another. For instance, the mathematical calculus specifies how quantities change, even at infinitesimal intervals, but does not specify the direction of change. Formulas that describe things as accelerating as they fall also describe things decelerating as they rise. Similarly, calculating the time it takes to drive between New York and Los Angeles does not specify which way one travels. The world as Newton described it is reversible and time symmetrical. This is summed up in the statement that every action has an equal and opposite reaction. In Newton's view, there is everywhere a present moment moving through time as a ship moves through the waves.

The laws of motion described by Newton, one of the two men mainly associated with the development of the mathematical calculus, posited perfectly balanced, symmetrical action and reaction. Action and reaction are simultaneous and exactly opposed, and thus zero-sum. They balance out to no net effect. Since there is no net effect, the idea of cause and effect or past and future can hardly apply. The Newtonian dynamics or "mechanics"[1] of motion lead nowhere, only around in circles or ellipses. Categorical reasoning uses circular logic, too. It proves itself! A poet wrote, "Beauty is truth, and truth beauty."

A children's seesaw demonstrates zero-sum interaction. One side cannot go up further or more often than the other side goes down. An economic example would be someone paying a dollar for a candy bar. The candy bar and the dollar have changed places, but overall there is no net change in value. If two baseball teams play, one wins and the other loses. Winning is +1 and losing is -1 in the league standings. Combining +1 and -1 yields zero. At the end of the season, the average winning percentage of all the teams in a league is .500. Newton would readily recognize the assumptions underlying the mathematics of social sciences such as economics, sociology, and psychology.

So far, I have used "monism" to refer to the world as Newton understood it, as a perpetually repeating system of symmetrical, reversible, zero-sum interactions. Yet Newton might have known that he was describing motion in a vacuum. On earth, there can be no perfectly balanced interaction, no perpetual motion machine. A factor called friction slows things down and unbalances symmetry.

Newton's laws ignore the fact that we ordinarily perceive time as asymmetrical. Time seems to us to proceed from the past through the present to the future. We do not ordinarily perceive simultaneous and symmetrical action and reaction. Rather, we perceive asymmetrical cause and effect, in which cause must come before effect. To account for the apparent forward motion of time, a new insight was necessary. The scientific idea of "time asymmetry" was born when the new science of thermodynamics proved mathematically that one cannot burn the same fuel twice. With thermodynamics, scientists figured out that friction meant that time could go only in the direction of using up fuel, for example to overcome friction.

A quantity called "increasing entropy" was postulated to represent spent fuel in any closed system that can never be used again. This is the famous Second Law of Thermodynamics, the principle of increasing entropy, as a result of which there can be no perfectly renewable, energy resource. Since the energy is stored in the molecular order of fuel, increasing entropy means progressively less order and more chaos everywhere in the universe that anything happens. Energy on earth depends for its renewal upon energy that arrives on earth from our sun.

Newtonian action-reaction is zero-sum, but thermodynamic interactions are *not* zero-sum. The past yields to a future of increasing entropy. The present

---

[1] The science of Newtonian motion is described as "mechanics," referring to the effects of forces on systems, such as of those that set objects in motion.

moment was therefore proven to be different from the past not because of the creation of some new work of art, but because every action no matter how creative causes more chaos than order. All that lives on earth must die. Here at least and at last, was a scientific sense of cause preceding effect. Gunpowder explodes before the bullet flies. The gun recoils instantaneously, as Newton would predict, but the gunpowder cannot be used again, a fact that Newton did not account for.

Returning to the matter of travel from New York to Los Angeles, we can now understand time asymmetry: we used fuel to get there. The only way, it seems, to be conscious of time, at least on earth, is that we are burning fuel every second of our lives. Everything we do and everything that happens uses up fuel.

Returning to the idea of zero-sum barter exchanges, we encounter a new way to understand profit. Business depends upon the generation of profit just as natural actions generate increasing entropy. So, profit can hardly be understood as a fuel, and in fact, having "too much" money produces stock repurchases by companies and early retirement by individuals, not renewed action. We leave considering the implications of this idea for another time.

1.6 From Monism to Monadism

Now, back to dualism and monism: we encounter a problem. If we try to consider hierarchy and interaction or dualism and monism to be symmetrical, that is of equal importance, we see them as dualistically distinct. This would, however, elevate dualism over monism, because to perceive them as separate but equal is dualistic. The idea of time asymmetry arrives just in time to solve our problem.

To solve the problem, we put dualism and monism together in a way that also preserves their difference. Hierarchy has elements both of symmetry and asymmetry, while monism is symmetrical. Hierarchy is asymmetrical in that one thing must be above another; otherwise there is equality. *One can therefore distinguish hierarchy from interaction as asymmetry from symmetry.* As asymmetry versus symmetry, dualism and monism may combine. All we need is the idea of time asymmetry. That the past comes before the present does not necessarily mean that the past outranks the present.

With respect to cause and effect, there is an asymmetry of past and future. The past may affect the future more than the future may affect the past. Thermodynamics is therefore monism *not* in distinction to dualism. Thermodynamics includes both the asymmetry we attribute to hierarchy *and* the symmetry required by Newton's laws. The asymmetrical hierarchy of category and specific gives way to the temporal asymmetry of past and future. Thermodynamics thus represents monism with increased explanatory power taking over some of the domain originally occupied by dualism. Newtonian monism could explain the motion of the planets; thermodynamics proved that the universe could not be understood without accounting for cause and effect.

We need a new word to indicate the "new monism." The other man associated with the development of calculus was Gottfried W. Leibniz. He used the word "monad" to represent a metaphysical or subjective substance upon which all that objectively exists is predicated. His "monad" was an infinitesimal, *metaphysical* interval, rather than an infinitesimal, *physical* interval of time or space. Over the centuries, writers in fields ranging from philosophy to computer science have adopted the word "monad" for various purposes. Adopting "monad" for our purposes will help us in the quest to perceive dualism and monism as equally fundamental.

I use the word "monism" to refer to words that imply zero-sum interactions. I use the term "monad" to refer to words that suggest cause and effect. This replicates what happened when Newtonian science met thermodynamics. An example of "a monism" versus "a monad" is "communication" versus "expression." Communication is an interaction, and expression is an action. Communication between people does not imply at any moment who is talking and who is listening. However, expression implies a vector, such as the transfer of information from one person to another or the performance of musicians at a concert for an audience.

I reiterate: a monad differs from a monism because a monad incorporates the asymmetry previously owned exclusively by dualism. By "a dualism," again, I mean something categorical, and that may mean subjective. What we mean by "subjective" is something knowable firsthand only by oneself. Consciousness, perception, affection, guilt, depression, grief, and even "self" are all subjective terms. They may be studied objectively in other people only as their brains light up in a neuroscience laboratory, or as they report the experience. They may be understood as responses or as reactions, but not as interactions.

The first computer word processors announced that they produced documents. At that time, I thought of nothing less than the Magna Carta as a document. But in the world of computers, a document simply documents (or evidences) something, as does a passport. The Magna Carta was a document in a "role" sense of the word, an embodiment of ideals, while computer documentation is a document in a "rule" sense, a simple description. New computers arrived with documentation, rather than an instruction manual. The documentation typically produced no instructional effect upon the baffled user; it was simply description.

Communication and documentation are examples of monisms. They imply no cause and effect. Expression and instruction manuals are monads, as I employ the term, and they imply cause and effect, and action passing from A to B.

History has proceeded and is proceeding from myth and religion to mathematics and science, from feudalism and dictatorship to egalitarianism and democracy, and from monism to monad. In history and in perception, dualism precedes monism. From the psychological standpoint, the dyad of parent and child precedes the monad of the developed individual. However, as I trust I have demonstrated, saying that dualism precedes monism does not mean that dualism outranks monism.

Part 2: Dyad and Monad
2.1 Playing to Tie

In my work as a family and marital psychotherapist, I sometimes offer this advice: "If you play to win, you lose. If you play to lose, you lose. If you play to tie, you win."

This advice applies to a current, global problem. Dualism and monism are now at war in the world in the form of fundamentalist religion versus political democracy and scientific evidence, as they have been in one form or another throughout history. These are essentially wars between believers in ranks, roles, and categories on the one hand, and, on the other, believers in rules and numbers (for instance, the number of votes or scientific data). That Western science has slighted the role of categories has intolerably injured the emotions of religionists, because they view categories such as good and evil and sacred and secular as reasonable. Meanwhile, scientists know that the mind employs categories and that emotions exist. Something is missing in math and physics in that categories and emotions cannot be accounted for, even though they are demonstrably useful to the mind.

Dualism and monism represent equally important and fundamental elements of human knowledge. Yet, recalling that the distinction of dualism and monism is still dualism, one sees no possible resolution to the struggle between fundamentalist religion and political democracy. Indeed, both in this example and in general, neither side is right or wrong, and neither side can or should win. *The problem is that they are not integrated into one structure.* A third model, something "monadistic" will be necessary to integrate them.

2.2 The Question of Equality

Let us pause for a review. My premise is that there are two distinct, opposed, equally important and vital ways of knowing, called dualism and monism. Dualism and monism are recognizable as roles versus rules, hierarchy versus interaction, and subjective versus objective. (Note that the word subject literally means "thrown under" and object means "thrown against.")

Recall that dualism is asymmetrical, because dualism implies hierarchy, and because hierarchy is asymmetrical. Recall that monism is symmetrical because *inter*action is symmetrical. Dualism and monism are equally important, and equally embedded in the psyche as how we know the world, and ourselves. Insisting upon the equal importance of dualism and monism may be controversial. Religious reasoning is categorical and hierarchical, and distrusts the ethos of democracy (the Church, after all, is not and never has been a democracy) and distrusts the insights of objective science, because these are interactive and egalitarian. Meanwhile, objective science considers unproven claims of religion as invalid ways of gaining knowledge about the world. The schism between fundamentalist religion and objective science represents the archetypal, seventeenth century, clash of dualism versus monism.

Attempting to treat dualism and monism as separate but equal immediately raises a logical problem: to distinguish dualism from monism is dualistic. Thus, dualism would seem to triumph! Monism in distinction to dualism is still dualism! Precisely because it is still dualism, precisely because it is defined in dualistic distinction to dualism, "classical monism" cannot fully describe the physical world. As we saw in Part 1, classical monism cannot account for the everyday experience of the asymmetry of time. Along came the science of thermodynamics. This science challenged the universality of Newtonian ideas of reversibility, zero-sum interactions, and the conservation of everything. A quantity called entropy was proven to increase with time in any complete system. Thus, unlike reversible Newtonian interactionism and its idea of symmetrical time, thermodynamics was not zero-sum with respect to time. The past is different from the future because one cannot light the same match twice.

The notion of a monad represents monism *not* in distinction to dualism. A monad is monistic, in that past, present, and future are perceived as a continuous flow. A monad nevertheless has something of dualism in it, namely the asymmetry that hierarchy implies. In dualism, asymmetry means that category outranks specific. In "monad-ism" the past outranks the future. That is, the past has more effect on the present than does the future. So, a monad need not be perceived to exist in distinction to dualism, or in the context of dualism. It can exist on its own.

So, instead of comparing dualism and monism, we may now compare dyads and monads. Every dualism is a dyad. But wait, isn't the distinction of dyad and monad just another dualism? Indeed, isn't dualism itself the dualism of dualism and monism? No, because time asymmetry rescues us. Just as in the actual history of science, we can travel from dyad to monad—they are not discontinuous, as are category and specific. The dyad is the past, and the monad is the future. Psychologically, this is to say that the mother-and-child dyad is the past, and individual death is the future. Historically, this is to say that hierarchical social systems like feudalism are the past, and interactive social systems like secular democracy are the future. Dyad and monad are continuous but absolutely distinct.

One may pass psychologically and intellectually from dyad to monad, but not the reverse.

To pass back and forth *ad lib* between dyad and monad would make them perfectly interactive, and therefore classically monistic. However, to distinguish dyad from monad as I have done is not dualistic, because one can travel intellectually from dyad to monad, but not the reverse.

So, dualism and monism are perceptible as both distinct and unified, just not at the same time. These are complementary perceptions. The trick is to understand that dualism always precedes monism. First, one perceives distinct dualism and monism. Then, one perceives monads. Perceiving one before the other, dualism and monism are both distinct and linked. Linked means that you can get from one to the other; distinct means that you cannot.

2.3 Infinite Regress or Not?

We turn to the problematic idea that dualism is the dualism of dualism and monism. If the perception of dualism *is* the perception of distinct dualism and monism, then the latter dualism just referred to must also be made up of, or may be said to break down into, another dualism-and-monism dyad. This new dualism must also be made up of, or may break down into, another two-ness and one-ness, and so on. *Any dualism can yield yet another dualism-and-monism dyad.* Might this open up an infinite regress? Yes and no.

If you hold up a hand mirror to a wall mirror, and catch the hand mirror's reflection in the wall mirror, you will see a series of mirror images cascading toward infinity. That is an infinite regress. Might every dualism leading to another dualism and monism yield such an infinite regress? Let's see.

In Roles and Rules terms, if any dualism may be made up of, or may break down into, a dualism and a monism, then this is to say that every role implies both a role and a rule.

For a simplified, but not trivial, example, let us consider the self-other physician-patient dyad, or role pair. (I write from the physician perspective.) The role of physician may break down into healer (dualism) and treatment (monism). Yes, the physician applies the treatment, but this is technique. The license to practice medicine identifies the physician in the role. "Healer" is the compassionate role a physician plays for a patient; treatment is the rule-driven application of technique that describes the interaction of physician and patient. The physician plays the healer role for free; treatment must be paid for. Treatment does not break down into a self-other dyad. Treatment may imply any number of techniques and applications. The role of healer, however, may be imagined to break down into compassion and intellectual investigation. The role of compassion may break down into . . . We stop here.

The problem of infinite regress is resolved in the Periodic Table of the Psyche in the following section. As you will see, it incorporates the Newtonian idea that things, such as planets, tend to circle around each other, rather than to fly off in all directions. For that reason, the dyad column starts at "self and other" and arrives at "other and self."

Part 3: A Periodic Table of the Psyche
3.1 Introduction

In this section we present a table that illustrates the concepts from Parts 1 and 2. The table shows how psychological components and attributes develop and combine into what we may call the structure of the psyche. It may be hard to imagine that something as diffuse or subjective as the mind or the psyche may have a structure, but I hope it will be easier to imagine by the end of this section.

The table, in Figure A-1, consists of three columns. The first is a double-file column, titled Roles. It lists descending dualistic-monistic dyads. The second, single-file column begins at the bottom where the first, double-file column ends, is single-file, and is titled Rules. The Rules column progresses upwards as it lists monads. At each level, the monad expresses in one term the sense of the two-term dyad at its left. The monad represents the monism as if it contained the dualism the way a body might "contain" a mind. Arriving at each new level from the monad below, you may judge whether or not the word I have selected is apt; perhaps you can imagine a better one. The third column is titled Structure. There will be more to say about structure later.

Descending along the Roles column, there is a progress—or a regress—of dualistic-monistic pairs. Each new dualism in the pair will spawn another dyad of dualism and monism. Each dualistic Role element is subjective and hierarchical, and thus does not describe anything in the objective, "real" world. Each Rule element will describe something objective, interactive, and quantifiable. All of this dualism and monism is still dualism. We have not left the mind and entered the world of cause and effect. You may recall from high school science that, scientific objectivity is an idealization that requires the elimination of the scientist as an agent. Objectivity exists in the mind of the subjective scientist. A scientist must imagine the objective world as if the scientist did not exist and was merely an observing subject, outside of space and time. Who would have thought that objective science was so mystical? Nevertheless, it is. When the interaction of scientist and world cannot be completely factored out of the equation, some degree of uncertainty must apply.

When the leaders of the Church and the founders of objective science faced off against each other, each side had an idealization to defend. Newton's laws are idealizations in that they do not account for time asymmetry; they operate eternally. Not until the Second Law of Thermodynamics did science leave the heavens and consider the earth. Increasing entropy makes the future uncertain. Our Roles and Rules columns repeat that sequence.

The downward, double-file Roles or Actor column and the upward, Rules or Agent column together describe a cycle. At the bottom of the Roles column, one moves across to the beginning of the Rules column. Now, the mind is a monad entering the world of cause and effect as an agent. Moving up the Rules column traces developing individuation toward its fulfillment in action (or, perhaps, actualization). By the top of the Rules column, one has acquired "free agency." As a free individual, one may freely accept a role, which means to choose to become an Actor, and to resume the cycle in some new way.

The fulfillment of individuation in action completes the cycle. A man or woman of action is ready to play his or her roles in life. We'll discuss the drama—the structure in which dualism and monism, Roles and Rules come together—in the third column.

Figure A-1: A Periodic Table of the Psyche

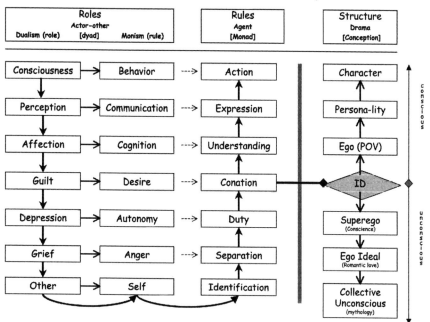

Note that Figure A-1 charts the psyche and the mind, not the body or the brain, and so does not need to be correlated with gross anatomy. Please take this table and my comments on it as heuristics or metaphors for understanding the functioning of dualism and monism, or Roles and Rules, in the psyche.

3.2 The Roles (Actor) Column

We start from the premise that every dualism is a dyad. That is, every dualism breaks down into another dyad of dualism and monism, and might hypothetically continue to do so ad infinitum. One enters the chart at the upper left as one enters life: in a role as a conscious person. In this section, I shall comment briefly upon each of the dyads in the double-file Roles column, beginning with the first concept, the Role or Actor.

At this point it should be clear that Role breaks down into Actor and Other. The actor is subject to the role and is the subject of the role; the other is the object of the role, meaning the person for whom or the purpose for which the role is performed. Actor is a dualism, which spawns another dyad of dualism and monism, which I identify as consciousness and behavior (in the top two boxes in the first double-file column). The category called consciousness breaks down into perception and communication. Perception breaks down into affection and cognition, and so on as we move down the double-file Rules column.

Role (Self and Other):

We start where psychological life begins, with one's recognition by around six months of age of "self" and "other," the latter of course, being mother. By six months, when breast-feeding becomes a relationship as well as nutrition, an infant seems to recognize self and mother. As baby recognizes the mothering "other," one's "self" forms as well.

While baby may not be aware of it, enrollment as a self usually starts right away, with baby in the role of "good sleeper" or "good eater" or "having eyes like Aunt Shirley." I use self to represent the sum of all one's roles in life, starting with the role of baby. I distinguish self from ego, which I take to mean a sustained point of view (POV) in an interaction. I call the dyad column Actor, because acting implies consciousness of the other for whom one plays a role, even if one is not conscious of the actual role one is playing.

Consciousness and Behavior:

I break the role of self into consciousness (consciousness of self) and behavior. In other words, consciousness and behavior are the dualistic-monistic dyad that the role of self breaks down into. Behavior is not necessarily conscious; it may be automatic, instinctive, or impulsive. Heightened or reflective consciousness, as occurs in psychotherapy, meditation, or reading, requires suspending behavior and attending to input. Behaviorist scientists understand behavior as interaction within a conditioning environment. Behavior is thus neither necessarily conscious nor intentional, but it is definitely measurable and predictable, and therefore monistic.

When brain scientists write about consciousness, they are necessarily muddled. Objectively one can speak only of the brain; the only consciousness of which one may be conscious is one's own. We can only infer that others are like oneself; much selfish, human behavior implies that such inference is easily lost. Perhaps consciousness is the role that the mind plays. There are social roles that market the idea of consciousness. Gurus, priests, teachers, world leaders, and even parents are supposed to represent wisdom and enlightenment.

Perception and Communication:

If we take consciousness to be a role, then we may imagine that the dualistic and monistic aspects of consciousness are perception and communication. Perception plays a role beyond registering sensations like hot and cold. Perception recognizes categories of (emotional) meaning like love and mother, and develops brand loyalties. Awe-inspiring politicians and artists play to collective perception when they evoke overwhelming emotions in their audiences rather than actually "communicate" with them.

Communication is an interactive notion that seems intrinsic to human consciousness. The science of linguistics can account for communication purely mathematically, without regard to semantic meaning. Other mammals may use sounds that qualify as words, but they lack the capacity to use syntax, and so lack the human capacity for creative communication in language.

Affection and Cognition:

Perception breaks down as affection and cognition. Affects are the conscious registration of emotions. What we perceive plays a role in our affections. Our affections may dictate which roles we play and how we play them.

Emotionality may easily overwhelm cognition, as in states of hysteria or mob action. Yet cognition routinely processes sensory data without emotionality. Sensation exists at the boundary of body and world, for instance in our fingertips. One's fingertip senses the velvety texture of the fabric covering the chair; the fabric stimulates the nerve endings in the fingertip. But one cannot and need not distinguish between what the fingertip senses and what the fabric stimulates. What matters is how the brain perceives the chair.

Guilt and Desire:

Next, we have guilt and desire. Guilt hovers in the background of all emotion, especially if one feels what one is not supposed to feel. "Bad" or "inappropriate" feelings lower self-esteem, which is the sense of the social rank or status in which one holds oneself. Guilt may overwhelm and negate desire, just as emotion may overwhelm logical cognition, and as perceptual awe silences communication.

Desire is a special case in that it points the way across the chart from self-other consciousness to psychological or psychic structure. Desire is the center of it all. The mythic origin of Western civilization is a tale of desire. The story of the founding of Rome leads to European Christianity and to the present day. The story of the founding of Rome starts with the earlier, legendary overthrow of Troy. The Trojan War was fought in epic because the goddess Aphrodite, later known as Venus, cheated. She bribed the handsome young man named Paris to choose her in a beauty contest. In return for choosing her, Aphrodite gave to Paris she who would become Helen of Troy. Hers was "the face that launched a thousand ships," because Helen's Greek husband objected to the kidnapping of his wife and invaded Troy. So, "romance" is a word inherited via the Roman Empire from the Trojan War, and Paris, France is enshrined as the romantic capital of the world.

Although it feels like a cause to action, desire is no such thing. Desire is a passion, which means that desire is suffering (as in "the passion of Christ"). Desire aims at something inherently as out of reach to an individual as a category is out of reach to a specific.

Depression and Autonomy:

Sooner or later, as the weight of guilt at some level inhibits desire, one gets depressed. Under the influence of guilt, one struggles for autonomy. It may be depressing to have no one else taking care of one anymore, but sooner or later one has to learn how to feed and to clean oneself, whether one likes it or not. When parents criticize messy teenagers who are struggling with autonomy, the teens often respond with rage—or sink into depression.

Autonomy is not the same as independence. A child's bedroom may be an autonomous zone, but the child is not independent. The Commonwealth of Massachusetts is autonomous, but not independent—it has no foreign policy. The State of Israel and the People's Republic of China have threatened to go to war with Palestine and Taiwan, respectively, if those entities declare themselves to be independent states, rather than autonomous territories.

Where We Are, and Where We Are Going:

We started at self and other, and are drilling deeper into what makes up the self. We are headed toward grief, the emotion of separation and loss of other that it is necessary to endure if one is to enter the world sufficiently identified with other people to develop into a loving adult. Behavior, communication, and cognition are easily understood as monistic in the classically monistic sense. However, when affection has split off from cognition, and breaks down into guilt and desire, one has left the interactive world. Desire, autonomy, and anger all ache for the world, but they cannot reach it. As the table shows, once having entered the affections, one can enter the world only as a self.

Grief and Anger:

Depression breaks down into grief and anger. Grief centers on loss, and one must somehow come to terms with it by "letting go." But in this case anger holds on and does not fuel constructive aggression, which might help a football player tackle an opponent or a hunter bring down a buffalo. This anger goes around in circles as one blames oneself, obsesses over failures, and nurtures hurt feelings.

Grief then breaks down into other and self. Anger holds on, but grief lets go. It is easy to understand grief as the affect of "letting go" when there is bereavement. Grieving is the letting go of a loved one who has died. Unsuccessful, prolonged grief often seems to be due to anger at the person who has died, as though anger could keep the other around until one has settled the matter.

Grief is also an element of normal development. One must let go of one's childhood, of one's parents, of failed loves, of one's own children, of many wishes and expectations, and finally of oneself. Before that last act, however, wholesome grief acknowledges that one is separate and whole. As a separate and whole being, one may identify with other people, who are like oneself in that they are also separate and whole beings. Successful separation means understanding that others are not extensions of one, and that one is not entitled to exploit others. To a child, this may be a grievous recognition.

Other and Self:

Originally, one is a self only in the context of other. One may wish only to play the role of "good child" that parents have in mind. By the bottom of the first, double-file, dyad column, in the greater or lesser shock of grief, one lets go of other. One no longer lives for another or to please another, or to dominate or exploit another. One no longer derives one's identity from the other, because the love for and of the other is internalized, and one may love oneself as one is loved.

All of this has tumbled out of the idea of self. When self can identify with other, one enters the world *as a self*. Incorporating the other within oneself effects the transition into the monadic, Agent column by means of identification with the other.

3.3 The Rules (Agent) Column

In the double-file, first column of Roles and the single-file, second column of Rules, we have two distinct columns that are connected in one direction only via identification. The two columns—Roles/Actor and Rules/Agent—retain their incompatibility at this point because the link between them is asymmetrical. *The dyad precedes the monad, just as the pregnant mother precedes the child.* Note, however, that the dyad precedes the monad, but does not outrank it as it would in dualism.

Actor and Agent seem a natural pairing, don't they? (They certainly are in Hollywood.) Agency refers to exerting power or to causing an effect. At the top of the Agent column is action, which is the realization of individuation. Individuals exercise agency; professional agents act as individuals, negotiating for those who are more identified with roles than rules. Actors must surrender some of their individuality to identify with a role and to develop a dramatic character. An actor is just the kind of person who needs an agent!

The idea of monad stems from our discussion of thermodynamics in Part 1, in which I used monad to combine the hierarchy of category and specific and the reversible interaction of monism. In that monad the asymmetry of hierarchy, of category and specific, transposes to the time asymmetry of cause and effect. In the Table of the Psyche the monad in the Rules/Agent column does exactly what was implied in that discussion of thermodynamics. Each monad combines the corresponding dualism and monism.

We continue our examination of the Periodic Table of the Psyche in Figure A-1 by reading the Rules/Agent column from the bottom up.

Identification:

The first monad is identification, the most important word in psychology. Identification is the monad that signifies the self embodying other. Rocks do not identify with other rocks. Computers cannot identify with each other, or with their users. We can, however, infer identification from the behavior of animals; birds of a feather do flock together. We assume that identification is more developed in humans because of their complex family and social patterns. (The idea of "god" may represent identification in its purest form, since the notion imagines a consciousness identified with the entire universe.)

Psychological life began in the self-mother dyad. That which passes back and forth between the newly separate self and mother was the affection known as identification. Mothering parent and babbling baby are crazy about each other; they see themselves in each other. This idealized identification makes tolerable the fact that mother-and-I are no longer blissfully one flesh, as one might feel briefly when suckling. A growing child separates in stages from home as identification is completed through adolescence.

The recognition of the other as not oneself sets identification in motion as a compensating response. Another person is not really your "right hand" or your "better half." There may be a loving wish to merge with someone, but identification is the next best thing—and the only real thing. An adult does not need others to "complete" oneself. One separates into an intact identity, which means that one is a whole person, like others.

Psychological development thus proceeds by stages of identification. We separate from those whom we love by becoming like those whom we love. In the case of parent and child, psychological identification is complete when the child is ready to leave home, to find love "out there," and eventually to create a new family.

In normal development, identification prepares one for eventual separation, for example from home. However, the shock of an unexpected, sudden death of a loved one places the separation before the identification. What we call grief is the process of accepting the separation by setting up the identification as well as one can, after the fact. While grieving, people may speak of keeping the spirit of the other alive. One may find oneself enjoying the departed uncle's favorite food or telling a joke as he would have. These are evidence of identification with the lost loved one.

In whatever context it takes place, the first stage of identification is idealization. Separation by identification, therefore, begins with idealization. Idealization is evident in the mother-baby dyad. It is also evident at funerals, where it is impolite to speak ill of the recently dead person.

Grief is also part of normal development. Many people find leaving home grievous and fearsome, especially if their sexuality has not developed as a motivation and compensation. A romance by late adolescence or early adulthood seems necessary for most people to go on their way. Indeed, the course of romantic love may be described as the progress of identification. Idealization as the first stage is obvious in the phenomenon of infatuation. Not so obvious is the progress of true love up from idealization to mirroring, the more difficult task of loving and understanding each other when idealization eventually fails, as it will in normal development.

By the last stage of identification, one has internalized the other sufficiently not to need the other to complete oneself, and one may speak of psychological separation within a relationship. A separate person wishes to love more than he or she needs to be loved. Now, lovers may be partners, each more interested in the other than in completing oneself.

Anecdote: Feeding the Bunny

Identification with other during childhood is often indistinguishable from identifying with the role of the other. My favorite story on this subject centers upon a two year old girl whose working mother had to leave her in day care. The daughter was inconsolable, and wreaked havoc at the center. After two or three days of this, another mother of a child at the center spoke to the mother. "Why don't you do for your daughter what I did for mine? Give her a carrot to feed the bunny."

There was a rabbit in residence at the day care center. The next day, the little girl came to the center armed with a carrot, and without asking the bunny whether it was hungry, stuck a carrot in its mouth. Her anxiety vanished, and the bunny did not complain.

Why did this work so well? The little girl was no longer in the role of abandoned baby. She was now in the role of omnipotent mommy, and the bunny was the baby. She had identified with her mother's role, and assuaged her grief.

Everything up to this point has followed from the ideas of self and consciousness. Everything after this point continues to follow from self and consciousness, but from here on up everything also follows from and builds upon identification (at the base of the Rules/Agent column). Each new monad builds on the one that came before. Reading down the Roles/Actor column and up the Rules/Agent column reflects the fact that the dyads break down, and the monads build up.

Identification describes childhood, emotional development after about six months. The "feeding the bunny" story naturally brings us to separation, which is the next monad.

Separation:

The first separation episode happens at about 18 months. Childhood development specialists call it the rapprochement crisis. Up to then, life may have seemed all fun and games. Suddenly, however, a toddler seems to become aware that growing older is for real, and that it is frightening. This crisis comes just before the "terrible twos," when children struggle in earnest with parents for control of themselves.

I take successful separation over a lifetime to require anger to embody or contain grief. The feeding the bunny story exemplifies this in that "feeding the bunny" binds up the anger and the grief. As a separate person, one must learn that one may not always get what one wants, or what one needs. This is not the end of the world if one can learn to love from those who love one and find more mature equivalents of feeding the bunny.

As I said, the first separation episode takes place at about 18 months, but separation from home takes place at about 18 years. Feeding the bunny for a two year old is sexuality for a late adolescent. Perhaps sexuality may serve as identification with one's own conception, or with one's parents' relationship. We do not need to think so deeply, though. Sexuality simply withdraws emotion from one's family of origin and invests it in one's personal future. At age 18, grief and anger are among the affects that one must bear as one pursues romance and succeeds or fails. Survival after separation from one's family of origin requires that one can love and compete with others and defend oneself.

However, regulating anger and controlling impulses is a major problem. In the popular film, *The Empire Strikes Back*, the character playing the role of consciousness, Yoda, instructs the young hero Luke in the ways of The Force. During a practice saber fight with an image, Luke gets angry and cuts off his opponent's helmeted head. Removing the helmet, he sees his own face. Yoda then cautions Luke about striking out of anger rather than out of serene resolve; otherwise, one only harms oneself.

Duty:

On the next line we find depression, autonomy, and duty. When autonomy can contain depression, one has a sense of duty. One does what one must, even if reluctantly. One has duties that come with the roles one chooses in life, such as friend and parent. One has not chosen to be a child of one's parents, and duties toward parents are difficult to perform when one feels very ambivalently toward them. The issues that interfere with the wholesome performance of duty have to do with whether or not parents have supported autonomy, since duty threatens autonomy, especially if one is depressed.

Conation:

Next up, we find a word that has fallen from common use, but fits perfectly here. That word describing desire-embodying-guilt is "conation," which refers to a characteristic will or striving, an inclination, impulse, or drive to act with a certain purpose. The philosopher Spinoza used "conatus" to mean "the tendency of a thing to persist in its being." A beaver's conatus might be to build its dam; a shark's might be to keep swimming forward; an artist's might be to create.

Here, guilt might be imagined to keep desire in check, so that, for example, no pig would ever wish to grow up to become a sheep dog, as took place in the film, *Babe*. (Babe was free to create an individual identity, apparently because Babe's mother had gone off to be slaughtered.) In human terms, guilt might ensure that someone will grow up and leave home rather than live off one's parents forever.

Understanding:

When cognition embodies affection, or emotion, one has understanding. One might use the word insight here, but I prefer understanding because "understanding" and "substance" share root words. "Under" is the Latin equivalent of the Greek "sub." So, "substance" (note the word *stance*) means that which stands under. Thus, I take understanding to be mental substance. The more one understands, the more substance one has and the more one becomes.

Expression:

When communication embodies perception—in linguistic terms, when syntax meets semantics—one has expression. Abstract expressionist art in the 1950s was also known as action painting. It attempted to capture the artistic gesture itself, devoid of any perception behind it. (Think Jackson Pollack's "drip" paintings.) The pop-art movement that followed reacted to abstract expressionism with concrete perceptualism, notably in Andy Warhol's utterly inexpressive soup cans. Expression cannot escape perception for long.

Action:

When behavior includes consciousness, one may speak of action. Pigeons and rats behave, but human beings act. Action is different from behavior because action is conscious and, I might add, dramatic. A person of action is an actor, and is eligible to play a role.

The cycle is now complete, and may begin again.

Agency:

The chart has so far illustrated a cycle that starts from the role of self in the self-and-other dyad. This is psychological development. The role of self is fulfilled as one separates from other because one can identify with other. Once identified with other, one is a whole person and can individuate. As a free individual one may consciously, voluntarily, and wholeheartedly play a role. Thus, consciousness progresses from identification, through separation, duty, and so on up to action.

The process of separation by identification can and does go awry. Some people are not particularly identified with others, and thus either idealize or degrade others. They spend their lives worshipping or exploiting others. Autism is probably the most profound condition of developmental non-identification. Sufferers from autism have no sense of themselves as like others, to the extent of complete social incomprehension.

The cycle may repeat at different stages of life and describe the development of consciousness and sense of self in the various life roles one undertakes, such as friend, spouse, colleague, manager, owner, and so on. However, cyclicality does not necessarily imply development. Cycles can simply repeat, with the elements of the cycle flowing into one another, each leading to the next, and so on. Therefore, another concept—structure—is necessary to describe how an individual might fully develop. Structure carries the implication of something that can grow, as itself and in relation to other structures, and differentiate itself creatively.

In the next section, we imagine a mental structure. To do so, we adopt words that other theorists and writers have used to imply psychic or psychological structure, and show how structure may arise by combining a dyad and a monad into a conception. This third column will portray the psyche as a whole.

3.4 The Idea of Structure

Referring back to Figure A-1, which I've reproduced here, we direct our attention to the column on the right, labeled Structure. By structure, I mean something integrated, something that is unified, and that does not pass away or flow into something else.

The structure column is also labeled Drama. This does not mean any particular type of story, such as comedy or tragedy. Rather it means that characteristic psychological or psychic elements play themselves out in the human story, by projecting themselves onto the world. For this reason, it will be natural to consider social arenas such as business using the arrangements of the table.

By now, we have both a descending column for "dyads" and an ascending column for "monads". This gives equal weight to viewing the psyche dualistically and monistically. There is one more step to take, and it is a big step. If we think of dyad and monad as feminine and masculine, then we may imagine the two meeting as a conception. *As a structure, a conception can develop creatively on its own terms, much as can a person.* I'll discuss this further in subsequent charts. In this discussion, I will adapt to our purposes certain terms that Freud and other theorists have used to describe psychological structure and explain my use of these terms.

Figure A-1

A Periodic Table of the Psyche (reprised)

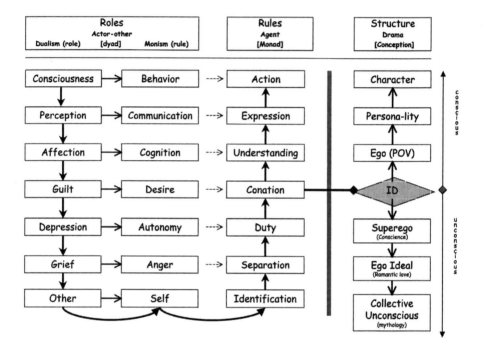

The It (The Id):

The third column starts in the middle and extends upward and downward. It begins with and develops from the it or the id, Freud's wonderful term for the representation in the mind of the needs and the impulses of the body. Eating, sleeping, breathing, and sexual urges are all subjective "drives" from which psychic structure differentiates.

One conceives of the id by simultaneously considering the dyad of guilt and desire on the one hand, and, on the other, the monad of conation (again, in Spinoza's formulation, "the tendency of a thing to persist in its being"). From this core representation of the body in the mind, we may differentiate further structures as we consider other dyads and monads. The arrows pointing upward from the Id aim at structures in everyday consciousness, and the arrows pointing downward aim at structures that comprise the unconscious.

The I (The Ego):

Proceeding up from the id, one finds the ego, which Freud called "the I" to distinguish it from the id. Ego in this sense has nothing to do with vanity; it only represents the establishment of an individual point of view. In other words, the ego constitutes the unique point of view (POV) of a person in this world. The ego and super-ego (see below) develop together through the grammar school years, during which one learns, plays, studies, competes, and loves one's friends.

Personality:

As one approaches puberty, the ego has developed quite a bit. One can read, think, present and respond to requests, and collect things. However, the slings and arrows of nascent sexuality may set any of us spinning at any moment. At around puberty a new structure matures to help meet the challenge. This is personality, the device that must work if one is to survive adolescence well.

Personality is the capacity to engage in affectionate exchange, that is, the capacity to bring out the best in others and to represent oneself in the best possible light. Personality stems from "persona," which is from the Greek for "sound-through." It referred to the masks actors wore and spoke through in ancient Greek drama.

Character:

After high school and perhaps college, one takes on life roles for real by deciding how to earn a living, whether and whom to marry, and so on. If one's personality can fit into the roles one must play or chooses to play, and one can play those roles for others rather than only for oneself, then one develops character. By character, then, I mean the capacity to play a useful and positive role in the lives of others.

Super-ego:

One level down from the id is the super-ego. Of course, super-ego means "above the ego," so what is it doing below the ego? I'll return to that question in a later section. The super-ego is what most of us understand as the conscience, meaning whatever it is that keeps us playing by the rules.

Ego Ideal:

Continuing down, one finds the ego ideal. This is what we are playing to obtain, either fairly or not. The original ideal was, of course, mother—or perhaps not mother *per se*, but the state of wholeness and happiness one may have felt with her in early infancy. One pursues this ego ideal fairly, that is, by playing roles for others and respecting the rules in life's various arenas if one has developed a super ego, and unfairly if one has not.

Collective Unconscious:

Below what we might take to be a personal unconscious is the history of our culture that we all share and learn about during childhood from stories and legends. This is the stuff of shared myths and beliefs, language and culture, purpose and meaning, and it forms a rich background that both informs and contrasts with the individual lives that play out against it.

3.5 The Elements of Structure

Figure A-2 depicts two triangles facing each other across a gap, with the id hovering between them. This figure represents the elements before they come together in a unified structure, that is, in the psyche.

The column from the far right of the table in Figure A-1 is reproduced on the left of Figure A-2. That column represents the structural elements proceeding away from the id in two directions, upward and downward, but in one dimension, a line. We need a richer representation, to depict an integrated structure. Clearly, the three conscious elements go together as do the three unconscious elements. So, they may be represented as segments of the two triangles on the right, with the id hovering between them:

3.6 Psychological Conception

Here in Figure A-3 is The Psyche, Incorporated. That is, here is a conception of a psyche in a mind and body. Notice that in the merger, super-ego is where it literally should be, above the ego. Hence, one's ego, that is, one's point of view, is subject to a conscience. In the center is a diamond that articulates the relations among id, ego, and super-ego at the core of psychological individuality.

Figure A-2

Elements of Structure

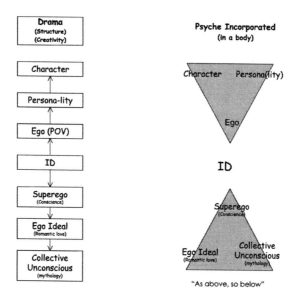

Figure A-3

The Psyche, Incorporated

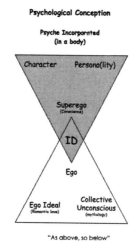

This is only a beginning, however, because this picture presents character and personality, and ego-ideal and collective unconscious, at too great a distance from the ego and super-ego, the dual dynamo that when combined with the id drives individual life.

The True Picture:

The final depiction of the structure of the psyche in Figure A-4 presents each structural element as equally distant from the center. This depiction of the structure is thus less ego-centric, as it were. It takes into account that the ego, even with its conscience as a guide, is awash in other psychological attributes that are unconcerned with individuality.

Figure A-4

A Star Conceived

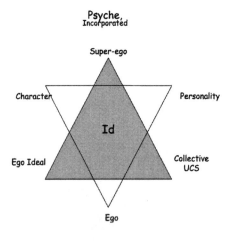

To develop fully as an individual, one must understand a lot more than reading, writing, arithmetic, and sports. One must understand culture, history, science, and the arts—or else the often brute demands of life may overwhelm any chance for an individual to be more than a stereotype.

At this point and in keeping with the subject of this book, we are ready to address the application of the Maieutic Method to the task at hand. We turn to the keep-versus-sell decision that a family business creator must make at the end of his or her working life.

Part 4: The Business Chart
4.1 The Role of Owner

Figure A-5 A Periodic Table of a Business depicts the structural elements and structure of the social institution we call a business. Each word in each position in the table in Figure A-5 below corresponds to the word in the analogous position in Figure A-1, A Periodic Table of the Psyche. This is to say that the mind and the world as we know it are one, as would be expected given that there are two ways of knowing about the world, which come together in consciousness. It is also to say that we create social structures that resemble ourselves, one class of which is the business enterprise.

Figure A-5

A Periodic Table of a Business

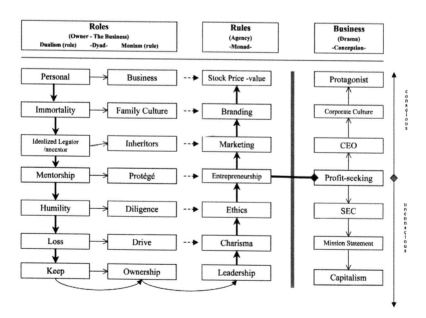

As the founders or owners of a family business approach retirement, they face important decisions about the future of the business and the family. Shall the elders try to pass along the enterprise intact to the next generation? Or would everyone be better served by converting the assets to cash for distribution to the heirs?

We approach the keep-versus-sell question even-handedly, given that it is a roles versus rules decision. Not incidentally, a decision to sell the business and distribute the proceeds renders the table irrelevant. To sell obviates any role considerations and in effect turns the matter over to the accountants and attorneys who will employ the rules of their professions to value the business, structure the sale, and sell the enterprise or assets. In contrast, the decision to keep raises the emotional considerations of ownership that one must take into account. This requires an understanding of the role that the founder must play for the successors in the transfer of the business to them.

We enter the table at the top of the first, double-file column, and prepare to circulate downward and upward as we did in the psychosocial chart. Again, please bear in mind that this, too, is a heuristic and not a doctrine.

Personal and Business:

An Owner-Actor's decision to keep the business, which means to play the owner role, may take place for personal or business reasons. Business reasons usually center upon the expected continuing profits from, and financial viability of, the business. Those are rules-based considerations. We proceed down the dyad column to consider what drives personal reasons, which the owner should be conscious of in order to play his or her role well.

Immortality and Family Culture:

Personal reasons may break down into a wish for symbolic immortality and the expression of that immortality in the family culture of the future. If the business has your name on it and your picture might hang in the reception area, you may enjoy the prospect of haunting the next generation, or at least of symbolically keeping an eye on them.

Idealized Ancestor and Inheritors:

The wish for immortality breaks down into, or is made up of, the idealized ancestor role that may live on in the minds of one's heirs and successors. That idealization can occur only in the minds of the inheritors, the corresponding monism.

Mentor and Protégé:

What are the dualistic-monistic, or Roles and Rules, components of ancestor worship? One imagines that the next generation would idealize the previous generation as mentors, as selfless teachers who fostered the authentic development of their progeny. The word 'protégé' extends this mentoring ethic into and beyond the biological family.

Humility and Diligence:

What are the dualistic-monistic components of mentorship? A mentor must have guilt at his or her disposal, so the protégés will want to please the mentor or live up to the mentor's standards. Failure to live up to those standards arouses a sense of inadequacy in the protégés, which they can assuage only by diligently doing their best.

A sense of humility in the business table corresponds to depression in the psychological table. A good mentor does not encourage the narcissistic vanity or greed of protégés, but rather the humility that will lead them diligently to do their duty.

Loss and Drive:

In the psychosocial chart, depression breaks down into grief and anger. In both business and psychological contexts, grief centers upon letting go. In the business context, grief recognizes the inevitability of retirement and succession.

Even in business, loss generates grief. What causes more business grief than the loss of money? There is more to lose and to grieve over than money, of course. There is the loss of control that one fears upon nearing retirement, and the loss of esteem as one assumes a powerless, emeritus status. Many elder owners, in a poet's words, do not go gently into that good night, but rage, rage against the darkening light. They hold on too long, and their drive contains their anger at the passing years and looming loss.

Keep and Ownership:

In the psychological chart, grief breaks down into other and self. In the business case, the "other" is one's successor, the recipient of the keep decision. To keep the business, the owner has to let go of the business, perhaps even before death and certainly in death.

4.2 Entering the Monad Column

Here, at the bottom of the next, single-file column, we enter the world of rules, as they are monads, elements of goal-directed action in the business. We have traveled along the bottom columns from owner to new owner. The *monistic* counterpart is ownership, and new ownership is not yet a role but only a rule, as defined in the legal and business rules of succession. The Rules/Monad column may tell us how the *new* owner may rise to the occasion and play the ownership role well.

Reaching this stage, the testator has successfully conveyed the proceeds of a lifetime as a living structure. Succession creates a new generation of owners, and passes along the ethos of ownership.

Leadership:

When ownership is purely financial, one hires others to manage. When a manager or owner-manager has a sense of ownership and acts upon it, there is leadership.

Charisma:

When drive can acknowledge loss, one creates charisma. For example, Ronald Reagan had the drive to become president of the United States, elected at least as much for his charisma as for his intellect. He was in office at the time of the first space shuttle crash, and no one could have portrayed grief more sincerely than he did as he consoled the decedents' bereaved families on the White House lawn. Too, President Reagan had a successful career as a film actor before being elected governor of California and president. He truly understood the *role* of president.

Ethics:

When one performs one's duty with diligence and humility, one has ethics. Every once in a while an avoidable business catastrophe, such as the failure of Enron Corporation, reminds us of the importance of ethical behavior in business, which precludes unjustly enriching oneself at the expense of others.

Entrepreneurship:

When a protégé has internalized what the mentor has passed along, the result is a leader with an entrepreneurial spirit. The business leader will have the confidence to innovate and to grow the business, and perhaps to diversify its activities or holdings as opportunities present themselves. (This is, to look ahead to the business Drama column, sound, desirable, profit-seeking behavior.)

Marketing:

Successful marketing includes conveying to the marketplace the corporate identity, which includes the history and legacy of the company. For instance, many family businesses such as car dealerships and restaurants market themselves as such, to the point of crafting sales messages stating that they treat customers like members of the family.

Branding:

As branding consultants continually remind us, the brand captures the company identity in a symbol, logo, or slogan. The company stands for something, and that something lives on in the brand and in the business behind the brand.

Shareholder Value:

The most widely accepted definition of management's mission is to maximize the long-term value of the company to the owners. Successful leadership therefore focuses on growing the business, increasing its value, and avoiding decisions and actions that undermine the growth of the value of the business.

At this point in the table, at the top of the Rules/Monad column, the leader is playing the ownership role to the fullest, and he or she will someday have a keep-versus-sell decision of his or her own to make.

But wait, there's more.

Development of the Business Structure

Now we can see the kind of business structures we may generate by putting together the dyads and monads we have delineated in discussion of the Periodic Table of a Business.

Figure A-6 presents the structure (or Drama) column and the triangles from both the psychosocial table and the business table, so we can easily compare the terms and understand the corollaries.

We start from the center of the first and second columns in Figure A-6. What represents the id of a business corporation? The requirement for profitability. As many observers have noted, a business exists to make a profit and literally cannot remain in existence for long unless it does so. The profit motive and its imperative very much corresponds to the id.

Figure A-6

Development of Structure - Introduction

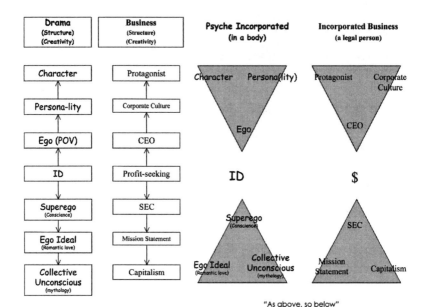

"As above, so below"

That is why, moving downward into the behind-the-scenes aspects of the business, the corporate conscience must be situated in the larger society. This conscience-in-society would be found in government regulation, here represented by the Securities and Exchange Commission, which I'm using to represent government regulation in all its forms.

Again, moving downward, the ego ideal of a company is its mission statement and its values. As do individuals, companies strive to reach and live up to these ideas but continually fall short. The company codifies its ideals in its mission statement, which unfortunately in many cases amounts to a paragraph of high-minded aims that hang in the background on the cafeteria wall, beyond the employees' consciousness.

What is the collective unconscious, or mythic story, that underlies business? Capitalism itself. In world history, this is a high time for capitalism, with communism either gone or going and national boundaries melting as the global economy develops.

Moving upward in the Business Drama column, what in the company might correspond to the ego? The CEO, who represents (in a multitude of ways) the company's point of view.

The "personality" of a company would be the corporate culture. Companies are actually known for their personalities in ways that at times resemble the budding personalities of high-school students, such as brainy, innovative, muscular, aggressive, sophisticated, or international.

Protagonist corresponds to character. We defined character as the ability to play a role for others. A business, any business, actually has a social role to play in its community and, if it becomes large enough, on the world stage. In a sense, companies choose whether to play their roles only for themselves or for their stakeholders and the larger society, either spreading prosperity or pillaging resources as protagonists in the business drama.

Figure A-7 simply compares the psychosocial and business structures, as they are about to come together.

Figure A-7

Development of Structure in Business - 1 - Preconception

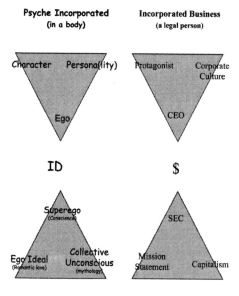

"As above, so below"

Figure A-8 depicts the coming together of the psychic structure and of the business structure. Just as the psychic structure places the super-ego over the id, the business structure places government regulation over the CEO. Psyche Incorporated places the psyche in a body, while the corporation is often described as a "legal person" that can make contracts, engage in transactions, and launch and defend itself against legal actions.

Figure A-8

Development of Structure - 2 - Conception

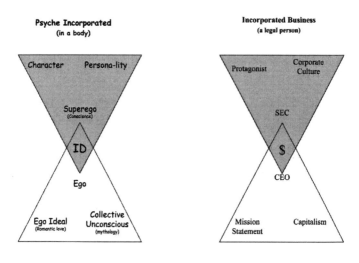

The mission statement and capitalism itself are core markers of identity that are taken as deep background on a daily basis by those in the business.

And, finally, Figure A-9 shows the two structures—the psyche and the business—presented parallel to one another for easy comparison. As structures, both the psyche and a business are capable of creative development.

Keeping track of the parallels, this would seem to be the optimal business structure for the organization's creative differentiation. Just as an individual mind, as a structure, results from the two ways of knowing (dualism and monism) and dyad and monad and Roles and Rules, the structure combines the personal and business elements, the Roles and Rules aspects, into a profit-seeking social structure regulated by society and guided by a chief executive officer.

Figure A-9

Development of Structure in Business - 3 - Differentiation

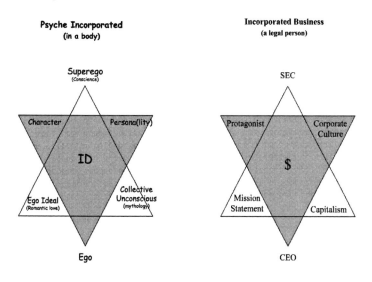

"As above, so below"

Some readers may be surprised to note "ego" and CEO at the bottom of the diagram, with super-ego and SEC at the top. Most of us take for granted that the situation as it exists is upside down, with the "ego" or CEO on top. However, all that may imply must await another book.

Conclusion

This appendix provides, in Parts 1 and 2, what might be termed deep background on the derivation and development of Roles and Rules as a psychological model. In Parts 3 and 4 it shows the implications of the model, that is, the implications of these "two ways of knowing," for, respectively, the psyche and business organizations.

As you may imagine, the model holds implications for many other areas of human activity and endeavor. At the macro level, these include politics and international relations, economic policy, education policy, organizational development, and the full spectrum of social policies. At the micro level, they include all aspects of personal development and interpersonal relations, particularly individual development and maturation, and marital and family relationships.

Again, this volume applies Roles and Rules to the challenges of succession and estate planning for family businesses, and for families with significant assets, and difficult family dynamics. However, that is only one application of this psychological model.

My greatest hope is that other professionals, both inside and outside the fields of mental health and business, will find this model useful in their work and develop both the model and applications of the model in new, creative, and beneficial ways.

APPENDIX B

Issues Affecting Attorneys Regarding Professional Conduct and Client Relationships

> *Note*: This appendix is adapted from "Risky Business: Family Business Succession and the Rules of Professional Conduct" by John W. Ambrecht, Esq. and Elyce Pike, PhD, a journal article which was published in *California Trusts and Estates Quarterly* (Vol. 12, Issue 2, Summer 2006), and which covers these issues in greater depth.

Attorneys using Roles and Rules or, for that matter, other "best practices" in succession and estate planning should be aware of several issues relating to professional practices and client relationships. Two key issues in these areas center upon rules of professional conduct and client identification. As noted in this book, the attorney's client is typically the testator (or the first generation, G1), but Roles and Rules can call for an attorney to deal with family members (G2, G3, etc.) and the family business in ways that extend beyond the scope of the typical client relationship.

Indeed, attorneys' rules of professional conduct can pose risks for attorneys who are using—or not using—Roles and Rules. For example, the California Rules of Professional Conduct (CRPC) may actually tend to hinder the transfer of a family business from one generation to the next because of ethical issues affecting attorneys, unless those issues are properly addressed. (In this appendix, we use the CRPC to represent rules of professional conduct for attorneys in general, while realizing that specific rules vary from state to state.) How could rules designed to protect the public undermine family business succession? The answer is found in a discussion of family business succession issues, client representation models, risks to estate attorneys and their clients, and ways of addressing the situation created by this confluence of factors. This appendix presents such a discussion and explores issues of client identification and professional relations for attorneys interested in applying Roles and Rules to succession and estate planning.

A Bit of Background

Recall the three factors that contribute most to the high rates of breakdown in the family business succession process:

1. 60 percent of typical breakdowns arise from relationship issues or "how we get along"
2. 25 percent of typical breakdowns arise from heirs lacking competence and being unprepared
3. 10 percent of typical breakdowns arise from tax and traditional estate planning issues.

This means that, in practice, estate planners and business owners spend most of their succession and estate planning time on activities related to 10 percent of the causes of succession breakdowns rather than on those accounting for 85 percent. Also, attorneys' skills in tax and governance do not address family relationship issues or the needs of heirs who are unprepared to assume their new duties. Given this, it may be useful for estate planners and business owners to adopt a broader view of, and more comprehensive approach to, the succession and estate planning process, such as Roles and Rules. In fact, it's possible that rules of professional conduct may actually "require" attorneys to acquire the appropriate skills or "associate with, or where appropriate, professionally consult[ing] another lawyer reasonably believed to be competent" as stated in the CRPC. Yet, ironically, limitations imposed by the CRPC may preclude them from broadening the scope of their representation. Indeed the lawyer (and even the client) may be at risk if the lawyer tries to "do the right thing."

In keeping with succession and estate planning best practices, Roles and Rules employs constant communication and feedback to and across the family and the family business—the two "systems" in any family business. (The term "family business" here broadly includes real estate and other assets requiring active management.) Such communication raises issues relating to rules of professional conduct and client relationships, so we begin with a brief review of client representation models.

Five Representation Models

The legal literature generally recognizes five basic models for a lawyer representing a client:

Single Client or "Hired Gun" Model

Most people assume that the single client or "hired gun" representation model, with its exclusive emphasis on the client, has always been the primary form of legal practice. Although it now dictates most aspects of legal representation, this model became dominant relatively recently, gaining sway in the 1950s and 1960s "rights revolutions," which shifted the primary objectives of the law from maintaining the purity of the legal system toward advancing individual rights.

Essentially, the single-client model fulfills clients' legitimate expectations—and attorneys' key duties—of confidentiality for, and loyalty to, the client. This model also fosters vigorous advocacy, which is currently deemed essential to our adversarial system of justice. Reflecting this model, key rules in the CRPC include the duty of confidentiality, the duty of undivided loyalty to the single client by avoiding conflicts of interest, the duty to diligently represent a client to the exclusion of all else, and the duty not to communicate with other lawyers' clients.

Joint Multiple Representation Model

In jointly representing multiple clients, the lawyer focuses on achieving the common objective of the clients. This model emphasizes elements that unify, rather than divide, the clients. For example, in joint multiple representation the same lawyer can represent a husband and a wife, and confidences whether relevant to the joint representation or not that are disclosed to the lawyer will be shared with the other spouse. If a conflict develops between or among the clients in this form of representation, the attorney will most likely be forced to resign from representing all of the clients unless a new written waiver of the conflict is signed by the clients.

Separate Multiple Representation Model

In separate multiple representations, the same lawyer represents both a husband and a wife but each is regarded by the lawyer as his or her separate and distinct client. Under this model, the lawyer is governed by the rules of the single client or "hired gun" representation model with respect to each client, subject however, to the rule that if a conflict does develop between or among the clients, the lawyer will most likely have to resign from representing the clients unless a new written waiver of the conflict is signed by the clients.

Reasonable Expectation or "Intermediary" Representation Model

A lawyer acts as an "intermediary" when he or she represents two or more parties with potentially conflicting interests. The concept of a lawyer as "intermediary" has its origins with Justice Louis Brandeis's concept of the role of a lawyer as "counsel for the situation." This concept attempts to balance the rights and obligations of each party in order to arrive at a solution equitable to each party. But before a lawyer may act as an "intermediary," five conditions must be met:

1. The lawyer must obtain informed written consent from each client after explaining the advantages and disadvantages of common representation.
2. The lawyer must "reasonably" believe that *potentially* conflicting interests identified by the lawyer can be resolved with terms compatible to the clients' best interests, and that,
3. Each client will be able to make adequately informed decisions in the matter, and that,
4. There is little risk of material prejudice to the interests of any of the clients if the contemplated resolution is successful.
5. If an actual conflict develops, then each client must give a new written consent before the attorney can continue to represent them.

In this model, having concluded that the requisite conditions described above are "reasonable" and having obtained the clients' consent, the lawyer may act as an "intermediary."

Single Entity Model

Sometimes the single entity representation model is associated with an earlier concept of the lawyer as a generalist representing the whole family—the "family lawyer"—but this is erroneous. The single entity representation model draws on the notion of the organization as client, with the client in this case being "the family unit." The lawyer represents the clients in and through their unit as a family. Instead of representing the clients as separate individuals with shared or conflicting interests and objectives, the single entity model returns us to the rules applicable to a single client. A lawyer representing a single entity maintains a client-lawyer relationship with the entity only and does not owe a duty to any individual member or members of the entity. However, caution must guide the lawyer using this representation model because a family member may mistakenly believe that the lawyer represents him or her individually, in which case the lawyer may be removed from further representation of the entire family unit in the event that conflicts occur.

The joint multiple representation model and reasonable-expectation/ intermediary model both require informed, explicit consent by the client to demonstrate genuine understanding and agreement when there is a potential conflict and again in the case of an actual conflict. Under the single entity model, implied individual consent suffices without individual consent, but extra steps may be necessary to avoid confusion among clients as to their being individually represented, as mentioned above.

Risks to the Family and the Lawyer

Again ironically, the CRPC can expose both families and lawyers to risks in family business succession situations.

Risks To The Family

If a lawyer works with a family using Roles and Rules as a "best practice," even assuming that the lawyer may have used the proper multiple representation letter with proper consents and waivers, one family member may still be able to remove the lawyer from further representation of all of the other family members as well as from the family business itself. If the lawyer is removed, negative consequences may result for the family, including the following:

- Money spent by the family to educate the lawyer about the family and business may be lost, and family members and the business may lose a trusted advisor.
- Family relationships may be strained, tainted, or destroyed for subsequent generations, and economic losses for the family may occur.
- Family members and the family business may have to hire separate lawyers, significantly increasing future legal fees.
- Succession may be delayed, perhaps indefinitely, with the risk that the issues will never be solved without court action.
- New lawyers may use the "hired gun" model and increase the probability of feuds fueled by adversarial approaches and their need to take sides because they lack knowledge of the complexities of the family and the business.

Risks To The Lawyer

The risks to the lawyer for even a "de minimis" violation of rules of professional conduct are real and include the significant possibility of losing the client and being named in a malpractice suit. For instance, the CRPC state that, "it is clearly established in California that the violation of an ethical rule may give rise to causes of action for legal malpractice, breach of fiduciary duty and consequent damages."

That said, a lawyer has a responsibility to protect his client in every possible way, which would imply use of best practices such as Roles and Rules (and others developed in fields such as management consulting, conflict resolution, and psychology) to facilitate a smooth and orderly succession and/or transfer of assets. Thus a lawyer may be forced to use a supplemented "hired gun" model (explained below) in order to fully fulfill his broad duty to the client.

Best Practices and the Estate Planning Attorney

Can, in serving their clients' best interests, attorneys employ best practices developed by other family business succession professionals? The answer may appear to be "no" at first blush. Central to best practice approaches, including, as noted, Roles and Rules, is communication with many, if not all, members of the family business system with the goal of balancing the family system and the business system. This may conflict with rules of professional conduct and tenets of representation models. If it does conflict, what can an attorney do about it?

We've found that the attorney should begin by explaining what happens if conflicts of interest arise among family members if the attorney is to represent more than one family member. This is necessary under the existing professional rules, but some attorneys believe, with good reason, that it somehow holds the potential for negative inferences right from the start. It certainly suggests that conflict is "bad" and, with a new client, that conflict may be expected during the representation. Given that some conflict is natural in families, these attorneys may feel constrained or handicapped in that they want to avoid worsening tense situations, yet they are being forced to disclose potential negative implications of conflict during the work even before the work has really begun.

From the best practice perspective, in contrast with the legal perspective, conflict is neither "good" nor "bad" but rather a natural and expected part of the family business system. From the best practice perspective, when conflict arises it is treated as "information" from the system and viewed as symptomatic of issues requiring resolution in the family and family business. This conflict represents an opportunity to work through the issues, reframe the conflict by understanding its meaning and normalizing its existence, and restructuring, to some extent, the family dynamics and business.

All of that said, several questions, which we take up below, remain for the lawyer interested in using a best practice approach to help family businesses through the succession process.

Client Identification Issues

The key questions the attorney and client must answer, particularly when the lawyer may be talking to other family members, are:

1. Who will be the client?

The answer to this question is typically clear in that the usual fee and representation agreement are prepared by the lawyer and presented to a particular, identified client, usually the senior generation power holders if at all possible. Waivers of confidentiality should also be requested so that the lawyer can work with all of the family members.

2. What if other family members also consider themselves clients?

If another family member is considered an actual or implied client, then the attorney must follow all rules of professional conduct relative to such a person. This includes the rule of confidentiality and avoidance of potential or actual conflicts with the other clients of the lawyer. Thus, if another family member were a client within the rules, then he or she would have the right to object to the lawyer's continuing to represent any other family members at any time.

How could a family member be considered a client when there's no formal agreement with the attorney and the attorney does not consider that person the client? The California State Bar has issued an opinion stating how an attorney-client relationship may *impliedly* occur and thus require the lawyer to act in accordance with all rules relative to that "implied" client. The opinion states, in part that,

> "An attorney-client relationship, together with all the attendant duties a lawyer owes a client . . . may be created by contract, either express or implied. In the case of an implied contract, the key inquiry is whether the speaker's belief that such a relationship was formed has been reasonably induced by the representations or conduct of the attorney."[1]

The Opinion goes on,

> "Whether the attorney's representations or conduct evidence a willingness to participate in a consultation is examined from the viewpoint of the reasonable expectations of the speaker. The factual circumstances relevant to the existence of the consultation include: whether the parties meet by pre-arrangement or by chance; the prior relationship, if any, of the parties; whether communications took place in a public or private place; the presence or absence of third parties; the duration of the communication; and, most important, the demeanor

---

[1]   *California State Bar Formal Opinion No. 2003-161 (hereafter* "Formal Opinion")

of the parties, particularly any conduct of the attorney encouraging or discouraging the communication and conduct of either party suggesting an understanding that the communication is or is not confidential."[2]

Thus, in order to avoid the risks to the family and to the lawyer discussed above, the lawyer representing a client with a family business and trying to work with the entire family must clearly state in writing who is and who is not a client. In this regard, it's suggested that the attorney ask the other family members to sign a non-representation letter acknowledging that the attorney is not his or her attorney. The attorney may even consider requesting the family member periodically to sign the letter again.

3. Even if a family member is clearly not a client, may the lawyer still owe a duty of confidentiality to that family member during discussions with that family member?

The simple answer is "yes," the lawyer may owe a duty of confidentiality to a non-client, which can result in the lawyer's being disqualified from representing any other family members. The above-referenced Formal Opinion No. 2003-161 provides, in part,

"Even if no attorney-client relationship is created, an attorney is obligated to treat a communication as confidential if the speaker was seeking representation or legal advice and the totality of the circumstances, particularly the representations and conduct of the attorney, reasonably induces in the speaker the belief that the attorney is willing to be consulted by the speaker for the purpose of retaining the attorney or securing legal services or advice in his professional capacity, and the speaker provided confidential information to the attorney in confidence."[3]

The Opinion goes on,

"The obligation of confidentiality that arises from such a consultation prohibits the attorney from using or disclosing the confidential or secret information imparted, except with the consent or for the benefit of the speaker. *The attorney's obligation of confidentiality may also bar the*

---

[2]   *Id.,* Formal Opinion.
[3]   *Id.,* Formal Opinion.

attorney from accepting or continuing another representation without the speaker's consent."[4] (Emphasis added)

Thus, the lawyer will have to clearly state that the family member is not a client and that any conversations with that family member will not be confidential. Such a statement may be added to the non-representation letter suggested above for all family members occasionally to sign.

Blending Best Practices with the Classic Models of Representation

Which models of representation, if any, can the attorney use to minimize the risks to the attorney and the family and the risk of succession failure?

We believe that generally neither the single client/hired gun model nor the various multiple representation models fully allows the attorney to completely implement a best practice approach such as Roles and Rules for the family business client even with the written waivers. It is, however, possible to supplement the single client approach to better balance the needs of the family and the attorney so that the attorney can implement the best practice approach at least to some extent.

Accommodating the Best Practice Approach: A Summary

In summary, for a lawyer to help a family business make the transition to the next generation with implementation of the Roles and Rules model, it may be best for the attorney to use the best practice of actually being able to communicate with all members of the family business system to various extents. To achieve this goal the attorney can supplement the classic single client model, within the rules of professional conduct, as follows, bearing in mind that each family business system is unique:

- Represent only one client, usually the senior generation (G1). This avoids the risk in the multi-representation models that an unhappy family-member client may disqualify the attorney from representing any family member, no matter which waivers have been signed.
- Have the client waive the lawyer's duty of confidentiality at least for the members of the family business system and the consultant (discussed below). This allows the lawyer to communicate freely with anyone in the family business system and eliminates the risk of the lawyer inadvertently discussing confidential information.

---

[4]   *Id.*, Formal Opinion.

- Have each person in the family business system (except the client) sign a letter that clearly states that the attorney does not represent any of the other family members and that no conversations between the family member and the attorney are confidential. In addition, the letter should suggest that the family member consult with his or her own attorney before signing the letter acknowledging the non-representation acknowledgement and confidentiality waiver.

- Consider the use of a consultant or facilitator or appoint someone to that role. The attorney should consider recommending that the family agree to use a consultant to implement aspects of the best practices approach, as explained in Chapter 4 of this book. (The consultant could, if properly informed and advised about the attorney's role in the Roles and Rules process, be another advisor to the family, such as a CPA, trust officer, company comptroller, insurance specialist, or other financial advisor.) This consultant does not necessarily face the ethical practice obstacles attorneys do in representing family business clients and therefore can function more as a participant, observer, and mediator and communicate the "big picture" to all family members. Also, if there are multiple attorneys involved, then the consultant can act as a mediator among the family members to ensure that the adversarial approach doesn't take hold. In this way, the consultant can address the needs of the family as a single entity and attend to individual and group needs. (Note, however, that just because an attorney indicates that he or she represents only G1, it does not become necessary to find another legal representative to "help" in the succession process.)

In sum, it's probably best for the lawyer representing a family business system to, first, discuss the advantages and disadvantages of each representation model and various options, such as those discussed in this appendix, with the client and, second, to let the client decide which model of representation and approach the attorney should implement, and document the decision accordingly.

Appendix C

Sample Communication Rules

The following is a proposed set of ground rules for communication at family meetings concerning business. These are closely modeled on sets of rules we have developed and used with client families. Bear in mind that these are business meetings at which each participant is expected to function in the role of business person, and that these rules aim to help them understand and function in that role.

Ground Rules for Family Business Discussions

1. Listen respectfully to every other speaker and don't interrupt.
2. Focus on issues, not on people or personalities.
3. At every meeting, all attending family members should address each other as peers, at least at some point.
4. It is okay to disagree with other family members, and for them to disagree with you.
5. When you disagree, use language that does not invite a defensive reaction. For instance say, "I have another view," or "Tell me more about what concerns you."
6. Use "I" statements rather than "you" statements. For example say, "I often feel that I am not part of the big decisions," instead of "You leave me out of the big decisions."
7. Assign a "referee" or timekeeper for particularly emotionally charged discussions.
8. Remember that no one is always right or wrong in everything he or she suggests.

9. Instead of trying to win, try to create the spirit of give-and-take that results in win-win solutions. Try to find a middle ground that meets everyone's minimum requirements (a compromise approach) or, better yet, try to find a solution that satisfies everyone's needs (a collaborative approach).

10. Keep anything told to you confidentially in confidence or else get the person's permission (in private) to share the information or viewpoint with others.

11. Respect each person's talents and intelligence, and use them for the benefit of the business.

12. Listen to other suggestions for achieving good communication, and incorporate the ones that everyone can agree to into these rules.

Signed:

_____   _____

_____   _____

_____   _____

_____   _____

_____   _____

_____   _____

We have the family members sign these agreements and then we distribute a copy to each member. As simple as that sounds, we have found that people take these rules more seriously when they have literally signed on to use them and have their own copy signed by all participants. Remember too that the family, with our guidance and coaching, develops these rules, which further heightens their cooperation. While nothing will guarantee their cooperation, these rules help and, equally important, provide a frame of reference for keeping discussions on track.

APPENDIX D

Issues in Estate Taxes, Gift Exemptions, and Exclusions

Many lay people are understandably mystified about estate taxes, so this appendix will help clarify things (at least as of this writing). Here we will leave aside income taxes, which we all deal with annually. We will also leave aside the political aspects of the estate tax, except to point out that those aspects exist and, as a result, in the United States the following major changes have occurred over the past 200 years or so: An estate tax or inheritance tax was instated in 1797 (to help develop the navy), repealed in 1802, instated in the 1860s (to help finance the Civil War), repealed in 1870, instated in 1898 (to help pay for the Spanish-American War), repealed in 1902, instated in 1916, and modified with exemptions and deductions at various times since then. As we write this, the estate tax is scheduled to be phased out in 2010, then reinstated in 2011. So, whatever your views on tax and fiscal matters, history shows that estate taxes will be periodically instated, modified, and repealed.

For our purposes, the key considerations are estate taxes, gift taxes, and the generation skipping tax, all of which are subject to periodic modification by legislative bodies. This appendix addresses a key element in these taxes: the amount of assets in the estate that are exempt according to the tax laws in effect at the time of the testator's death. As noted several times in this book, advantageous compliance with tax law stands among the chief aims of sound estate planning. That means minimizing the amount of taxable assets in the estate, which is achieved by maximizing the use of deductions, gifts, valuation discounting, and exemptions. Another important element is the ability to leverage and grow assets in certain tax exempt trusts, which we also cover in this appendix.

The Marital Deduction and Estate and Gift Tax Exemptions

First, let's cover the marital deduction, which is straightforward. The marital deduction is the amount of assets in the estate that an individual can transfer to his or her spouse, during life or upon death, completely free of estate or gift taxes. The marital deduction was created in 1948, when it applied to 50 percent of the adjusted gross estate. With the Economic Recovery Act of 1981, the marital deduction became unlimited. (If the surviving spouse is a non-US citizen, special considerations apply.)

Often a testator wants to give assets to the surviving spouse under the marital deduction so no gift taxes will be due, but not give them outright. Sometimes the testator wants to give assets in a way that preserves both the marital deduction and control of the assets. This can be achieved through trusts as explained in Chapter 7 and below in this appendix.

Gift taxes differ from the estate tax, as do the exemptions to gift, estate, and generation skipping taxes. The exemptions that apply to estate taxes and generation skipping taxes are coordinated, but gift tax exemptions are not. An estate tax exemption means that a certain amount of the value of the assets in an individual's estate is exempt from any estate taxes (separate from the marital deduction). Technically, that amount is called the applicable credit amount.

Up until 2001, gift tax exemptions and rates paralleled those of estate taxes. In 2001, the estate tax laws were changed to gradually increase the amount of assets exempt from estate taxes. But Congress didn't want to lose the gift tax revenue, and wanted to help preserve the income tax rules, so they stopped extending the estate tax exemption to assets subject to gift taxes. In other words, they kept gift taxes in place and uncoupled them from estate taxes as far as the exemptions apply.

As of 2006, the estate tax exemption (the applicable credit amount) was $2.0 million, and was scheduled to increase to $3.5 million in 2009 and to become unlimited in 2010, which represents the phase out of the estate tax—but only for that year. As of this writing, the exemption is scheduled to return to $1.0 million, which was its 2002 level. (But again, history shows that anything can happen.)

These exemptions apply to the estates of individuals. That means that with a $2.0 million exemption a husband and wife wouldn't pay any estate taxes until their estate reached $4.0 million in assets; under a $3.5 million exemption, they wouldn't pay estate taxes until $7.0 million in assets, and so on. That's because the marital deduction allows a person to pass assets to his or her spouse free of taxes, while protecting their estate tax exemption in a bypass trust.

For example, if, under a $3.5 million estate tax exemption a couple's estate is over $7.0 million, then the unlimited marital deduction kicks in and there is no tax. The deceased spouse's estate will then be kept in a bypass trust and then when the surviving spouse dies, the assets in the bypass trust will not be included in the estate of that second spouse to die. If instead the entire $7.0 estate went to the surviving spouse *without* the use of the bypass trust, then the estate of the surviving spouse would be $7.0; in that case there would be no tax upon the first spouse's death, but there would be tax upon the second spouse's death. (Again, the marital deduction and the estate tax exemption are separate: the former is unlimited, while the latter is now being gradually increased as described in the preceding paragraph.)

In a situation with a $2.0 million estate tax exemption, if Jack passes $5.0 million to his wife Janet, no estate taxes are applied at that point, because of the unlimited marital deduction applied to the $3.0 million, and the $2.0 million would go into a bypass trust to secure the estate tax exemption. Then, when Janet dies, assuming that she has no other assets, $3.0 million of the assets in her estate are exempt from estate taxes (thanks to her $2.0 million exemption and Jack's $2.0 million exemption being kept in the bypass trust). Upon Janet's death, still assuming a $5.0 million estate, $1.0 million of her assets would be subject to the estate tax. (Note, too, that the $3.0 million in assets could be placed in a QTIP trust for control purposes.)

Sound estate planning and the use of trusts aim to remove assets from the estate proper and bring the value of the assets in the estate to within, or as close as possible to within, those exemptions. Estate tax exemptions are a powerful means of preserving wealth and should be used to maximum advantage.

The Generation Skipping Tax

In times past, the senior generations of wealthy families could put their assets in trusts that essentially would last forever. Their children would become life beneficiaries of these trusts, and as each successive generation died *their* children would become life beneficiaries of these trusts. Each generation would receive all or part of the income and have varying degrees of control over the assets, depending on the provisions of the trust.

Under this system, when children died, nothing in that trust was included in their estates, because they had only an income interest in the trust, which terminated upon their death. When the child died, the grandchildren would then have that income interest in the trust for their lives. When the grandchild died, the great-grandchildren would have that income interest, and so on with none of the assets in the trust included in their estates. Of course, if you don't have to pay estate taxes or gift taxes as the trust passes along, the growth of the assets in the trust, as compared with that if taxes had been levied, is substantially larger.

Seeing this and looking to social and fiscal policy, Congress established the rule against perpetuities, which basically states that a trust cannot last indefinitely.

More specifically, the rule against perpetuities states that you cannot create an interest in a trust if it extends beyond the lives in existence at the time the trust is created, plus twenty-one years. In this way, the rule against perpetuities limits a testator's power to give gifts to unborn descendants. Note, however, that this rule has been repealed in certain states, including Delaware; in such cases, if the generation skipping tax exemption is allocated to the trust, the trust will forever not be subject to GST taxes.

The generation skipping tax limits a testator's ability to pass assets to future generations without taxes when those assets exceed the GST exemption amount, which is coordinated with the estate tax exemption amount. These are two separate exemptions. Here's how this works: when the donor makes a gift that extends two or more generations below that donor's generation, the gift is subject to a flat tax equal to the maximum estate tax rate, if the gift exceeds the GST exemption amount. This means that when mom and dad set up a trust for their child or their child's spouse, and it's designed so that the assets go directly to their grandchild, there will be no estate tax when the child (or the child's spouse) dies, because ownership resides with the grandchild. The assets stay in trust for the life of the child, and the generation skipping tax will apply to the assets whenever one of three events occurs:

1. A taxable distribution, which occurs when the assets in the trust pass from the child of the trustor to the grandchild, and anytime the grandchild gets income or a distribution from the trust; the distribution or the income from the trust would be subject to the generation skipping tax
2. A taxable termination, which occurs when the grandchild dies and there are assets in the generation skipping trust; those assets would be subject to the generation skipping tax
3. A direct gift, which occurs when the senior generation directly gifts a grandchild with assets, which do not go through a trust; the amount of the gift would be subject to the generation skipping tax.

Actually, both the generation skipping tax and income taxes would apply to any distribution to the grandchild, that is, in situation #1 above. The distribution to the grandchild would be subject to the income tax and to the generation skipping tax—to the extent that the assets in the trust exceed the generation skipping tax *exemption*, which is equal to the estate tax exemption.

Although it largely stands apart from the Roles and Rules aspects of estate planning, estate, gift, and generation skipping taxes and the applicable deductions and exemptions are important matters, given the traditional aims of estate planning and the desire and need to preserve family wealth.

The Gift Tax Exemption and Exclusion

With gift taxes, two key mechanisms come into play: the gift tax exemption and the gift tax exclusion.

- The gift tax *exemption* is the total amount that you can give over your lifetime without incurring the gift tax; as of this writing, that amount is $1.0 million.
- The gift tax *exclusion* is the annual amount that you can give to a person without incurring the gift tax or using any of your gift exemption amount; as of this writing, that amount is $12,000 (increased from $11,000 in 2006 and previously from $10,000 in 2001, because the exclusion amount is indexed to inflation). Under the gift tax exclusion, a husband and wife can give away twice the individual exclusion amount to any one donee, which would be $22,000 as of this writing, even in a separate-property state.

Gifts of up to $12,000 per year per donee do not count against the $1.0 million lifetime exemption. However, the amount of gifts *over the exclusion* do count against the lifetime exemption. So, for instance, if in one year you gave $100,000 to each of ten people, you would give away a total of $1.0 million. But because of the $12,000 exclusion you would use only $880,000 of your $1.0 million exemption (= $1,000,000-$120,000, with the $120,000 = $12,000 x 10 donees).

Gifting Caveats

Gifting can be a powerful tool for getting assets out of the taxable estate and for transferring both wealth and control over assets, especially over the long run. However, a valuation issue often arises regarding shares in LLCs, family limited partnerships, and other business entities. After all, the $12,000 exclusion, even indexed for inflation, is a relatively small amount, although it can and will add up over time, and the valuation issue remains. For example, a business owner could give away, according to her appraisers, $800,000, yet the IRS can still contradict that and contest the value as exceeding $1,000,000 and levy taxes. So it's important to have accurate, defensible appraisals of family businesses and any other assets not valued by a known market price, as is the case with government securities or stocks or bonds of public companies.

In addition, gifting assets has implications regarding the tax basis of the assets involved and this can result in capital gains taxes for the recipient when the asset is sold. So again, as with all estate planning matters, gifting strategies must be carefully planned and reviewed with a qualified advisor for soundness and for all legal and tax implications *before being implemented.*

Leveraging Assets into an Exemption Trust

An exemption, bypass, or generation skipping trust can be set up so that a couple's child has an income interest in that trust, and that exemption trust can be allocated assets in the amount of the generation skipping tax exemption ($2.0 million, as of this writing). That way, when the child dies, that trust is not included in the child's estate which then passes to the grandchild. When the grandchild dies, or when there is a distribution—because that trust is exempt for generation skipping tax purposes—distributions to the grandchild from that exempt trust will be tax free to the grandchild for generation skipping tax purposes. (The grandchild must still pay income tax on the distribution of any income associated with the assets.)

However, the assets in that trust will be exempt from generation skipping taxes for the grandchild, the great-grandchild, and the great-great-grandchild. Once the assets in the trust are exempt, they will continue to be exempt from the generation skipping tax as the trust passes from generation to generation *even if those assets increase due to appreciation.* For example, if you use the $2.0 million to buy stock that rises to $10 million, $15 million, or any other value, the entire amount is exempt from the generation skipping tax. Note that some states limit how long the asset may remain in such a trust and other states do not.

It's best to place assets that may realize high appreciation into this kind of trust, for instance ownership interests in a family business, so you get it out of the estate tax system. For example, let's say you put $2.0 million into the bypass trust and allocate your generation skipping exemption to that trust. You then take that $2.0 million and buy a single-premium life insurance policy of, let's say a $10 million, on the parent. Then when the parent dies, that generation skipping trust suddenly holds $10 million instead of $2.0 million. Then you can take that $10 million and buy $10 million of assets in the family business. You then place that ownership interest in, say, an LLC or a family limited partnership, into the bypass trust or irrevocable life insurance trust. This is an extremely effective way of leveraging your exemptions. You have insurance money in the estate to pay estate taxes, and you've packed the membership interest in the business into the bypass trust or irrevocable life insurance trust.

Now, if you can take that $2.0 million and make it grow to $10 million or $15 million or more, what about the rule against perpetuities in the United States? As noted, that rule states that the trust can generally remain in effect for all the lives that exist at the time the trust is first established plus 21 years. So at some time the trust has to end, at which point the assets are distributed out and go back into the transfer tax system. However, several states have recently done away with the rule against perpetuities. In those states under the law as of this writing, those exemption trusts can be set up to last forever. Of course, as indicated at the start of this appendix Congress may override those state laws.

APPENDIX E

Modifying Trusts with Multiple Trustees to Enhance the Trusts' Stability

As noted several times in this book, when a senior generation begins the estate planning process or passes away and leaves assets in trust for the next generation, a Rules Crisis ensues. Gone are the roles that parents played for children and which more or less kept sibling issues in check. Even in cases of highly successful parenting, siblings can find themselves unprepared to manage their natural rivalry and to deal with disappointments that may arise around the provisions of the estate plan.

Rules, such as those in a trust agreement, cannot by themselves promote peace, security, and prosperity. Rules play out in a context of roles. People in the role of police officers on the streets, umpires in stadiums, and judges in courtrooms keep people playing by the relevant rules. Their roles are those of parties interested only in the application of the rules of the game, not in the stakes of the game.

The law itself serves to regulate interactions among parties, as is the case in agreements and contracts. For instance, the equal legal status afforded to parties to a contract assures that interactions can be fair. Contracts and agreements are rule-defined and rule-driven, and thus operate such that parties may affect one another to an equal, equivalent, or reciprocal extent. In this sense, the interactions of the parties are symmetrical.

Yet the law sometimes recognizes asymmetrical relationships that are role-driven rather than rule-driven. Asymmetrical or nonsymmetrical relationships are also hierarchical, which means that one party may affect another more than the reverse, as occurs in rules that define the guardian and child relationship.

Trustee and beneficiary is another hierarchical, role-driven relationship. A trust agreement defines the manner in which a trustee or trustees shall act in the interest of the beneficiaries. This gives trustees power to make decisions on behalf of beneficiaries, even against the expressed wishes of some or all of the beneficiaries. Such trustees are quite literally in loco parentis, since they carry out the will of a parental generation.

A curious situation occurs when beneficiaries may also be trustees. While rules may define conflicts of interests among parties to contracts and agreements, there has been no definition of a "conflict of roles." Yet a potential role conflict exists when the same person may be both trustee and beneficiary. This is analogous to someone being both guardian and child at the same time. The guardian-child, trustee-beneficiary hierarchy of roles thus collapses.

The rules of a contract cannot be assumed to ensure the discharge of all parties' duties when conflicts of interest exist. However, it is generally assumed that the trustee-beneficiary relation may be regulated by the terms of the trust and by pertinent law even in the presence of a conflict of interest and a conflict of roles. This assumption is unwarranted, and it generates instability in trusts with multiple trustees and beneficiaries.

Trusts with Multiple Trustees Are Inherently Unstable

Let's turn to the way in which a typical trust is structured when multiple trustees govern it. Multiple trustees may include professionals, individuals, and individuals who may also be beneficiaries, or any combination thereof. In general, unless otherwise directed in the trust instrument, trust law provides that if there are multiple trustees, they all have the same powers, duties, and responsibilities to work in the interests of all the beneficiaries. Administering such a trust creates a situation in which there is no hierarchy among the trustees, because they all have the same role and the same powers. That all the trustees are to work on behalf of all the beneficiaries diffuses responsibility, generates subjectivity, and invites litigation.

Taken in the context of the Roles and Rules model, current trust law thus directs trusts to be structured in an inherently unstable manner. This can lead to costly court action in which parties turn to a judge to enforce the rules and restore hierarchy to the system. (Of course, if there is one trustee and that trustee is not a beneficiary, the hierarchy built into the structure will allow for a potentially stable situation from the Roles and Rules perspective, in which case no changes need to be built into the trust document. However, even this configuration is itself no protection against an irate beneficiary suing a trustee.)

There is a distinction to be made between trustees who are only trustees and those who are also beneficiaries. As noted, the hierarchy of trustee to beneficiary collapses when some or all trustees are also beneficiaries, and the in loco parentis function of trustees cannot hold. Conflict of interest is well-understood, but conflict of roles such as occurs here is not recognized. As a trustee, one has obligations to *all* the beneficiaries; however, as a beneficiary, one might logically seek to accrue maximum benefits for oneself. Merging trustee and beneficiary is tantamount to merging the roles of guardian and child. One cannot expect rules, such as the rules of trust law, to regulate an adversarial role situation such as this any more than hockey players can referee their own games. The presence of beneficiary-trustees thus increases the potential for litigation, again to seek the application of rules by a judge.

How can a trust instrument be modified to avoid the fact that traditional trust structures with multiple trustees (with or without beneficiary-trustees) are inherently unstable? Trustees must administer the trust according to the trust instrument and, except to the extent the trust instrument provides otherwise, according to the relevant state's trust law and public policy. The tenet that the trustees must follow the terms of the trust instrument is so strong that some courts have said,

> *"Thus, in general, trustees are bound by the terms of the trust and possess only that authority conferred upon them by the trust." (The California Supreme Court in Crocker-Citizens National Bank v. Eckstrom 4 cal. 3d 202 (1971) ("Crocker")).*

Can trust drafters modify the standard trust law that provides that all trustees have the same powers, duties, and responsibilities in administering a trust? Can they modify it to provide that some trustees have different powers, duties, and responsibilities in administering the trust? If trust drafters can provide for different powers in the trust instrument, then a trust can be designed with distinct roles for the various trustees to play. In fact, the Crocker court goes on to state,

> *"Of course, the terms of the trust may provide that certain powers shall be exercised by one trustee and other powers by another (citations omitted)."*

Thus, a trust drafter has great latitude in drafting the terms of the trust. It is therefore possible to build into the trust instrument the Roles and Rules required for more stable relationships among multiple trustees by governing their interactions more precisely. This can reduce or obviate the motivation for people to resort to litigation in order to seek the missing hierarchical role in a judge.

Sample Trust Provisions Incorporating Roles and Rules

There are many ways to build into a trust document hierarchical roles for multiple trustees. The following example in this appendix represents only one option. Simply stated, in this example we add special provisions to the standard trust instrument in the form of a new article that modifies the trust terms by adding a new role for one of the trustees. This establishes a single trustee—whom we call the Managing Trustee—with additional powers over the other trustees.

Specifically, we give the Managing Trustee a power to veto the decisions of all of the other trustees at any time; this, of course, effectively gives the Managing Trustee a higher rank than the other trustees. However, we also provide a way for the veto of the Managing Trustee to be overridden if that is deemed appropriate; this adds another level of rank in the trust situation without resorting to the court. Thus, the trust with multiple trustees is no longer unstable from the Roles and Rules perspective; instead, it has both Roles and Rules (rather than rules alone) built into its operations.

Again, the following trust operating provisions and procedures are one example of a way to incorporate the Roles and Rules approach in a trust document for multiple trustees. *This sample and its language are not intended for use in their present form; such provisions must be designed for the specific situation. Please consult legal counsel for proper inclusion in documents.*

Sample Article
Additional Trust Operational Procedures

1. *Purpose and Intentions of the Trustors.* The Trustors understand that when their children (or any successors to the children) assume responsibility as successor Trustees that certain conflicts may naturally arise by and between the children in their new role as successor Trustees and/or as trust beneficiaries because the Trustors' parental role with its attendant powers will have been permanently changed. When the Trustors' roles do change, such a transition creates a "Rules Crisis" or "shock" wherein the successor Trustees suddenly become entrusted with, and therefore obligated to administer, the trust according to the terms/rules outlined in this Trust and under trust law in general, a responsibility and task that none of them had heretofore ever faced. The Trustors also understand that when the successor Trustees assume their roles and consequent duties and responsibilities as Trustees that trust law in general is not sufficient in and of itself to help monitor, regulate, and guide the relationships and behaviors by and between the successor Trustees themselves, without possibly resorting to costly court actions. Therefore, the Trustors have supplemented and modified the duties of the successor Trustees as provided in this ARTICLE and, as such, it is the Trustors' specific intention and direction that these additional duties and responsibilities be carefully followed and implemented by the Trustees according to their intentions and directions as herein set forth.

In order to facilitate the implementation of these supplemental duties, the Trustors have, both as a courtesy and as a way to help to enforce these new supplemental duties, provided the successor Trustees a copy of this ARTICLE, either before its inclusion into this Trust instrument or after its inclusion but prior to the "Date of Implementation" (as hereinafter defined). In either case, the successor Trustees will have had the opportunity to review, comment upon, and edit these supplemental duties prior to their implementation. Therefore, the successor Trustees shall in all respects be considered to have affirmed these new duties and will have agreed to carry out such additional duties. Given that the successor Trustees have affirmed these supplemental duties, it is hoped that any court or arbitrator shall, if so requested, consider that such supplemental duties and responsibilities be enforced as hereinafter provided and so directed by the Trustors.

Notwithstanding the above, when no "Family Business" (as hereinafter defined) is owned jointly with any other sub-trusts that may have been created by the terms of this Trust or upon the exercise of any powers of appointment granted to any beneficiary herein, then the provisions of this ARTICLE need not be implemented with regard to such sub-trust(s).

2. *Definitions and Selected Additional Duties and Powers*

A. "Family Business". As used in this Trust, the term "Family Business" refers to the interest of any sub-trust created under the terms of this Trust, including any sub-trust created by the exercise of any power of appointment herein granted, to jointly hold any real estate or any non-publicly traded interest in a sole proprietorship, partnership, corporation, limited liability company, or any other similar business structure in any state or foreign country.

B. "Family Committee". All references to the "Family Committee" shall refer to all of the then acting Trustee(s), all of the "Panel Member(s)" (as hereinafter defined), and any and all current and remainder beneficiaries over age thirty (30) (hereinafter collectively referred to as the "qualified members"). Voting by the members of the Family Committee shall be as hereinafter set forth. Notwithstanding the above, the qualified members of the Family Committee may be modified, limited, or changed as provided in Paragraph 4, following.

C. "Managing Trustee": "Election", "Term", Resignation and Removal.

    1. "Election" of Managing Trustee. The Managing Trustee shall be elected, from a group consisting of the then acting Trustees, by a majority vote (or by unanimous vote if only two persons are acting

as Trustees); provided, however if no such nomination and election to the office of Managing Trustee should occur within 30 days after the Date of Implementation, then by a majority vote of the Family Committee except that the vote of any Trustee who may also be a trust beneficiary shall be counted only as a Trustee vote. Any person who is nominated or is interested in being nominated as the Managing Trustee shall also be entitled to vote in the election. If within forty-five (45) days from the Date of Implementation, no Managing Trustee is elected by the Family Committee, then the Managing Trustee shall be selected by _____ [name(s) of specific party or parties].

2. "Term". The initial nominee selected as the Managing Trustee shall serve for a term of five (5) years from the Date of Implementation. Within sixty (60) days before the anniversary of the Date of Implementation or, if applicable, the five (5) year anniversary of any successor thereto, a successor Managing Trustee shall be nominated (for which any presently acting Managing Trustee will also be eligible) to serve for a subsequent term(s). If no new successor is nominated within the sixty (60) day period above referenced, then the then acting Managing Trustee shall continue to act as Managing Trustee for another five (5) year term. Any newly nominated Managing Trustee shall accept such nomination in writing within five (5) days of such nomination; otherwise, the election process above referenced shall be re-instituted to name a new successor Managing Trustee.

3. Resignation or Removal of Managing Trustee. The Managing Trustee may resign at any time by providing all of the Family Committee members with a written notice of resignation, which shall be effective not less than thirty (30) days from the date of the delivery of the notice of resignation to the Family Committee members. A Managing Trustee may be also removed as Managing Trustee if the Managing Trustee should be deemed to have "Failed to Comply" as defined in Paragraph 2.G. following, or solely upon the unanimous vote of then acting Panel Members; provided, however, that if the Panel Members remove the Managing Trustee, the Managing Trustee may institute the appeal procedures set forth in Paragraph 2.I., "Appeal Rights After a Notice of Failure", following.

D. "Trustee Meeting(s)". Reference to a "Trustee Meeting" in this ARTICLE means a meeting of the Trustees in which Family Committee members and any and all other beneficiaries, current and remainder, are invited to attend (unless otherwise agreed in writing at least fifteen (15) days in advance of said Trustee meeting by the Trustees), but no Family Committee members nor any other beneficiaries in attendance may vote on any matter but may express their opinion as may be recognized by the Managing Trustee.

E. "General Trust Meeting(s)". Reference to a "General Trust Meeting" in this ARTICLE means a meeting of Trustees, and all Family Committee members may vote in the manner hereinafter provided.

F. "Voting" by Trustees, Family Committee Members, and Managing Trustee Veto Power.

1. "Trustee Voting Limitation". After Trustors' death and creation of one or more sub-trusts at any time, all of the then acting Trustee(s) of any particular sub-trust (including the Administrative Trust, if it should then be in existence) shall have only one (1) vote as among all other Trustees of other respective sub-trusts. However, if the Family Committee members decide by majority vote, an equal number of votes may be assigned to each respective sub-trust in proportion to the greatest number of Co-Trustees of any one sub-trust; e.g., if there are five sub-trusts total and three of them have one trustee, one sub-trust has two co-trustees and one sub-trust has three co-trustees, then each of the five sub-trusts may be assigned three votes, to be exercised by the respective trustees and co-trustees, and with respect to any sub-trust with two or more co-trustees said co-trustees shall agree amongst themselves how to allocate the three votes, by a majority vote, or if two trustees, then unanimously.

2. Voting at Trustee Meeting(s). Subject both to the Trustee Voting Limitation and the Managing Trustee's Veto power (as hereinafter defined), during any Trustee Meeting, the Trustees may vote and the majority vote shall control, notwithstanding that any other members of the Family Committee may also be present. No Trustee may vote through a proxy; however, voting may be done through the delegation rules provided in Paragraph ___ of ARTICLE ___.

3. Voting at General Trust Meeting(s). During any General Trust Meetings, the majority vote of the Trustees, as above defined, and the majority vote of the Family Committee members (except that the vote of any Trustee who may also be a trust beneficiary shall be counted only as a Trustee vote) in attendance shall control subject to the Managing Trustee's Veto power. All decisions of the Family Committee members shall control whether or not a quorum of the Family Committee members is present at the time of the vote. No Family Committee member(s)' vote shall be counted who may be

absent from the General Trust Meeting unless a written proxy is submitted to the Trustees and accepted before the beginning of the General Trust Meeting.

4. "Managing Trustee Veto Power". During any Trustee Meeting and/or any General Trust Meeting, the Managing Trustee shall have the power at any time and from time to time to veto any and all decisions made at any such meeting.

5. "Override" of Managing Trustee Veto. At any time within five (5) days after any veto by the Managing Trustee, all of the other then acting Trustees, and/or by a majority vote of the Family Committee members (except that the vote of any Trustee who may also be a trust beneficiary shall be counted only as a Trustee vote) may revisit the vetoed decision and "reframe" said decision, then vote again on the matter, subject, however, to the Managing Trustee's veto. If no new decision is made after any such veto within the five (5) day period and accepted by the Managing Trustee, then the Managing Trustee within ten (10) days from date of the first veto date, may request in writing that the Panel Members re-frame the decision, and then by the unanimous approval of the Panel Members and the Managing Trustee, all within twenty (20) days from date of the first veto, shall be final and conclusive on the matter. If the Panel Members and the Managing Trustee cannot agree for any reason within the twenty (20) day period, then the decision of _____ [name(s) of specific party or parties] shall control and be final.

G. "Failed to Comply". In the event any Trustee including the Managing Trustee fails to follow the provisions of this ARTICLE and the provisions of this Trust in general, or if any Trustee fails to cooperate with the other Trustee(s) in order that the other Trustee(s) may comply with the provisions of this ARTICLE and/or the Trust terms in general, said Trustee(s) will be deemed to have "Failed to Comply" within the meaning of this paragraph, and thereby be subject to the provisions of Paragraphs 6. and 7., below. A Trustee shall automatically be deemed to have Failed to Comply if, after the Notice of Failure of such failure is final as hereinafter set forth, any of the following should occur:

1. Managing Trustee. The Managing Trustee fails to comply with his or her duties as hereinafter set forth more than three (3) times during his or her Term.

2. Minutes. Any Trustee assigned to keep the meeting minutes and provide a copy of said minutes to all of the Trustees and Panel

Members at least one (1) week prior to the next Trustee meeting, fails at least three (3) times during any two (2) year period beginning with his or her assignment and acceptance for such responsibility.

3. Payment of Expenses. Any Trustee who fails to pay or direct payments of his, her, or its share of the compensation of the Panel Members unless otherwise agreed in advance by all of the Trustees shall be deemed to have failed to comply.

4. Communication. Any Trustee who is responsible for communicating with any or all of the members of the Family Committee and who fails to so communicate at least two (2) times during any two (2) year period.

5. Failure to Attend Trust Meetings. If a Trustee, after notice as hereinafter provided, fails to attend any Trustee Meeting or Family Committee Meeting in toto at least two (2) times in any two (2) year period or at least five (5) times in any four (4) year period.

H. "Notice of Failure". Any time a Trustee (hereinafter referred to as the "Subject Trustee") fails to follow any of the provisions of this ARTICLE and in particular the provision of Paragraph 2.G., above, or any other provisions of this Trust in general, then any of the other then acting Trustee(s), Panel Members and/or any three of the members of the Family Committee together, may present to the Subject Trustee a "Notice of Failure" to follow the provisions of this ARTICLE; provided, however, that no person shall present a Notice of Failure to the same Subject Trustee more than one time in any three (3) year period.

I. "Appeal Rights After a Notice of Failure". After presentation of the Notice of Failure to the Subject Trustee, said Subject Trustee, within five (5) days after receipt of such Notice, has the right to appeal in writing the content of such Notice in accordance with the provisions of Paragraphs 6. and 7., following. If the Subject Trustee fails to appeal the Notice within said five (5) day period, such Notice shall be deemed to be final and binding and said Subject Trustee shall be deemed to have failed to comply with his or her duties herein set forth.

J. "Panel Members": Election, Duties, Term, Resignation, Removal, Compensation, and Indemnification.

1. Appointment. There shall be two (2) Panel Members who shall be approved by unanimous vote of the Trustees (unless a majority vote of the Family Committee members at a meeting called by any two of the Family Committee members determines that either more or fewer Panel Members are appropriate). If the Trustees cannot select

the Panel Members or any successor to any Panel Member within ten (10) days from the Date of Implementation or the resignation or removal of a Panel Member, then a vote of sixty (60) percent of the Family Committee members shall control and be final and conclusive. If the Family Committee members cannot agree within twenty (20) days from the Date of Implementation or the resignation or removal of a Panel Member, then the Trustees or any one of them shall request that the court make such decision. The Trustors suggest, but do not direct, that the person(s) selected to be Panel Members have at least fifteen (15) years extensive experience in areas similar to the type of business or "niche" in which the Family Business may be so involved, and/or extensive experience as a mediator or facilitator. Notwithstanding any other provisions of this ARTICLE, the Managing Trustee shall not have a veto power over any decision made with regard to the selection of a Panel Member.

2. Purpose and Responsibilities of Panel Member. The Trustors' purpose in appointing Panel Members to participate in any and all decisions of the Trustees and/or Family Committee members is to provide a mechanism whereby problems or issues that may arise incident to the co-ownership of any Family Business by any sub-trust can be identified, discussed, and analyzed, and that any and all controversies and disagreements which might impede the efficient and profitable operation of the Family Business can be resolved in a satisfactory and mutually beneficial manner, and that creative courses of action which are conducive to the efficient and profitable operation of the Family Business can be developed and implemented. Notwithstanding any other provisions in this Trust and/or any other provisions in Trust law in general, a Panel Member shall not be considered nor treated as a fiduciary when he or she acts (including any required voting) as may be directed in this Trust.

3. Term. A Panel Member shall be appointed for a term of one (1) year and shall be reelected to another one (1) year term or notified by the Managing Trustee at any time before the year anniversary of the Panel Member that that Panel Member's services are no longer required. Notwithstanding the power of the Managing Trustee to remove a Panel Member, by a majority vote of the Family Committee members at a meeting called by any Trustee or any two Family Committee members in writing within ten (10) days before the date of the removal of the Panel Member, the Managing Trustee's notification of removal may be overridden and the Panel Member shall continue to act as a Panel Member for another term.

4. Confidentiality Agreement. Each Panel Member shall execute a confidential disclosure agreement prepared by the Trust attorney and approved by the Trustees prior to being accepted as a Panel Member.

5. Resignation. Any Panel Member may resign at any time upon sixty (60) days prior written notice to the Trustees and members of the Family Committee.

6. Removal of Panel Member. Any Panel Member may be removed at any time and replaced by an unanimous vote of the Trustees and the other Panel Member not being removed and/or at least sixty (60) percent of the members of the Family Committee, so long as a replacement Panel Member has accepted the position prior to the removal of a currently acting Panel Member.

7. Compensation of Panel Members. Each Trustee shall be responsible, out of trust funds, for a pro-rata portion of the compensation based on a fraction, the numerator of which is the value of the real estate and/or other business interests owned by the sub-trust, and the denominator of which is the value of all such real estate and/or business interests owned by all of the sub-trusts or as otherwise agreed by majority vote of the Trustees.

8. Indemnification of Panel Members. No Panel Member, whether then-acting nor having ever acted at any time as a Panel Member, shall be liable for any acts taken or any failure to act in any manner, and shall be fully and completely indemnified (including attorneys' fees and other litigation costs) for any liability and expenses incurred by acting as a Panel Member. Any and all costs incurred by the Panel Member may as directed by the Panel Member be paid in advance of such costs that may be so incurred (for example but not limited to responding to the challenge). All such costs incurred by the Panel Member shall be paid first from any sub-trust of which the person instituting the challenge may be a Trustee and/or a trust beneficiary, and, next, from the sub-trust for the benefit of his or her sibling(s) and/or parent. The Trustors intend and therefore direct by this instruction that no Panel Member shall be liable or be required ever to pay any costs in any manner for any actions taken by him or her as a result of acting at any time as a Panel Member.

K. "Date of Implementation". Except as otherwise provided in Paragraph 1. of this ARTICLE, after the death or incapacity of both Trustors (or sooner if otherwise directed in a written statement signed by either or both of the Trustors and delivered to either all of the other then acting Trustees or the successor Trustee(s)), during the term of any sub-trust created in accordance with the terms of this Trust, the then acting Trustees or successors shall operate any such sub-trust in accordance with the provisions of this ARTICLE (hereinafter referred to as the "Date of Implementation").

L. "Rules of Communication". The Trustees are requested to prepare and review with all persons in attendance at any and all of the Trustee Meetings and Family Committee Meetings a written set of communication guidelines ("Rules of Communication") that all attendees agree to follow while at any such meeting.

3. *Trust and General Trust Meeting Requirements.*

A. Presiding Trustee at All Trustee and General Trust Meetings. The Managing Trustee shall preside over all Trust Meetings and General Trust Meetings in accordance with generally accepted business practices including but not limited to implementing "roughly" Roberts Rules of Order for all discussions and appropriate resolutions for all Trustee and Family Committee decisions. However, the Managing Trustee may delegate his or her authority to preside over any such meeting(s) if the other Trustees and Panel Members approve of such delegation in writing at any time and from time to time but prior to the meeting itself.

B. Frequency of Trustee Meeting(s) and Power to Call General Trust Meetings.

1. The Managing Trustee shall set at least three (3) Trustee Meetings each year unless otherwise agreed in advance by a unanimous vote of all of the Trustees and Panel Members, and the Managing Trustee shall call a General Trust Meeting at any time that a vote is required by the Family Committee members as set forth in this ARTICLE or as the Family Committee members may request as hereinafter provided.

2. By a written Notice of a Proposed Family Committee Meeting ("Meeting Notice") submitted to the Managing Trustee which is signed by at least twenty (20) percent of the Family Committee members, the Managing Trustee shall set a meeting of the Family Committee but no sooner than sixty (60) days from the date of the Meeting Notice by the Family Committee members provided, however, that such a Meeting Notice and call for a Family Committee Meeting be not more than one (1) meeting per year. The Managing Trustee shall prepare an Agenda in the manner as hereinafter provided for any Family Committee Meeting(s).

3. Postponement of Meeting. Any Panel Member may, for any reason, direct the Managing Trustee to postpone the scheduled meeting if the Panel Member notifies the Managing Trustee and the other Panel Members at least fourteen (14) days in advance of the scheduled meeting. If a meeting is postponed, the Managing Trustee shall immediately (within two (2) days) notify all Trustees, Panel Members, and Family Committee members of such postponement and shall also set a new date for the postponed meeting within twenty-one (21) days of the originally scheduled meeting date.

C. Conduct of Meetings.

1. Agenda. The Managing Trustee shall prepare a written agenda of items to be discussed at the next Trustee Meeting and/or General Trust Meeting. The agenda may include, but is not limited to, any issues related to the Family Business, any real estate, accounting problems, development of long range plans for the Family Business, ways to enhance communication between the Trustees and/or the Family Committee members, anticipated problems between the Trustees and/or the Family Committee members, suggestions for procedures to settle any conflicts between the Trustees and/or Family Committee members, etc. (Each and every agenda shall include a review or modification of the Rules of Communication and minutes (as defined below) of the previous meeting.) The proposed agenda shall be delivered to all Trustees, Panel Members, and all Family Committee members via facsimile or by other generally accepted methods of delivery at least fourteen (14) days before the scheduled meeting (the "original due date"). The Trustees, Panel Members, and/or Family Committee members are encouraged to submit to the Managing Trustee any other suggested agenda items before the agenda is sent out which items shall be included in the agenda at the discretion of the Managing Trustee.

2. Attendance at Meeting(s). All Trustees and Panel Members are required to attend all Trustee Meetings and all General Trust Meetings. A Trustee, including the Managing Trustee, and Panel Member may participate in a meeting through the use of a conference telephone or similar communications equipment including video conferencing, so long as all persons participating in such meeting can hear one another. Participation at a meeting pursuant to this subparagraph constitutes presence in person and attendance at such meeting.

3. Waiver of Notice Requirement. In the event a Trustee Meeting is required and "time is of the essence," the fourteen (14) day notice requirements set forth in Paragraph 3.C. (1), above, is not required provided that (1) all Trustees and Family Committee members are given notice of the date, time, and place of the meeting as well as the general nature of the business to be discussed, whether by telephone, email, fax, or in writing, and (2) a majority of the Trustees and all Panel Members sign a "Waiver of Notice" prior to the commencement of the meeting.

4. Written Consent to Action. Any action(s) which may be taken at a Trustee Meeting and any action that is required to be taken by the Family Committee members may be taken without a meeting and without prior notice if authorized by a writing signed by all Trustees ("Written Consent to Action by Trustees") and, where applicable, at least twenty-five (25) percent of the Family Committee members and the unanimous approval of the Panel Members. If applicable, a copy of the Written Consent to Action by Trustees as signed shall be delivered within seven (7) days of signing to the Trustees, Panel Members, and Family Committee members.

5. Minutes of Meeting. A Trustee shall be assigned the responsibility for taking minutes of the meeting or shall appoint another person to so act. All minutes shall be in accordance with standard business practices and the original minutes shall, after approval at the following meeting, be retained in a _____ FAMILY TRUST Minute Book which any member of the Family Committee, Trustee, or Panel Member may at any time review provided however that such review is approved by the Managing Trustee at his or her sole and absolute discretion. No Family Committee member may request a review of the minute book more than one (1) time per year.

4. *Modifications of Trust Operational Procedures.*

A majority of the Trustees, with the unanimous written approval of all Panel Members, may alter, amend or change any and all of the provisions for the operation of the Trust or any sub-trust as set forth in this ARTICLE at any time after two (2) years from Date of Implementation and not more than once every five (5) years thereafter by providing all of the Family Committee members with a written copy of the proposed changes at least thirty (30) days prior to the implementation of said proposed changes. If more than forty (40) percent of the Family Committee members should disagree with the proposed change(s), said Family Committee members may then institute the mediation and arbitration procedures set forth in Paragraph 7., below, provided that such procedures are begun within twenty (20) days after the notice of the proposed change(s) is sent to the Family Committee members. If such action is not taken within the twenty (20) day period by the Family Committee members, then the proposed change(s) to the provisions of this ARTICLE shall thereafter be implemented if approved by the Trustees at a Trustee Meeting.

5. *Resolution of Disputes.*

Any and all disputes by and between the Trustees, and by any one or more of any trust beneficiaries, and/or among any one or more of the trust beneficiaries and the Trustees or any one of them shall be determined by mediation and arbitration in accordance with Paragraph 7., below. It is the intention and direction of the Trustors that any and all disputes shall be subject to the requirements set forth Paragraph 7., below, which shall be the sole remedy for any such conflicts and disputes.

6. *Consequences for a Trustee's Failure to Comply.*

A. Removal of Trustee. A Trustee who has Failed to Comply with any of the provisions of this ARTICLE and, in particular, the provisions of Paragraph 2.G., shall, at the conclusion of the "Removal Hearing" (hereinafter set forth), be subject to automatic removal of such Subject Trustee as Trustee from all sub-trusts established under the provisions of this Trust, even if such act is of a "dc minims nature." The initiation of such Removal Hearing can be by any one or more of the Panel Members, any Trustee, and/or at least twenty-five (25) percent of the members of the Family Committee. The Removal Hearing shall be conducted in accordance with the provisions of Paragraph 7, below. Any such removed Trustee shall be disqualified from acting as a Trustee of any sub-trust created as provided in this Trust for a period of four (4) years from the date of such removal.

B. Investigation. Any Trustee and/or Panel Member, and/or at least twenty-five (25) percent of the members of the Family Committee, at such Trustee and/or Family Committee member's own personal expense (provided that if a Panel Member institutes the investigation, the expenses will be charged to the Trust of such Subject Trustee), may institute an investigation of the Subject Trustee's actions to determine whether the Subject Trustee has failed to follow the procedures prescribed herein notwithstanding that such failure may be considered of a "de minims nature." In the event such a failure is discovered, then the mediation and/or arbitration procedure in Paragraph 7, below, shall be utilized first to determine whether the failure was inadvertent or intentional. If the failure was inadvertent, the Subject Trustee shall not be removed. However, if the action is found to have been intentional, notwithstanding whether or not such action was of a "de minims nature," the Subject Trustee shall be removed in accordance with the terms of this Paragraph 6.

7. *Mediation and Arbitration.* Any and all disputes by and among the Trustees and/or among Family Committee members and/or among the Family Committee members and the Trustee(s) concerning any aspect of the operation of the Trust (including any action to remove a Subject Trustee for a Failure to Comply) shall be determined by mediation or arbitration in the following manner:

A. Written Demand. Any Trustee, Panel Member, and/or at least twenty-five (25) percent of the members of the Family Committee may serve upon the other(s) (including any Subject Trustee) involved in the dispute a Notice of Failure (as defined in Paragraph 2.H. of this ARTICLE) by registered mail; written demand that the dispute, specifying its nature, shall be submitted to mediation or arbitration as may be indicated in the Notice of Failure. Within five (5) days after service of such demand, the parties in dispute may mutually designate in writing a single mediator or arbitrator, and if arbitration is selected, the decision of such arbitrator, made in writing and under oath, shall be final and binding upon the parties. If the Notice of Failure specifies arbitration or if the parties failed to agree on a single mediator, then within the above referenced five (5) day period the parties in dispute have not agreed upon a single arbitrator, then within five (5) days thereafter, each of the parties in dispute shall appoint an arbitrator and serve written notice by registered mail of such appointment upon the other party. The decision of the two arbitrators made in writing and under oath shall be final and binding upon the parties. If the two (2) arbitrators fail to agree within ten (10) days after they have been appointed, the arbitrators shall, not later than on the tenth (10th) day after the passage of the ten (10) day period above, appoint a third arbitrator. If the two (2) arbitrators fail to agree upon a third arbitrator within the ten (10) day period, application may be made by one (1) or more Trustees and/or at least twenty-five (25) percent of the members of the Family Committee, upon notice to the other(s), to any court of competent jurisdiction, for the appointment of a third arbitrator, and any such appointment shall be binding upon all parties. The decision of a majority of arbitrators made in writing and under oath shall be final and binding upon the parties. The arbitrators shall, by majority vote, if applicable, determine the place for hearing, the rules of procedure, and allocation of the expenses of the arbitration. Any decision made by the arbitrator(s) under this provision shall be enforceable as a final and binding decision as if it were a final decision or decree of a court of competent jurisdiction. In no event shall the arbitration or mediation process exceed ninety (90) days in time including any decision of the arbitrators. If for any reason any party delays the process either by missing the deadline for appointment of the arbitrator or mediator or not responding for any reason, then the other party shall be deemed to have prevailed in the action in all respects as if the arbitrators had so held, including the payment of the prevailing party's expenses as provided in subparagraph B., below.

B. Cost of Arbitration. The cost of arbitration, including any and all of the prevailing parties' attorney fees, whether reasonable or not as approved by the prevailing party, and other costs of the conflict, shall be borne entirely by the losing party and shall either be paid from the losing party's individual assets or deducted from his or her sub-trust (whether the losing party is Trustee or a member of the Family Committee), and added to the trust of the prevailing party; provided, however, if a Panel Member instituted the investigation, the cost shall be born by the Subject Trustee or his or her sub-trust in which the Subject Trustee is a beneficiary, if applicable.

8. *Business Judgment Rule For Family Business Decisions.* For purposes of all decisions regarding the Family Business, the Trustee(s) shall be subject to the "business judgment rule" afforded business decisions by corporate law and shall not be subject to the standard usually required of a Trustee acting as a fiduciary, oftentimes referred to as the "prudent person rule." Accordingly, the Trustee(s) and, as previously set forth, Panel Members, are exonerated from liability when they have acted in good faith and in an honest belief that the Trust's best interests have been served, provided that their judgments involve no issues of illegality, fraud, or conflict of interest except as otherwise provided in Paragraph 9., below.

9. *Conflicts of Interest.* The Trustors recognize that in the exercise of the above provisions as well as other powers and duties applicable to the Trustee(s) under this Trust or by law, a Trustee may be placed in a position where his or her interests, as a fiduciary, conflict with his or her interests, as an individual

or with those of any other trust beneficiary or Trustee. The Trustors intend and therefore direct that such conflicting interests shall not be a basis for denying any Trustee from participating in the exercise of such powers or for disqualifying or removing the Trustee. The Trustors' selection of the named Trustees was made with full knowledge that conflicts of interest may arise due to the powers granted herein, and, accordingly, a Trustee shall not be subject to surcharge or any other claim, by or on behalf of any person who may be interested in any sub-trust hereunder, arising out of, or claimed to arise out of, any possible conflict of interest based on the interest of any Trustee (whether individually or as a fiduciary of any estate or trust) in any Family Business or other property which is or may become trust property. The provisions of this Paragraph shall be liberally construed to the end that such Trustee (in his or her individual capacity and/or as fiduciary of another estate or trust) may deal with himself or herself as Trustee hereunder in matters pertaining to any property which is or may become trust property, as if he or she were a stranger to the sub-trusts established hereunder.

Side note: The drafters of the trust document may also want to consider the following additional points for inclusion in the document to reinforce the Trustors intentions:

1. Provisions, for a residence or other tangible property in any sub-trust, allowing a trust beneficiary to use such property while owned by a sub-trust.
2. Clarification of the powers (and, when applicable, *specific waiver* of any trust law requirements affecting decisions) (a) to retain investment property including any family business and therefore waive any duty to diversify trust assets, (b) to acquire interests in such family businesses, (c) to operate the family business at the risk of the family business and not the trustee, (d) to loan money to any sub-trust at fair market rates by any Trustee, (e) to allow a trustee to purchase assets from any sub-trust at their fair market value, (f) to allow the trustee to retain "unproductive" property (e.g, the family businesses) except as otherwise may be required to qualify for the marital deduction, and, if appropriate, (f) to waive any duty of impartiality.
3. Addition of a strong no contest clause.
4. Addition of an additional attorney fees clause.
5. Addition of a Trustee delegation clause.
6. Provision that majority vote of the trustees controls.

Appendix F

Sample LLC Operating Agreement Procedures

The following is only a selected sample of definitions and provisions and is intended to provide readers with ideas and language for definitions and provisions for LLC operating agreements that define and reinforce a Roles and Rules approach. *This sample and the language herein is not intended to be used in its present form.* Please consult legal counsel for proper inclusion in documents.

I. Selected sample definitions to be added where appropriate to an LLC Operating Agreement incorporating the Roles and Rules approach:

1. *Definitions:*

    1.04 *Purpose.*

        (a)   The purpose of the Company is to create an "organizational structure" for the management of SMITH INVESTMENTS, LTD., SMITH BROTHERS LAND, LTD. and WILLIAM SMITH FAMILY PARTNERSHIP, LTD. (or any other partnership or corporation or other entity that may acquire, merge with, or otherwise succeed to the business of any such partnership) by setting up "roles and rules" for family and business behavior that give each Brother or Sister and his or her family a clear understanding of their roles within and outside the business of the Company and related companies such as SMITH RANCH, INC. The Company's organizational structure, being the general partner for SMITH INVESTMENTS, LTD., SMITH BROTHERS LAND, LTD., and WILLIAM SMITH FAMILY PARTNERSHIP, LTD., will help direct family and business relationships towards productive work and respectful relationships. This in turn will help maximize the efficient use of the family properties that have been accumulated through the personal efforts of the Brothers and Sisters.

(b)   Besides the primary purpose as stated above, the Company may purchase or lease any real or personal property, make any investment, and engage in any other joint venture, general partnership, limited partnership, or other business activity approved by the Board.

2. *Definitions Continued:*

2.02   *Board* shall mean the board appointed by the Members pursuant to the provisions of Article VI below to manage the affairs of the Company.

2.03   *Board Approval Committee* shall mean the committee appointed by the Consultants, as hereinafter defined, and approved by the Board pursuant to the provisions of Article VI, Section 6.15.

2.04   *Board Qualification Standards* shall mean those qualifications that a Board member must meet before being appointed to the Board and set forth in Schedule B [not included in this Appendix], attached hereto. The Board Qualification Standards may be changed upon the recommendation of (1) the Consultants as hereinafter defined, (2) the Board Approval Committee, as hereinafter defined, or (3) by a majority vote of the Brothers and Sisters, provided that such Brother and Sister voting shall not be a Disqualified Person, as hereinafter defined, and such recommendation is either (1) approved by a majority vote of the Brothers and Sisters who are not Disqualified Persons, or (2) approved by the Family Units Voting Process, as hereinafter defined, and a majority vote of the Board.

3. *Definitions Continued:*

2.12   *Disqualified Person* shall mean a person who has committed a willful material breach of the terms of this Agreement, or, as determined by the Consultants and approved by a majority vote of the Board excepting the person under review, is guilty of such conduct as tends to affect prejudicially the carrying on of the Company's business or otherwise so conducts himself or herself in matters relating to the Company business as to render it not reasonably practicable to carry on such business, or such person has been adjudged Bankrupt, has been adjudged insane or incompetent in any judicial proceedings, has been committed to a mental institution, or is convicted of a felony crime or three (3) instances of Driving Under the Influence (DUI).

2.13   *John Unit* shall mean all the Membership Interests in the Company owned by John and Cheryl and/or any of his descendants or his Member Qualifying Trust(s) (as hereinafter defined).

2.14   *Ann Unit* shall mean all the Membership Interests in the Company owned by Ann and Phil and/or any of his or her descendants or his Member Qualifying Trust(s) (as hereinafter defined).

2.15   *Sam Unit* shall mean all the Membership Interests in the Company owned by Sam and Nancy and/or any of his descendants or his Member Qualifying Trust(s) (as hereinafter defined).

2.16   *Jane Unit* shall mean all the Membership Interests in the Company owned by Jane and Bill and/or any of his descendants or his Member Qualifying Trust(s) (as hereinafter defined).

2.17   *Ron Unit* shall mean all the Membership Interests in the Company owned by Ron and Sharon and/or any of his descendants or his Member Qualifying Trust(s) (as hereinafter defined).

2.18   *Manager* shall mean the person elected as such in accordance with Article VI, in such person's capacity as a Manager.

2.19   *Members* shall mean JOHN SMITH, ANN JONES, SAM SMITH, JANE RIGHT, and RON SMITH, in their capacity as Members, and any other person admitted as a substitute or additional Member in accordance with Article VII, in such person's capacity as a Member. In addition, JOHN SMITH, ANN JONES, SAM SMITH, JANE RIGHT, and RON SMITH are each sometimes individually referred to herein as an "Original Member" and collectively as the "Original Members," and any reference to the Membership Interest of an Original Member shall be deemed to be a reference to the Membership Interest that is, or was, owned by such Original Member.

4.   *Definitions Continued:*

2.22   *Qualifying Trust* shall mean a trust (A) which has at least one Trustee who (i) is a descendant of any Original Member who is at least twenty-five years of age, or (ii) is a bank or trust company, or (iii) a spouse of any Original Member or a descendant of any Original

Member, and (B) the terms of said trust provide that (i) all of whose income and remainder beneficiaries are descendants of any Original Member, or (ii) whose income beneficiary is the spouse of any Original Member or a descendant of any Original Member which spouse only has rights to income of the trust, but no rights to receive principal of the trust. Reference to a *Member's Qualifying Trust* or *Qualifying Trust of a Member* shall mean a Qualifying Trust.

2.24 *Unit* shall mean any of the units of the Original Members and *Units* shall mean all of said Units.

II. Selected management provisions in the LLC Operating Agreement using Roles and Rules and relevant reporting structures.

ARTICLE VI

MANAGEMENT: RIGHTS, POWERS, AND OBLIGATIONS OF THE MEMBERS

6.01 *Appointments to The Board.*

(a) *Initial Appointees and "Board Member Approval Process".* The Original Members or Brothers and Sisters shall each have the right to appoint one voting member for his or her chair (hereinafter referred to as the "*Chair*") to the Board during his or her life; provided, however, that such appointee by the Original Member must (1) meet the Board Qualification Standards set forth in Schedule B attached hereto, (2) be approved by the Board Approval Committee, and (3) not be a Disqualified Person (hereinafter the three steps are referred to as the "*Board Member Approval Process*") before taking the Chair; and further provided that such appointee may be changed at any time by the Original Member upon delivery of a written notice to the other members of the Board and the member being so changed.

(b) *A Brother or Sister's Unit Chair Recommendation Process and "Voting Unit Members".* After the Original Member's death, or upon the Original Member becoming a Disqualified Person, or earlier if the Original Member so requests, his or her family Unit Members over age 21, including the Brother and Sister's spouse (but not any other Unit Member's spouse) provided that he or she is not then a Disqualified Person (hereinafter referred to as "*Voting Unit Members*"), will be entitled to recommend a person to sit in that Brother and Sister's Unit Chair for confirmation for that Chair as provided in Section 6.01(c).

In determining how the Voting Unit Members will agree to select the person for its recommendation, the Voting Unit Members may use any one of the following methods to agree to the person so recommended within thirty (30) days from the time the vacancy occurred:

(1)   The Voting Unit Members may unanimously agree informally to recommend a person for consideration for the Chair (*"Informal Agreement"*).

(2)   If for any reason an Informal Agreement among the Voting Unit Members is not possible and at least eighty percent (80%) (rounding any fraction down to the closest whole number) of the Voting Unit Members so agree, then the Voting Unit Members may vote by secret ballot for a person so recommended, and the majority vote of such Voting Unit Members shall be that Unit's recommendation (*"Secret Voting Process"*). If, for example, there are two, three, or four Voting Unit Members and if one of the Voting Unit Members objects, then the Secret Voting Process will not be available. For another example, if there are six (6) Voting Unit Members, then, assuming that at least four (4) people (6 x 80% = 4.8) would like to vote, then the person must receive at least four (4) votes of the six (6) possible votes before that person is so recommended for the Chair. For a further example, if there are five, seven, eight, nine, or ten Voting Unit Members and if not more than two Voting Members object, then the Secret Voting Process will be available.

(3)   If for any reason the Secret Voting Process is not utilized, or if no person receives a majority vote of the Voting Unit Members during that process, or if a majority of the Voting Unit Members so agree, then the Voting Unit Members shall consult with the Board Approval Committee, and the Voting Unit Members shall discuss with said Approval Committee all of their possible candidates for the Chair, and then the Voting Unit Members shall try again to come to an Informal Agreement on a candidate. If the Voting Unit Members cannot come to an Informal Agreement, then the candidate will be selected by The Family Units Voting Process except that the Voting Unit Members who could not come to an agreement shall *not* provide a participant for The Family Units Voting Process.

(4)   Any other process that at least 90% (rounding any fraction down as followed above) of the Voting Unit Members so agree

to follow in writing. For example, the Voting Unit Members may agree that another person or persons make the decision, or the Voting Unit Members may agree to mediate their differences with an experienced mediator.

(5) If the Voting Unit Members do not agree to follow the provisions of this Section 6.01(b) or if the Voting Unit Members do not recommend a Qualified Candidate within thirty (30) days from the date the Chair becomes vacant, then they will lose their right to name a Chair and the nomination of the Chair shall be in accordance with the manner set forth in Section 6.01(c) as if the Voting Unit Members failed two times to gain approval of a recommended Chair.

(c) *Confirmation Process of Recommended Board Member, and "The Family Units Voting Process"*. After the death of a Brother or Sister or sooner if so requested by the Brother or Sister, the Brothers and Sisters intend that each deceased Brother's and Sister's Unit shall be entitled to recommend a person for the Chair of the deceased Brother or Sister in the manner set forth in Section 6.01(b) above; provided that appointee may take the Chair only after the appointee has been confirmed in accordance with the Board Member Approval Process; and further provided that a person appointed as the Chair by the Original Member may serve for a Term as hereinafter defined as if said person were just appointed the Chair. If the appointee is not approved in accordance with the Board Member Approval Process, then the deceased Brother's or Sister's Unit may recommend another person for the Chair and such new appointee may take the Chair only after the appointee has been confirmed in accordance with the Board Member Approval Process. If the new appointee is not thereafter confirmed in accordance with the Board Member Approval Process, then a third appointee is to be recommended by the Consultants whereupon such third appointee may take the Chair only after (1) being confirmed in accordance with the Board Approval Process, and (2) been approved by a secret majority vote of Units wherein each Unit names one person in the manner set forth in Section 6.01(b) above who shall be entitled to vote for that Unit (herein after an all Unit vote is referred to as *"The Family Units Voting Process"*). If the Units do not approve of the third appointee, then a fourth appointee shall be recommended by the Consultants whereupon the same process for approval shall again be undertaken. If the fourth appointee is not approved by a majority vote of the Units, then the Board shall recommend the fifth person entitled to take the Chair provided that such person is approved in accordance with the Board Member Approval Process. If such fifth person is not approved, then the Board still again recommend a person for the Chair until such person is approved in accordance with the Board Member Approval Process.

(d) *Voting Rights of Each Unit to Recommend a Chair.* The Brothers and Sisters intend that after the death of the Original Member or upon the Original Member becoming a Disqualified Person, the descendants of the Original Members continue to have the ability to recommend a person to take the Original Member's Chair in the manner provided in Section 6.01(b) only if such descendants of said Original Member retain a significant ownership interest in the Company (hereinafter referred to as *"Unit Members"*). Therefore, if, at any time after the death of an Original Member or upon the Brother or Sister becoming a Disqualified Person, if the percentage Membership Interest comprising the particular Brother's or Sister's Unit Members shall represent less than forty percent (40%) of the percentage Membership Interests comprising such Unit at the time of the Original Member's death (taking into account any bequests from the Original Member), or at anytime thereafter, then such Unit shall no longer be entitled to appoint a member of the Board and, any member then serving on the Board who had been appointed with respect to said Unit shall immediately cease to be a member of the Board and the Board shall thereupon have one less member.

(e) *Term of Board Member.* Each Chair after being confirmed in accordance with the Board Member Approval Process shall serve for a term of six (6) years unless reappointed to subsequent term(s) in the manner provide in Section 6.01(c), or, if sooner, is removed in accordance with The Family Units Voting Process; provided, however, removal shall occur immediately if said person becomes a Disqualified Person as determined by the unanimous agreement of the Consultants in their reasonable discretion.

6.02 *Decision-Making Process of the Board.* The Board shall meet no less frequently than annually each calendar year at the principal offices of the Company (or at such other times and places as a majority of the Board shall determine from time to time), and at such other times as called by the Manager or any member of the Board upon no less than thirty (30) days prior notice. The Board shall make all material decisions relating to the operation of the Company based upon a majority vote of the Board; provided, however, that at least an eighty percent (80%) vote of the members of the Board shall be required to sell any assets originally contributed to the Company or originally owned by any of the partnerships in which the Company is the general partner, namely SMITH INVESTMENTS, LTD., SMITH BROTHERS LAND, LTD., and WILLIAM SMITH FAMILY PARTNERSHIP, LTD. A member of the Board may be present at a meeting in person or telephonically. Any deadlock shall be resolved by binding mediation and then arbitration in accordance with the procedures set forth in Section 10.02 [not included in this Appendix].

6.03   *Consultants to the Board.* The Board shall appoint two or more non-voting members to serve as consultants ("Consultants") to the Board to assist the Board in its decision-making process and to facilitate the operation of the Company in such a manner as will facilitate making decisions in a businesslike manner after the death of three (3) of the Brothers and Sisters or sooner if so approved by a majority of the Board. One such Consultant shall have at least twenty (20) years significant experience in managing and/or investing in real estate with a thorough knowledge of other investment alternatives, and the other Consultant shall have had at least twenty (20) years of significant manufacturing operations experience. Such Consultants shall be invited to attend all meetings of the Board and shall be reasonably compensated. Any Consultant shall continue to serve as such until resignation or removal by the unanimous vote of the members of the Board and the other Consultant at a meeting called for such purpose. In no event shall a Consultant be a related party to any of the members of any of the family Units within the meaning of Code section 672(c).

6.04   *Rights and Powers of the Board.* The Board is hereby granted the right, power, and authority to do on behalf of the Company all things consistent with this Agreement which are connected with or incidental to the business of the Company, including, but not limited to, to assign to the Manager, agent, employee, or any other Member such tasks as it in its sole and unrestricted discretion shall determine; to cause the Company or any partnership in which the Company is the general partner to acquire and finance the acquisition of Property; to operate, manage, lease, encumber, or otherwise deal with all or any part of the Property; to borrow on a recourse or nonrecourse basis, including from a Member, and on such other terms as the Board in its sole and unrestricted discretion shall determine; provided, however, that any borrowing from a Member or a person related to a Member shall not be at an interest rate less than that required by the Code or Treasury Regulations, or more than two points over the prime rate as published in the *Wall Street Journal,* or its successor, as of the time of the borrowing; and to enter into, execute, acknowledge, and deliver any and all contracts, agreements, or other instruments necessary or appropriate to effectuate any or all of the foregoing. Notwithstanding the foregoing, neither the Board nor the Manager shall cause the Company to sell or otherwise transfer any assets originally contributed to the company or any partnership in which the Company is a general partner without complying with the restrictions regarding transfer of any assets imposed by any Partnership Agreement provisions associated with said asset as well as the provisions of Section 6.02.

6.05 *Appointment of Manager.* JANE SMITH shall be the initial Manager of the Company. In the event the Manager ceases to act as Manager for any reason, the Board shall appoint a successor Manager. The Manager shall serve for a one (1)-year term, or longer, if the Board fails to name a replacement. The Manager may be removed at any time by a recommendation of the Consultants and thereafter a majority vote of the Board, provided that a successor is named who agrees to assume the obligations of a Manager under this Agreement.

6.06 *Rights and Powers of the Manager.* The Manager shall manage and control the day--to-day ministerial operations of the Company and shall perform such other tasks as are assigned to the Manager by the Board. Subject to the terms of this Agreement, the Manager shall have all rights, powers, and obligations of a manager as provided in the Act and as otherwise provided by law, and any action taken by the Manager shall constitute the act of and serve to bind the Company. In dealing with the Manager, no person shall be required to inquire into, and all persons are entitled to rely conclusively on, the power and authority of the Manager to bind the Company.

6.07 *Compensation to Manager and Members of the Board.* The Manager and members of the Board shall be entitled to receive reasonable compensation for services provided hereunder. After the death of two of the Brothers and Sisters, said compensation shall be determined by the 80% vote of the Board; provided, however, that if, for any reason, the Board can not so agree, then the Consultants, acting alone, shall determine the compensation of the Manager.

6.08 *Expenses.* The Company shall not be required to reimburse the Manager or members of the Board for overhead expenses incurred in providing services to the Company but shall be required to reimburse any of such persons for reasonable out-of-pocket expenses incurred by any of them.

6.09 *Individual Investment Opportunities Permitted.* A Member shall not be restricted by this Agreement from engaging, as owner, investor, shareholder, partner, employee, or otherwise, in any other venture or investment of any nature or description, whether similar to or competitive with any investment acquired at any time by the Company, and no Member shall have any obligation whatsoever to offer any particular opportunity to the Company or other Member.

6.10   *Title to Property.* Title to Property shall be taken in the name of the Company or in the name or names of a nominee or of nominees designated by the Board.

6.11   *Indemnification.* The Company shall indemnify, defend and hold harmless any Manager, member of the Board, Committee Member, as herein after defined, or any Consultant (the "Indemnified Party") who is or becomes a party or is threatened to be made a party to any threatened or pending action, suit, or proceeding, whether civil, criminal, administrative, or investigative (including any action by or in the right of the Company) by reason of any acts, omissions, or alleged acts or omissions arising out of the Indemnified Party's activities as the Manager, as a member of the Board, or as a Consultant, on behalf of the Company or in furtherance of the interests of the Company against losses, damages, claims, or expense (including judgments, fines, and amounts paid in settlement) actually and reasonably incurred by it for which such Indemnified Party has not otherwise been reimbursed, including reasonable attorneys' fees incurred by the Indemnified Party in connection with the defense of any action, suit, or proceeding, which attorneys' fees shall be paid as incurred, so long as the Indemnified Party did not act in a manner constituting gross negligence or willful misconduct. The termination of any action, suit, or proceeding by judgment, order, settlement, or upon a plea of nolo contendere or its equivalent, shall not of itself create a presumption that the Indemnified Party's conduct constituted gross negligence or willful misconduct unless in any such action, suit, or proceeding the Indemnified Party was adjudged to, or admits to, having acted with gross negligence or willful misconduct.

6.12   *Liability of Manager, Member of Board, Consultant, or Committee Member.* A Manager, a member of the Board, Committee Member, or a Consultant shall not be liable, responsible, or accountable in damages or otherwise to the Company or to any of the Members, their successors, or permitted assigns, except by reason of acts or omissions due to gross negligence or willful misconduct. Any action taken in good faith in reliance upon and in accordance with the advice or opinion of counsel shall be conclusively deemed not to constitute gross negligence or willful misconduct.

6.13   *Manager is the Tax Matters Partner.* The Manager shall be the "tax matters partner" for purposes of the Tax Treatment of Partnership Items Act of 1982, and shall have the authority to exercise all functions provided therein for a tax matters partner, or in regulations promulgated thereunder by Treasury, including, to the extent permitted by such regulations, the authority to delegate the function of "tax matters partner" to any other person. The tax matters partner shall be reimbursed for all reasonable expenses incurred as a result of its duties as tax matters partner.

6.14 *Voting on Company Matters.* All matters upon which the Members are entitled to vote pursuant to this Agreement shall be voted upon only by the Members, including any substitute Members admitted to the Company pursuant to Article of this Agreement, or any Member holding the proxy of another Member. However, for purposes of voting on any Membership matter, in the event a Member assigns ("assignor Member") all or any portion of his or her interest in Company profits, losses, or Cash Flow to a third party who is not then admitted as a Member (and, consequently, has no right to vote on Company matters), such assignor Member's Membership Interest shall not include the percentage portion thereof that has been so assigned.

6.15 *Board Approval Committee.* The Board Approval Committee ("Committee Members") shall consist of at least three persons, selected by a majority vote of the Board and the Consultants. For example, a vote of four (4) by the Board and the Consultants will be sufficient for a person to be confirmed as a Committee Member. If the Board cannot agree, then the Consultants will be responsible for naming the three (3) Committee Members. In no event shall a Committee Member be a related party to any of the members of any of the Units within the meaning of Code section 672(c). One such Committee Member should have at least twenty (20) years of ranching and/or manufacturing experience. Another Committee Member should have a background in money management or financial analysis, and one such person should have experience in working with written documents to provide the Committee with a deeper understanding of the reasons the Board Qualification Standards were adopted.

III. Other Provisions in the LLC Operating Agreement would include but not be limited to the following in addition to the standard parts:

1. Right of first refusal to buy membership interests before sale to outside parties or other Disqualified Persons
2. "Put" provisions so that a Member may sell gracefully his or her membership of the LLC
3. Admissions of new Members procedures
4. "Calls" on a membership interest if a member loses his or her membership interest in bankruptcy or divorce
5. Agreement on determining the price for a Put or Call that is fair to all parties involved, especially the selling member.

ACKNOWLEDGEMENTS

Writing a book, particularly one on a subject as complex as succession and estate planning and family relationships, is truly a team effort. I therefore first want to thank my co-authors, Howard Berens and Richard Goldwater, for illuminating the relationship between the law and psychology and for their groundbreaking work in this field, and Tom Gorman for his invaluable contribution to this volume. I also extend my thanks to: Leslie Wright, Jim Reid, Jean Smith, Lorraine McBurnie, Cynthia Brittain, Dibby Green, C. Edward Crowther, Ken Kimball, Mark Aijian, Robert Lane, Chris Wong, David Peri, Bill Atha, Dana Goldinger, Darya Allen-Attar, Dorothy Hamilton, Ron Wolfe, Shana Warshaw, Craig McDonald, and Cheryl Wright for their ideas and assistance regarding various legal, financial, and business aspects of succession and estate planning; to Thomas H. Kenney and Ann Harris for their special insights into trust and tax law; to Richard Llewellyn III, Richard Albrecht, Jon Feder, and Henry Coopersmith for guiding me in the early work that led to this volume, and to Elyce Pike for reading early drafts of chapters and related articles. My thanks also go to Adele Demko and Jerry Jambretz for their interest, encouragement, and support of this project without which it may never have happened. I especially want to thank my parents, John F. Ambrecht and Dorothy Jean Ambrecht, my brother, Tom Ambrecht, and my wife Cheryl Ambrecht, for their unfailing support of all my endeavors.

John W. Ambrecht, Esq.

I first want to thank Richard Goldwater, who in developing Roles and Rules, and in our work together expanded my view and knowledge not only of psychiatry, but also of the nature of this world and our consciousness of it. I thank John Ambrecht for his work in applying the Roles and Rules model in the challenging area of succession and estate planning, and Tom Gorman for translating very challenging ideas into clear and lively language. Nelson Lerner and Tom Nash provided valuable insights into the implications of our work for trusts and trustees, and Ron Wolfe provided similarly valuable insights into the implications in situations involving real estate. Erlene Rosowsky, Psy.D. helped by means of an early article we co-wrote. Thanks also go to my friend and colleague Steve J. Samuel, Esq., for his support and encouragement. I thank my children Dylan and Jesse for their support for and interest in this project and for their excellent questions and comments as the book took shape. And I thank my patients and clients over the years, all of whom in various ways helped me become the practitioner I have become, as I trust I have helped them.

Howard Berens, M.D.

Ideas develop in practice. The work leading to this book began in my head more than twenty-five years ago, but has come to fruition here only because of my partners Howard Berens, John Ambrecht, and Tom Gorman. I also especially thank my colleagues, Tom Gutheil and Stephen Porter. I owe a debt of gratitude to my children and their friends with, and for whom, I have grown up: Jonah Goldwater, Micah Goldwater, Benjamin Lambert, Jon Liroff, and Marc Barron. My psychiatric teachers, including Christopher Gates, Halim Mitry, John Merrifield, Ed Rolde, and Shep Ginandes, gave me a foundation on which to build, and the tools I needed in order to keep building. The late Professor of English at Columbia University, Andrew Chiappe, gave me an understanding of Shakespeare that included the perception of distinct realms in each play, which represent what I have come to call Roles and Rules. The musical composers and performers J.S. Bach, Franz Schubert, Gustav Mahler, Benjamin Zander, and Shaylor Lindsay have made the sublime sensible to me. And I thank the clients with whom I've worked as consultant, as well as the patients for whom I worked as psychiatrist and who trusted me as a partner in their search for the meanings of their lives.

Richard Goldwater, M.D.

We also collectively thank Cheryl Ambrecht for her superb cover design and Tom Gorman, who in his writing provided as much substance as style and who skillfully guided the project to completion.

ABOUT FAMILIES
AND WEALTH, LLC

Families and Wealth, LLC works with families and family businesses, and with attorneys, trust officers, and other advisors to create and administer succession and estate plans in cases of difficult family dynamics. In general, our approach:

- Recognizes that difficult family dynamics arise naturally around succession and estate planning
- Employs Roles and Rules, a psychological model that promotes humane, objective, rational thinking about emotional issues
- Helps families address the Rules Crisis that occurs when family roles clash with legal and business rules
- Shows families how to move from decisions and behavior based on their family roles to decisions and behavior based on legal and business rules
- Helps attorneys and advisors to improve their practices, unfreeze stalled plans, and better serve their clients.

Families and Wealth, LLC is an interdisciplinary team led by John Ambrecht, Esq., and Howard Berens, M.D. Mr. Ambrecht, a fellow of the American College of Trust and Estate Counsel, offers thirty years of trust and estate planning experience. Dr. Berens has thirty-five years of work in private practice with individuals and families and in consultation with organizations, as does Richard Goldwater, M.D. Dr. Goldwater is the creator of the Roles and Rules model. He is also a founder and principal of the firm, as is general manager and director of business development Tom Gorman.

We welcome inquiries regarding our approach and our services.

Families and Wealth, LLC

West Coast Office:
1224 Coast Village Circle
Santa Barbara, CA 93108
Tel. 805-965-1329

East Coast Office:
1075 Washington Street
Newton, MA 02465
Tel. 617-558-5800

www.familiesandwealth.com

ABOUT THE AUTHORS

John W. Ambrecht has been creating and administering estate plans for families with businesses, real estate holdings, and other major assets for over thirty years. His practice focuses on sophisticated estate planning, domestic and international trusts, tax litigation, and business succession. Mr. Ambrecht, who began formally addressing family dynamics in estate planning the 1980s, is a fellow of the American College of Trust and Estate Counsel (ACTEC) and a founding member of California Trust and Estate Counselors (CALTEC). He has testified before the House Ways and Means Committee and the Joint Committee staffs and often speaks on succession and estate planning at institutes and conferences of attorneys, business owners, accountants, and bankers.

Mr. Ambrecht holds an MBA from UCLA, a JD law degree from Loyola of Los Angeles, where he was a member of the Law Review, and an LLM degree (tax law) from New York University.

Howard Berens, M.D. has, for more than 20 years, counseled family businesses and coached entrepreneurs, executives, and political candidates in leadership, personal effectiveness, management skills, and communications. He has consulted to family-owned businesses on goals, growth, organization, operations, and personnel, with a focus on the effects of family systems on the business. Over the past ten years, Dr. Berens, who maintains a private practice in psychiatry, has worked with Dr. Goldwater and business consulting clients to apply the Roles and Rules methodology to family business situations and, with John Ambrecht, to estate planning situations.

Dr. Berens was graduated from Albert Einstein College of Medicine and completed his psychiatric residency at Boston University Medical Center. His practice is based in Newton, Massachusetts.

Richard Goldwater, M.D. consults with family businesses and corporations and specializes in organizational behavior and coaching owners and senior managers in management, communications, and conflict resolution. One of the few original thinkers in psychiatry today, Dr. Goldwater developed Roles and Rules over the past twenty-five years as a theory of human identity and development. He employed the model first as a treatment modality for patients attempting to solve problems and achieve life goals. Later, in the 1990s, he found this approach tremendously useful in his organizational behavior consulting practice.

Dr. Goldwater, who also practices psychotherapy with individuals and families in Massachusetts, was graduated from Columbia College and Boston University Medical School. He completed his psychiatric residency at the Massachusetts Mental Health Center at Harvard Medical School.

Tom Gorman is a communications consultant and the author, collaborator, and ghostwriter of more than a dozen business books. These include volumes on leadership, customer service, technology, innovation, and sales process improvement, among others. A former marketing and operating manager at Dun & Bradstreet Credit Services and DRI/McGraw-Hill, Mr. Gorman has more than twenty years of management experience in companies of various sizes. As a former corporate trainer with Better Communications, Inc. he has extensive experience in facilitating workshops and seminars.

Mr. Gorman holds a BS in psychology from Fairleigh Dickinson University and an MBA from New York University's Leonard N. Stern School of Business.

INDEX

A

acting CEO, 76, 77. *See also under* facilitators
advisors, 12, 14, 48, 83, 91, 96, 109, 138, 150, 153, 155, 161, 168, 169
    helping testator and family, 165
    level of participation, 163
arbitration, 70, 71, 87, 245, 246
    cost of, 247
asset protection, 42, 132, 137, 140, 142, 146, 147, 152, 169
assets, 34, 36, 63, 81, 84, 143
    succession and transfer, 132
    types, 133
attorneys, 14, 17, 24, 63, 70, 138.
    See also lawyers
    practice-related issues, 85, 86

B

binding arbitration, 70
business, 13, 15, 28
    correcting failures, 117
    keep-or-sell decision, 14, 169
    roles, 16, 126, 127
    rules, 16, 117, 121, 127
    valuation methods, 135
business judgment rule, 247

C

California Rules of Professional Conduct, 213
California State Bar, 219
children, 28, 46, 180
client identification, 218
collaborative mediation, 71
collaborative negotiation, 71
communication, 182, 189, 191, 196
    rules, 66, 114, 115, 118, 121
conflict, 43, 63
    between business and trust, 41, 45
    family, 85, 150
    intergenerational, 42, 96, 107
    next generation, 95, 106
    senior generation, 95, 106
    within the business, 41, 43, 44
consultants, 13, 166, 250
consulting, 13, 34, 111
CRPC. *See* California Rules of Professional Conduct

D

Delaware, 48, 228
    law, 151
    trustees, 150
desire, 190

liquidity, 42, 147
LLC (limited liability company), 37
logic, 179

M

Maieutic Consultant, 79, 80.
See also under facilitators
management practices, 13, 72
management skills, 118
MBTI (Myers Briggs Type Indicator), 34
MC. *See* maieutic consultant
monism, 182. *See also* communication *and* documentation

N

Newton's law, 186
Newtonian monism, 181

O

ownership, 123. *See also under* rules

P

parents, 24, 28, 150
perception, 189
prudent person rule, 247
psychological development, 193

Q

QTIP (qualified terminable interest property trust), 143. *See also under* irrevocable trust
questions, 59, 60, 108, 115

R

revocable trust, 139. *See also under* trusts
Rockefeller, John D., 116
roles, 26, 28, 30, 56
Roles and Rules, 26, 31, 36, 52, 85, 86, 92, 111, 214, 249
  as a model of human identity and interaction, 20
  language of, 51
  major benefit, 41
  view, 48
rules, 29, 30, 118, 176
  as tools, 110
  basic, 120
  communication, 114, 223, 242
  executive team and reporting lines, 122
  finance and accounting, 122
  government and industry specific, 122
  human resources, 122
  operations, 122
  ownership, 121
Rules Crisis, 15, 36, 37, 40, 41, 43, 154
  dealing with, 155
  explanation, 50

S

structure, 52, 55, 61
succession, 12, 15, 33
successors, 167, 242

T

tax laws, 37, 140
testator, 42, 49, 52, 64, 109, 166, 168, 213, 226
  intentions, 51